Messengers
of Disaster

Messengers
of Disaster

Raphael Lemkin, Jan Karski, and
Twentieth-Century Genocides

ANNETTE BECKER

Translated by Käthe Roth

THE UNIVERSITY OF WISCONSIN PRESS

Publication of this book has been made possible, in part,
through support from the George L. Mosse Program in History at the University of
Wisconsin–Madison and the Hebrew University of Jerusalem.

GⓁM

GEORGE L.
MOSSE
PROGRAM IN HISTORY

The University of Wisconsin Press
728 State Street, Suite 443
Madison, Wisconsin 53706
uwpress.wisc.edu

Gray's Inn House, 127 Clerkenwell Road
London EC1R 5DB, United Kingdom
eurospanbookstore.com

Printed in the United States of America
This book may be available in a digital edition.

Library of Congress Cataloging-in-Publication Data
Names: Becker, Annette, author. | Roth, Käthe, translator.
Title: Messengers of disaster : Raphael Lemkin, Jan Karski, and twentieth-century genocides
/ Annette Becker ; translated by Käthe Roth.
Other titles: Messagers du désastre. English | George L. Mosse series in the history of
European culture, sexuality, and ideas.
Description: Madison, Wisconsin : The University of Wisconsin Press, [2021] |
Series: George L. Mosse series in the history of European culture, sexuality, and ideas |
Originally published in French as: Messagers du désastre : Raphael Lemkin,
Jan Karski et les génocides. | Includes bibliographical references and index.
Identifiers: LCCN 2021008855 | ISBN 9780299333201 (cloth)
Subjects: LCSH: Lemkin, Raphael, 1900–1959. | Karski, Jan, 1914–2000. |
Genocide—History—20th century. | Genocide—Europe—History—20th century. |
Genocide—Armenia—History—20th century. | World War, 1914–1918—Atrocities. |
World War, 1939–1945—Atrocities.
Classification: LCC HV6322.7 .B43513 2021 | DDC 940.53/180922—dc23
LC record available at https://lccn.loc.gov/2021008855

To the next generation: to Sarah

To Colombe and her baby Siné/Alexandra,
and to Sandrine, Cynthia, and Laurie, who adopted me
as a grandmother in their country, Rwanda

To Philippe

To Jan

Everything occurred as if most people were turning half-closed eyes on the surroundings of an exterior world that they disdained to notice.

—MARC BLOCH, "Reflections of a Historian on the False News of the War," trans. James P. Holoka, *Michigan War Studies Review*, 2013

CONTENTS

Messengers
of Disaster

Introduction

The Unnamable Is Unnamable

"So much cruelty." In July 2016, in Auschwitz, Pope Francis stood alone at the foot of the gate whose arch is inscribed with the words *Arbeit Macht Frei*. He expressed his sense of bewilderment in the camp's guest book in a way that conflated the tortures inflicted on the Polish coreligionists of his predecessor, John Paul II, in the concentration camp with the killings of Jews deported from Poland and occupied Europe at the extermination site in Birkenau. If this speaks volumes about the difficulty today of differentiating the Nazi oppression that fell upon everyone from the singular fate of the Jews, one can imagine how such a distinction was even more unthinkable between 1939 and 1945.

Yet, in 1941 and 1942, a handful of men recognized the specificity of the extermination of Jews amid the chaos of World War II. Among them were two Poles: a Jewish lawyer who had fled the Nazis and a Catholic student who had joined his country's resistance. The traces left by Raphael Lemkin and Jan Karski in the gigantic war-torn world and the reactions of their interlocutors both anonymous and well known open a window on one of the mysteries of recent history: how could it be that only a tiny number of people "saw" while others denied the knowledge of what was in front of their eyes? These messengers wanted to open people's eyes, to offer what they had seen and understood about the truth of the disaster, in the spirit of Charles Péguy's injunction "We must always tell what we see. Above all, and this is more difficult, we must always see what we see."[1]

❡

January 1945. The *Polish Review*, a New York journal linked to the Polish government in exile in London, published parts of the "spy novel" that was Jan Karski's memoir, *Story of a Secret State*,[2] as well as excerpts from Lemkin's *Axis Rule in Occupied Europe*, which was published in the fall of 1944; the preface was written in 1943, and chapter 9 is titled "Genocide."[3]

The hero of the resistance and the activist lawyer, neither of them well known at the time, accomplished their mission: to tell about what they had themselves witnessed in Europe—up to the winter of 1941 for Lemkin and up to October 1942 for Karski. The *Polish Review* was glowing in its praise of Karski's work: "This book is a cry from the abyss. Much more than that, it keeps the flame alive ... in the diabolical world of the Nazis." But no details were provided about the nature of this "diabolical world." Nor was it mentioned that Lemkin was Jewish; the crime of "destruction of a people" was noted in passing but without specifying that its goal was the extermination of Jews, even though the mass murder was extensively documented in its pages after 1943. Lemkin and Karski were among the first links in a chain of public testimony about the extermination. Starting in 1939–40, and especially between 1941 and 1943, they took on the task of transmitting what they knew about persecution of Jews to readers in France, then in Great Britain and the United States. Although some disseminated their ideas, while also gleaning information from other sources, most did not listen to, or did not hear, them.

"I know humanity, I know man, no, no, it's impossible." This cry of rejection was uttered in 1943 by Supreme Court justice Felix Frankfurter, himself Jewish and kept informed of all the dispatches on a daily basis. When Professor Karski was reminded of it in 1978, he answered, "I think he believed me, of course; I have no doubt he did his best, whatever he could have done. . . . Probably he wanted to show me that the world is unprepared, this is an unprecedented problem, a horrible problem."[4] The question therefore has to be shifted from "Who knew what?" or "Who denied what?" to "Why did no one believe what was said by those who took so many risks to spread the message?" Raymond Aron expressed it well: "The gas chambers, the industrial killings of human beings, no, I admit, I did not imagine them, and because I couldn't imagine them, I didn't see them."[5] The "engaged spectator" disengaged himself; he was neither the sole resister nor the only

Jew in London, in the United States, or in the world at war to refuse to believe the "vision" offered by the messengers of mass death who had come from Eastern Europe.[6]

I have always been struck by the impossibility of apprehending the extermination of Jews at the time that it was taking place, between 1941 and 1945. It seemed to me, as a historian of memories and repressions of World War I, that the rumors—especially those related to the German, Russian, and Ottoman atrocities—made the crimes of the following war, which was, in many respects, the first war's extension, opaque, from the atrocities of the invasions and occupations to the extermination of Armenians and the civil wars. Lemkin, born earlier, in 1900, and Karski, born in 1922, were also faced with the epistemological obstacle engendered by the preceding war and its perpetuation into the 1920s, but they broke through it.

In the 1920s, Lemkin had written a great deal about the tragedies of the Great War; he knew that the horrors of World War II were not without precedent in the recent past but that forgetfulness or alterations of memory could make knowledge of the crimes inaccessible. But how could those who felt that they had been duped by various false atrocity stories during World War I and had long forgotten the fate of the Armenians be made to believe in the specificity of the extermination? In this book, I answer that question.

A paradox remains: although the mental universe resulting from World War I and the 1920s and 1930s impeded, in most cases, comprehension of the specific fate of the Jews, it enhanced the precocious lucidity of those few who were conveying the indescribable. Lemkin and Karski were eyewitnesses who became moral witnesses, ready to take every risk to make their message heard.[7] Dante, whom they quoted often, wrote that hope comes to one man because another man brings the message.

The diplomat Varian Fry and the authors Franz Werfel, Arthur Koestler, and George Orwell also transmitted the scope and nature of the disaster that was raining down upon Jews in Europe; they drew upon their experiences of 1914–18 and between 1917 and 1938 in the Russian revolutions and the Spanish Civil War.[8] Aware that civilians were suffering, they described the hardships and deaths of families in great detail and tried to reconstruct the tragedy of persecution and then extermination. They chose to name the unnamable; few heard or understood them.

In this book, I retrace their paths through texts and images from British, American, French, Israeli, and Polish public and private archives, as well as those of the International Committee of the Red Cross in Geneva and the International Tracing Service in Bad Arolsen. Completing the picture are the accounts of historian-victims such as Simon Dubnow and Emanuel Ringelblum and of the Soviet war reporter Vassili Grossman, who was among those who discovered Treblinka.

Most of these sources were transmitted, verified, and cross-checked in real time in the offices of the Foreign Office in London, the State Department in Washington, DC, and the foreign affairs offices of the Polish and Czech governments in exile in London, as well as in the heart of liberated France and by Jewish organizations, and even in Mandatory Palestine. Articles, photographs, and drawings were published by the clandestine press, by newspapers, and in Jewish, British, American, Swiss, and other organs. Even given the war censorship in democratic countries, these documents were not confined to the circles of power, or at least not always; most of the information was within the reach of the general public. Who was reading, watching, listening; who might have known that an "ethnic and religious group"—a people—was being wiped out?[9]

Convinced that his personal grief would be possible only if it was borne by all of humanity, Lemkin applied his original thinking to the crimes against the Armenians and the Roma. The life of Karski, the resister, was thrown into upheaval by his discovery of the extermination of the Jews. A fervent Catholic, he related how his "self-Judaization" started after he donned, fraudulently, the uniform of a Ukrainian reservist. He felt his body and soul being defiled by what he saw, smelled, and heard in Izbica, not far from Belzec: the cries and atrocious deaths of human beings crammed into wagons into which quicklime had been poured.[10]

Karski was not able to return to Poland after his last mission in 1942–43. Like Lemkin, he took refuge in the United States. Both were refugees with the message of barbarism. Whereas Karski "made his report," Lemkin was simultaneously the "alarm" for the fire and its theoretician. He invented the term "genocide" and, in December 1948, was instrumental in getting the General Assembly of the United Nations to adopt the Convention on the

Prevention and Punishment of the Crime of Genocide—almost a miracle as the Cold War was dawning.

Lemkin always presented himself as a man who had had the premonition of a disastrous genocide (even before the word existed) when he was a child. He set to work in the 1920s, and the intellectual formulation to which he was committed was illustrated in 1941 and 1942 by the murder of his own family. After enduring all kinds of abuse in their shtetl of Volkovysk, which became a ghetto, his parents were gassed at Treblinka. We may accuse Lemkin of using tautology in his reconstruction of facts in order to prove his visionary foresight,[11] but we must acknowledge that he was one of the few to think the unthinkable: that during his lifetime, two peoples, the Armenians and the Jews, had been intentionally condemned to extermination.

Karski fought against the Nazis in the military; Lemkin conceived the "crime of crimes" as a legal scholar. Both men came from a Poland in which the relationships with power, territory, the nation, and minorities were different from those in Western Europe. When they arrived in England and the United States, they were faced with incomprehension. Messengers with an inaudible message, they perceived great resentment about it. But from the point of view of the Allies, didn't the extermination of the Jews, in 1944 and 1945, seem secondary, both in public opinion and in the view of the governments struggling against the Axis: shouldn't they first win the war and then punish those responsible for the crimes?

This book does not stop in 1945–46. It does not end in Nuremberg, where Lemkin was very disappointed that the concept of "genocide" was not integrated into international law, or in Washington, DC, where Karski returned to his studies while continuing his fight for a free and independent Poland. Although Lemkin died early, in 1959, his work continued thanks to the legacy of the 1948 convention, even when it became mined territory during the Cold War: some consigned "genocide" to the Nazi past, whereas others broadened it to other populations, following Lemkin's opinion. Unfortunately, the future bore out his vision, and so this book concludes with the genocide of the Tutsi in Rwanda.

Jan Karski, who became "Righteous Among the Nations" and an honorary citizen of Israel, continued his fight until his death, in 2000. Elie Wiesel and Claude Lanzmann brought him back into the public light; he was featured in Lanzmann's film *Shoah*, released in 1985. As a fictional character in Yannick Haenel's novel *Jan Karski*, published in 2009, even in posterity he revisited the question of true and false. And the debates that then arose around what had been known about the extermination of the Jews joined in an endless cycle with what I could read at the same time in the archives: starting in 1941 and 1942, eyewitnesses to the Nazi atrocities had crossed the Channel and the Atlantic, their reports had been analyzed, and they were not believed.

"Even words fail."[12] Samuel Beckett gave up on naming the unnamable, but Raphael Lemkin and Jan Karski did not.

1

Karski the Soldier, Lemkin the Lawyer

1939–40

> This war was waged by the Nazis not only for frontiers, but for the alteration of the human element within these frontiers.
>
> —Raphael Lemkin

In September 1939, certain Poles reacted to the defeat of their country with extraordinary courage and decisiveness. Among them were two men who had very little in common: Jan Kozielewski and Raphael Lemkin. The former, a young man, chose military action; the latter found a way to continue his work as a legal scholar.

Kozielewski, a Catholic student, was mobilized in eastern Poland, soon to be occupied by the Soviets following the signing of the Nazi-Soviet Pact. His determination to return to his homeland to fight saved him from probable death when he exchanged his officer's uniform for that of a simple soldier, as the Soviets were executing the elite of the Polish army in Katyn.[1] At the same time, Lemkin was trying to travel from Warsaw to the town of Volkovysk (near Bialystok), in the eastern part of the country, where his parents lived, and convince them to follow him out of their homeland. He, too, had to take on a different identity. He had been warned that his hands, the pale hands of an intellectual, would likely betray him—the lot of many Polish officers who tried to pass for peasants in order to escape captivity. These two men would come to resemble each other in two ways: both refused to hide reality, and both had to disguise their true identities in order to survive and fight.

Meeting up with the embryonic Polish resistance was not difficult for Kozielewski; his older brother, Marian, had been kept on as chief of the Polish police when Warsaw surrendered, on September 28, 1939. A World War I veteran who had fought in the Pilsudski Legion, Marian was in contact with the Polish government in exile in France and quickly converted his office into a headquarters for the early resistance. Created on September 30 and led by General Władysław Sikorski, the Polish government in exile was based in Paris and Angers and then, after the defeat of France, in London. It was to these three cities that Jan Kozielewski, who now called himself Karski, went on two courier missions. The first lasted from late 1939 to early 1940, after which he returned to the Polish resistance. The second took place in fall 1942 and was extended by an unplanned detour to the United States in 1943. Because this mission became public knowledge, Karski could no longer return to Poland.

When Poland surrendered, Lemkin, a thirty-nine-year-old Jewish lawyer, decided to leave for the Baltic states, which were not yet occupied, as a stepping-off point for Belgium. His ultimate destination was to be the United States, where he had long cultivated professional contacts. In Vilnius, Lithuania, and Riga, Latvia, he shared the fate of members of the Polish Jewish intellectual, religious, community, and professional elite, who had lost everything when they fled and now depended on charity. "Maybe I will be luckier now, as a nomad, than I was as a member of a sedentary society," Lemkin wrote in the notes that would later become his autobiography.[2] A fugitive in his own country, then a refugee, he had quickly realized that for him, an ambitious lawyer in Warsaw, and for his parents, shopkeepers in eastern Poland now under Soviet rule, life as they had known it was gone forever. His parents declined to follow him but supported his plans. As he was leaving Europe, he expressed his last qualms: "As long as I was in Europe, I had felt that I was watching over them. But it was only a geographical illusion. . . . When I was on the constant run, escaping from actual dangers, I called myself an escapee. But now that direct and immediate danger of losing life and liberty did not threaten me, I became a refugee. Now I was threatened with the disintegration of my personality through idleness, apathy, loss of self-esteem and assertiveness."[3] Taking inspiration from the poetry of Dante, also a fugitive, Lemkin wrote a detailed account of this time of wandering in search of a visa—the curse of refugees. Although he took an ironic tone, he was not unaware that most of those whose paths he crossed had been moved into ghettos, put into forced labor, mistreated in every conceivable way, murdered.

> A consulate at that time was the god and the supreme ruler of the race of refugees. They studied their gods, whose idiosyncrasies and habits of conversation they had learned from people who had already been received by them. The waiting rooms of the consulates were social meeting places for refugees. People would go there just out of habit. From there they would go to another meeting place . . . where they would report to their friends that they had just come from the consulate and that their visas had not yet arrived. For a long time the real relationship between a refugee and a consulate was just waiting.[4]

As he traveled from Poland to the Baltic states and Sweden, Lemkin met with many people and scoured libraries; he brought to bear in the struggle against "Axis domination" his knowledge about war and crimes against humanity garnered from his analyses conducted during the 1920s and 1930s and from what he had learned since the beginning of the war. His mission: to convince the world of the significance of the new territory being mapped out by the Nazis—or, at least, that is how he reconstructed it later: "This war was being waged by the Nazis not only for frontiers but for the alteration of the human element within these frontiers. This alteration meant that certain people were to be annihilated and supplanted by Germans. Their destruction would be irrevocable and their cultures erased forever."[5]

Lemkin, or the Weapons of the Intellect

The man who had fought briefly in the Russo-Polish War in 1920 now found himself banned from his homeland, Poland—a stateless Jew. The situation was paradoxical for a tireless legal scholar who had helped to write the Polish criminal code, as well as those of the Soviet Union and Italy. Just as ironic was that his major opus, *The Regulation of International Payments*, a study of the trade systems of fifty-four countries, was being published in Paris at that very time.[6] Lemkin was also interested in recent history: the disasters of World War I and the Russian Civil War, the conflicts that had crushed the Jews of Russia and Galicia—his people—and the Armenians. Fascinated by the rich Jewish cultural life in 1930s Poland, expressed in Yiddish and

Hebrew despite growing state persecution, he compared it to that of the Armenians: "These wretched and insecure people had a unique capacity to absorb and digest culture. It went straight into their bloodstream. In their cultural ability and receptivity there was also a great deal of resemblance between the Jews and the Armenians, who, in 1915, lost more than a million people by genocide in Turkey."[7]

"There is nothing new in the sufferings of Jews, especially in time of war"[8]

During his difficult crossing of a Poland defeated and occupied by the Nazis and the Soviets in the fall of 1939, Lemkin found refuge among his fellow Jews, who reflected all the complex facets of Judaism at the time—observant and secular, socialists of all types, leftwing and rightwing Zionists. Some, like him, had quickly realized that flight was the only solution in the face of imminent Nazi persecution. Yet, this remained to be achieved. Different, and even opposing, encounters, each of which revealed the state of Polish Jewish society at the time, touched him deeply. For, to start with, the Jews themselves had to be convinced.

In Dubno, Lemkin was given warm hospitality by his host, a strictly observant baker. The baker felt that Hitler and the new war would change nothing for the Jews, who had endured adversity for generations: "My grandfather used to tell me stories about pogroms by Kosaks. . . . In the last war, 1915–1918, we lived three years under the Germans. It was never good, but somehow we survived. I sold bread to the Germans; we baked for them from their flour. We Jews are an eternal people, we cannot be destroyed. We can only suffer." Lemkin attended Shabbat services in the shtetl, and he gave a sensitive description of his hosts' faith. Although he no longer shared it, as a former student in a *heder* (Jewish school), he understood it intimately: "This was where my host changed from a poor baker into a king." Recounting this episode often after he arrived in the United States, he spoke of it as both the culmination of his knowledge of Polish Judaism and the beginning of his mission; he apparently shared his vision of "genocide" with the incredulous baker: "He could not believe the reality of genocide [of course, the word did not exist in 1939] because it went against nature, against logic, against life itself. . . . There was not much sense in disturbing or confusing him with facts. He had already made up his mind. He had a private, bilateral covenant with

God. When born this contract devolved on him from his father. He was ready to take his punishment if he were to violate this covenant . . . he would not complain about it."[9]

The baker was living in the time of God; Lemkin was living in the historical present. He tried to bring the two together to convince his hosts that the Nazi aggression was something new: "It is not a war to grab territory so much as to destroy whole peoples and replace them with Germans. It is like Assur, which you remember from the Bible, who destroyed many nations and settled their lands with its allies."[10] The baker seemed unwilling to accept this comparison, even reinforced by the Bible, because he knew well that ever since the biblical confrontation between Jacob and Esau, the survival of the Jewish people had been guaranteed by scattering—and, above all, by faith.

An Orthodox Jew from the Warsaw ghetto responded similarly to the socialist Zionist historian Emanuel Ringelblum, who wished to amass as many documents as possible to archive the lives of Jews in Poland before they disappeared: "Jews have no history, all of it is only myth. . . . Only a myth will remain of the present time. Will it be the myth of Sodom or the myth of Abraham's charity?"[11]

Lemkin was both moved by such firmness and fervor and despairing about what he sensed was coming. In this, he shared the view of the historian Simon Dubnow, whom he met in Riga. As an intellectual, Lemkin had probably read the new edition of Dubnow's *Histoire moderne du peuple juif*, published in 1938, in which he took stock of the danger with remarkable prescience: "We are living at a turning point in world history, and this turning point, at present, is leading us toward the worst, toward the worst centuries in human history. . . . The theory of racism leads from humanity to bestiality."[12] However, Lemkin certainly had not read the article that Dubnow had sent to the editors of a Yiddish journal founded in Paris after the Munich Agreement and the failure of the Evian Conference. In his article, Dubnow observed that democracies had no intention of helping persecuted Jews by accepting more refugees and loosening immigration quotas: not the British in Palestine, nor the United States, nor Switzerland, nor Australia, nor France.

Dubnow referred not to Assur but to Haman and the Book of Esther: "And the letters were sent by posts into all the king's provinces, to destroy, to kill, and to cause to perish all Jews, both young and old, little children and women, in one day."[13] In 1939, Dubnow was eighty years old, and he knew Jewish history better than anyone else. He had grasped the uniqueness of what Hitler and the Nazis thought and planned to undertake: "We are witnessing the beginning of the obliteration of European Judaism. ... The hegemonic center of our people will have to be transplanted beyond the seas—to America or Asia." Dubnow used the word *khurbn*, "total destruction," reserved up to then for the destruction of the temple in Jerusalem—a word that would come to mean, in the following months and years, "extermination system" and "expulsion from Germany" of Jews by the Nazis— expressions that he was already using. Dubnow concluded, still in 1939, "It is their bodies that must be saved. First the Jews—and then the entire Yiddish way of life.[14] We must fight against the scourge of anti-Jewish hate in its Nazi form and against the plans to organize new expulsions and persecutions in eastern Europe."[15] Lemkin was obviously impressed with the elderly historian during their sole meeting; when he related their dialogue, he had found refuge in Washington, DC, and was aware that Dubnow had been murdered, along with all the Jews in the largest ghetto in Latvia, in the Rumbula forest in 1941. "In the city of Riga, Latvia, 8,000 Jews were killed in a single night. A week later 16,000 more were led into a woods, stripped and machine-gunned."[16] In just a few weeks, Latvia was rendered *judenfrei*.

"How can we comprehend this hate that rises from the abyss?" (Franz Werfel)

Other Jewish intellectuals, such as Franz Werfel, faced similar challenges and tried to analyze them. Born in Prague and having fought on the Russian front during World War I, Werfel, who wrote in German, had enjoyed some celebrity before the publication, in 1933, of *The Forty Days of Musa Dagh*, a novel about what was not yet being called the Armenian genocide. In 1932, he toured Germany reading excerpts of the forthcoming book. At that time he made public two chapters in which he reproduced excerpts of an interview conducted by Johannes Lepsius, a German Orientalist theologian who had taken the side of the Armenians, with one of the three people responsible for the genocide, Enver Pasha:[17] "'In our very own time, one of the oldest and most venerable peoples of the world has been destroyed, murdered, almost exterminated—and not by warlike enemies but by their own countrymen."[18] In chapter 5, the comparison between Armenians and Jews is more pointed. Lepsius observes that a great deal of information on the deportations of the Armenians was available in 1915 thanks to reports by Christian missionaries and Henry Morgenthau Sr., ambassador from the United States, which was still neutral, to the Ottoman Empire. "'Mr. Morgenthau,' said Enver brightly, 'is a Jew. And Jews are always fanatically on the side of minorities.'"[19]

In his talks, Werfel explained that in Germany in 1932, the SA and the SS were taking part in demonstrations during which they shouted the same kind of hate. He nevertheless thought that Hitler had no political future and was convinced that his book, in which he attacked what he called national fanaticism, would be very important in the struggle: "My book may be read symbolically, outside of time, because of current events: oppression and destruction of minorities by nationalism."[20] Werfel was naive: he believed, in 1933, that he could retain his membership in the literary section of the Prussian Academy, and he expressed the conviction that Roosevelt and the pope would ultimately get rid of Hitler. Culturally assimilated, he apparently thought that the Nazis had banned his book on the massacre of the Armenians because he was making a barely veiled attack against them by equating them with the Ottomans. In fact, his book was burned because he was Jewish.

In 1936, Werfel, basking in the success of his book, received a standing ovation in New York from three hundred members of the Armenian community during a gala dinner attended by Henry Morgenthau Sr., former US ambassador to Turkey. After the Anschluss, Werfel had to flee Austria, where he had been living, and he took refuge in France. And then 1940 came: "We're trapped," he admitted to other immigrants who hoped that his celebrity could be of use to them.[21] It was thanks to assistance from the Emergency Rescue Committee in Marseille, organized by the American writer Varian Fry, that he was able to reach Spain, accompanied by Heinrich, Nelly, and Golo Mann, via an exhausting march across the Pyrenees to Portbou.[22] He finally reached Portugal, then left for the United States. "Exile is a terrible disease," wrote his wife, Alma Schindler (who had previously been married to Gustav Mahler and Walter Gropius).[23] Meanwhile, Werfel's parents were unable to leave Marseille. His father died there; at the last minute his mother, again thanks to Fry's team, was able to join him in the United States.

When Werfel arrived in New York in late 1940, he was physically and mentally exhausted. Having meditated and written on the extermination of the Armenians, he found himself gripped by the situation, both similar and different, that Jews were facing. He wrote a remarkable essay, published in a German émigré journal, in which he explored the recent sufferings of Jews in the light of world history, religion, and human nature:

> How are we to comprehend this hatred from the abyss, which is massing more horrifyingly than ever around an ethnic group that has preserved its existence among the nations for several millennia now? . . . In earlier times, hatred of Jews was always parochial, limited in scope. Today, in our technical age, it is global. . . . It is the most monumental religious war of all time, a war that the human race is waging against the two-thousand-year-old paradox, against the spirit of Israel, the biblical spirit in all its manifestations. . . . But if Israel's God and spirit are to vanish from this planet, the physical vehicle of this spirit— the Jewish people—must first be annihilated, down to the very last man.

Werfel was even more despairing when he looked beyond Nazism: he was convinced that humanity was entering a new age that he called the "motorized golem" that "dreams with strange fanaticism of a value-free, spiritless, and soulless world that resembles a technically elaborate frozen hell."

As 1940 drew to a close, only the British were waging war in Europe; would the Americans join the fight? Werfel was increasingly prophetic as he took stock of the catastrophe: "We Jews are fighting today for more than the continued existence of our communities in the Diaspora, for more than the development work in Palestine, yes, for more than our lives. We are engaged in God's struggle for the salvation of the entire world."[24]

Some had read *Mein Kampf* and listened closely to the speeches given by Hitler and his henchmen, and they sounded the alarm. Others had closed their eyes to the whole thing. All had been massacred. Lemkin had had conversations with an erudite historian and a devout baker. One might say that he and Dubnow were intentionalists ahead of their time, but that would be to grant too much significance to references that no longer made much sense. In light of what they had perceived, they agreed with the most innovative present-day historians of the extermination of the Jews, such as Omer

Bartov and Peter Longerich: from the start, anti-Jewish policies had been the tie that bound the Nazi racial community together, and the transition from rhetoric to implementation of the extermination was inherent to Germany's will to transform the demography in the eastern territories that it now occupied.[25]

In the 1950s, Lemkin instrumentalized Dubnow's moral and intellectual unction: he had likely told Dubnow in 1939 about the great work that he was planning. Dubnow acknowledged that it was "strange how initiatives taken by dictators fascinate and even paralyze statesmen of democratic nations, and how easily they let them get away with such bold actions." Lemkin then told him about his plan "to outlaw the destruction of peoples." Dubnow's "reaction was vivid: 'The basic value of your plan lives in the criminal character of the act,' he said. 'Obviously if killing one man is a crime, killing of entire races and peoples must be an even greater one.'" Lemkin responded, "'Murder of a whole people must be recognized as an international crime, which should concern not just one nation but the entire world.'"[26]

Was this really the content of their dialogue? Did Dubnow really say this in 1939? He suffered to the end for being an intellectual—his library was confiscated when he was confined to the Riga ghetto—and would have encouraged survivors to write history. And this was true up to his last breath: during the *Aktion* of December 1941, he was killed by a bullet probably fired by a Latvian militiaman. He supposedly called out, as he lay dying, "'Write it down, write it down!' It was a historian's testament."[27]

Like Ringelblum, who took inspiration from him when he created the Oyneg Shabes archivists' group in the Warsaw ghetto in 1941, Dubnow had felt since the late nineteenth century that history was the means by which the Jewish people would resist and survive.[28]

Fleeing, Making History

Lemkin wanted to make history. That is why he sought exile in the United States: there, it would be possible to work toward punishing mass murderers. But how would he reach North America?

In the 1930s, Western democracies, jointly and separately, closed their borders. For Poland, the war and the double occupation made the situation catastrophic. Anti-Semitism was nothing new; the rebirth of Poland in 1918 had been accompanied by a nationalism that took an aggressive stance toward the "Jewish problem"—a minority seen as too large. Especially after the death of Marshal Pilsudski in 1935, the country instituted a state policy of anti-Semitism: bans on professionals—of which Lemkin was a victim in 1933—quotas or even outright bans on students, separate seats for those still taking courses, boycotts of Jewish businesses, expulsions. The Catholic Church expressed full-throated support for the ideology of exclusion promulgated by nationalist political parties that used anti-Semitism as both program and strategy.

Edward Raczynski, the Polish ambassador to London and a future minister of foreign affairs for the government in exile, stated in January 1939, "There exist in Poland great numbers of Jews who far exceed the power of economic absorption of that country and whose rapid rate of natural increase has already for many years past subjected them to a necessity growing ever more urgent of considerable and continuous emigration."[29] Both hardline and moderate anti-Semites agreed with the Zionists' solution: emigration. Yet, "emigration" meant "Palestine," and Palestine was under British mandate. Not only were the British limiting the number of Jewish immigrants to Palestine, but they preferred the persecuted German Jews who had been seeking refuge since 1933, who were deemed more assimilated and therefore more assimilable. The British concurred with the Poles' attitude toward "their" Jews.

Starting in the summer of 1939, Polish Jews found themselves in the same predicament as German Jews—or worse. There was no longer any question of emigrating; they had to find refuge from horrible persecution at a time when the world war was further restricting border crossings. And yet, the government in exile and the British authorities were always thinking about the future in terms of emigration, one result of which was this surreal note written by Frank Roberts, one of the Foreign Office diplomats in touch with Karski in London, on May 13, 1941:

> Since there are some three million Jews in Poland (ten per cent of the population of prewar Poland) and many of these are not very well assimilated, any Polish government must inevitably aim at finding some solution of this problem by emigration. Since, however, no other country is willing to accept Polish Jews, and the absorptive capacity of Palestine is strictly limited, it is not in the interest of H.M. Government to encourage such a policy on the part of

the Poles. All we can do is express the pious hope that the Poles will in fact do their best to assimilate the Jews.[30]

In June 1941, Operation Barbarossa and then the mass extermination of the Jews in Eastern Europe obviated any political move by the Polish, British, and other governments. There would soon be no more Polish Jews.

The British, dogged by the Palestine question, nevertheless continued to reflect upon refuge as a solution. The Home Office, Aliens Department, met with the High Commissioner of the Refugee Bureau of the League of Nations on January 6, 1942. What would the refugees—and, in particular, the most numerous among them, the Jews—choose to do after the war? There had to be agreement on acceptable guarantees for them in their countries of origin so that they could return to them. Otherwise, "the long-term refugee pb [problem] would then become insoluble."[31] The solution to the "Jewish problem" devised by the Nazis was called death.

Karski Encounters Poland's "Jewish Problem"

As Raphael Lemkin was fleeing east through Poland, passing through his hometown of Volkovysk, Jan Karski was starting his first mission in that part of Poland. The young activist had been dispatched by his brother, Marian, and his resistance organization to convince the various underground movements to unite—a mission made trickier because Poland was occupied by the Nazis to the west and the Soviets to the east. Sent to Lvov in the fall of 1939, Karski entered the Soviet zone with help from someone in the Jewish resistance who smuggled people in when they were convinced that they would be safer there than in the Nazi-controlled zone.

In early 1940, Karski traveled to France to give an account of what he had seen. He was physically strong, spoke many languages, and proved to be dependable, accurate, and discreet. He relied for the first time on what he would later call his "photographic memory." His debriefing dealt essentially with the conditions under which the resistance was operating in the two occupation zones, which were of particular interest to the government in exile: what was really going on in Poland? Karski's report took another form when the minister of the interior, Stanislaw Kot, asked him to put down in writing everything he had seen, listing the different themes—military, political, social—that should be discussed; a secretary would encrypt his notes to guarantee his safety and that of people whom he might quote. Did Kot choose the theme of the "Jewish problem," or was it Karski's initiative? Karski barely mentions the report in his memoir. Yet, in 1940, he wrote some ten detailed pages on the situation of the Jews. The ardent young patriot had eyes only for Poland and for the men, like his brother, who had made it possible for Poland to be resurrected after World War I and who had immediately committed themselves to ensuring that it would not disappear again. Although the fate of the Polish Jews was a secondary concern, his report nevertheless included a remarkably pointed analysis.

The historian David Engel unearthed the report in the archives of the Polish government in exile at Stanford University's Hoover Institution. He asked Karski about it, and Karski confirmed its provenance in 1982. Engel then translated and published it in 1983.[32]

This fascinating ten-page document describes the discovery by the Polish Catholic majority of the tragedies of the occupation; Karski took exception to certain discriminatory measures that most people considered legitimate, at least in 1936, when they oppressed the Jewish minority. In the view of the core members organizing the underground state, the nation now needed everyone, Jews included, at a time when defeat had exacerbated nationalism. How were things going in the field? Karski described the "Jewish Question . . . in the homeland," a homeland now divided into three zones: the regions annexed by the Reich; the Generalgouvernement, in which Warsaw was situated; and the territories occupied by the USSR. He noted that he had not written about the Nazi-occupied regions because "the situation of the Jews in these territories is clear, uncomplicated, easy to understand." They were officially destined, "through the use of force, law, and propaganda, for destruction or removal. . . . The intent is toward the complete cleansing of this area of the Jewish element. . . . The tendency is toward a resettlement of all Jews from the annexed territories to the Generalgouvernement."[33] In the Germans' view, these territories, "essentially German but disgracefully Judaized by the Poles," had to be re-Germanized—that is, populated with *Volksdeutsche* (ethnic Germans), Germans of the Reich, and wiped clean of their Jews. In the majority "Polish" zone, now designated the Generalgouvernement, there was "the impression that the Germans would like to create . . . something along the lines of a *Jewish reservation*" (emphasis in original). In particular, Jews expelled from the annexed territories were resettled in the

Lublin region and "all wear stars or patches . . . which indicate that they are Jews." For "in the territory of the Generalgouvernement . . . 1) there are more Jews here; 2) Jews cannot be sent farther away from there. . . . The Germans nevertheless are attempting suitably to 'organize' the Jews here, 'to teach them [how to] work,' 'hygiene,' and 'respect for Nordics and Aryans in general,' to ruin them materially and to limit their life to an extremely narrow range." Karski sanitized his description of public sessions of torture and humiliation, speaking instead of forced gymnastic exercises and the cutting of beards of observant men. "Forced physical labor for Jews is organized on a large scale—mainly for the purpose of 'cleansing' Warsaw and other cities of garbage."[34] Well aware of how the Nazis reified the Jews— they had become malodorous trash that had to be disposed of by the master race—he wrote, "The 'Master Race' is really a nation of madmen, of brutal haters and heartless beings."[35] He carefully distinguished between the "legal" violence inflicted on Jews and the cruelties superimposed on this violence to increase their suffering and the enjoyment of their torturers.[36]

Although the first few pages of the report give a glimpse of Karski's compassion for the Jews persecuted in the Nazi zone, the tone changed when he described the Soviet zone. There, Jews "do not experience humiliations or persecutions," as the occupiers made "no distinctions . . . among nationalities or religious groups." Not only did Jews feel "at home" there because of their "ability to adapt," but they became members of political cells and took over "the most critical political-administrative positions." Because of his anti-Sovietism, understandable in a young soldier who had just escaped from Soviet prison camps and had been instructed on Judeo-Bolshevism through an atavistic anti-Semitic lens—he noted without batting an eye their supposed power over money and sex—Karski did not hide his disgust for Polish Jews who adapted to the Soviet system and who "are involved in loan-sharking and profiteering, in illegal trade, contraband, foreign currency exchange, liquor, immoral interests, pimping, and procurement."[37]

Karski knew that the zone annexed by the Soviets presented a complicated situation. First, he adopted the Polish doxa that likened the Jews there to communists who had betrayed their homeland by welcoming the occupiers with "baskets of red roses," but he nevertheless made "certain distinctions." The Jewish proletariat saw its situation improve "*structurally*": its members had "formerly been exposed primarily to oppression, dignities, excesses, etc., from the Polish element," and the fact that they "responded positively, if not enthusiastically, to the new regime" seemed, to Karski, "quite understandable."[38]

Karski began to use the first-person voice at this point in his text. In giving his opinion, he no doubt came to conclusions that went far beyond what his interlocutors could have imagined. For, in his view, if Jewish communists had frequently betrayed the Poles, other Jews, among the intelligentsia and the well-to-do, were persecuted by the Soviets to the point of undergoing "collective liquidation"[39] and had proved loyal to the homeland. They wanted to revive a democratic and independent Poland within which they would be welcomed. Karski was speaking here of Jews to whom he felt socially and politically close, even though he used the usual anti-Semitic slurs: "Of course, a certain calculation of self-interest is involved in all this."[40] It went without saying, in Karski's view, that the Jews, including the most respectable, "counted" everything, which included weighing the value of supporting the homeland. They would have no one to blame but themselves if their "devotion" to the Bolsheviks brought upon them the vengeance of the Poles!

Testimonials by Jews confirmed and fleshed out Karski's portrait. With the Soviets, Jews may have felt that they had escaped not only the Nazi horror but also Polish anti-Semitism. This was the sense in Volkovysk, Lemkin's native shtetl, where many members of his family still lived; they did not want to exaggerate the Soviet danger when he suggested that they flee with him. His father told him, "I have been living in retirement for more than ten years because of my sickness. I am not a capitalist. The Russians will not bother me." His brother added, "I gave up my store and registered as an employee before it was taken over by the new government. They will not touch me either."[41] The *Volkovysk Memorial Book* includes accounts of the long history of terrible relations between Polish and Jewish communities, which were made worse by the war. When the Polish army withdrew before the Soviet advances in this region, some residents, assisted by soldiers, organized a pogrom during which they pillaged, robbed, and murdered people, including Jewish fighters. "Who knows what cruelties the Poles might have accomplished? The Soviets entered the town and ended the anti-Semitic depredations. . . . The Jews began to breathe again. Many, such as the old shoemaker who climbed on a Red Army tank crying victory, even greeted the Soviets with great joy." The *Memorial Book* then related how the man was "rewarded": the "anti-Semite who had led the pogrom" had him arrested by the Soviets, who shot him dead.[42]

When the Soviet troops entered Luck, the Zionist Moshe Kleinbaum saw some young communist Jews applauding them. Such gestures could not hide the convoluted emotions experienced by everyone: "'We were condemned to death, but our sentence has been commuted to life-long imprisonment.' The Nazi danger meant the death penalty for the Jews. The Red Army came and rescued a million and a half Jews from a sure physical and civil death, but the Red Army rescued no more than the bare lives of Jews. . . . Life continues, but with nothing more than black bread and water, and people are no longer free. . . . At least 80 percent of the Jews think that way, and . . . they accepted Soviet rule first with a sigh of relief, because of the weeks of anxiety regarding the threat of Nazi invasion, and then with a sigh of deep concern: What will the morrow bring us?"[43]

In Otwock, near Warsaw, Calel Perechodnik expressed this stark lack of options even more directly: death for some, a gagged life for others. "Although I had been against communism throughout my life," he wrote, "now I begged God that the Bolsheviks would occupy the area up to the Vistula. I was ready to lose [everything] in order to be able to live as a free man, without any racial restrictions. Still, I did not jump for joy at the sight of Soviet tanks."[44]

Indeed, the Soviets were still Soviets. In Volkovysk, citizenship was offered to residents and many refugees from Nazified Poland; those who refused were sent to Siberia. And yet, the *Memorial Book* ends, in 1946, with, "Ultimately, this decree was a godsend for thousands of Jews from Poland and Lithuania. It saved their lives."[45]

"Repayment in blood"

Karski's handlers were keenly interested in what Poles thought about the fate of the Jews during the early months of the double occupation. The question turned out to be so complex that Karski rewrote his account three times, either on his own or according to requirements. The text was no doubt intended for the Allies: after the German-Soviet Pact was signed, they were eager for any criticism of the "Bolsheviks." And yet, Karski did not hesitate to expose Poles' mistrust of Jews, who apparently did not resist the Germans' orders but seemed capable of fleeing to the Soviet zone at any instant: "The Jew here would rather commit suicide than resist the Germans."[46]

In the first version of the report, Karski noted, "It would be advisable were there to prevail in the attitude of the Poles . . . the understanding that in the end both peoples are being unjustly persecuted by the same enemy." This was no doubt his own position, and he was aware that it was the exception: "Such an understanding does not exist among the broad masses of the Polish populace. Their attitude toward the Jews is overwhelmingly severe, often without pity. A large percentage of them are benefiting from the rights [over the Jews] that the new situation gives them. They frequently exploit these rights, and even abuse them. This brings them, to a certain extent, nearer to the Germans."[47] It is understandable why a different version of this paragraph was written—one in which the Poles were presented as being in the process of changing "under the influence of what is happening" and discovering "visible sympathy" for the Jews "given the unbounded bestiality of the Germans."[48] If the original version were to fall into the hands of the British and French allies—this was in February 1940—it might have a terrible effect: how could it be stated so plainly that the defeated Poles found a certain satisfaction in seeing Jews mistreated and hoped to profit from it? For, Karski specified, the Germans not only mistreated the Jews but hoped to use their anti-Jewish policy to "win over the Polish masses." The persecution by the Poles was intended, in part, to extort as much as possible from the Jews, as one way to "solv[e] the Jewish Question in the Generalgouvernement . . . [and] it must be admitted that they are succeeding in this. . . . The Polish peasant[s] . . . proclaim: 'Now then, they are finally teaching them a lesson.'—'We should learn from them.'—'The end has come for the Jews.'—'Whatever happens, we should thank God that the Germans came and took hold of the Jews.'"[49] As might be expected, this section also had a different version: "[The Germans] are attempting to play upon as many and various conflicts as possible within Polish society . . . probably not assuming the fact that the mass of Polish society is not anti-Semitic. . . . But the Polish populace more and more frequently [is] thinking out loud: 'This is already too much.'—'These are not people.'—'This must end with some horrible punishment for the Germans.'"[50]

Karski understood the trap that Germany had laid for the Poles: to play on their visceral anti-Semitism in order to encourage them to collaborate by hunting down Jews and pillaging their goods, after which it would turn against them. Although his new version softened the wording, it was clear to Karski that Germany's perfidious solution took advantage of Polish anti-Semitism.

The government in exile, which was trying to unify the early resistance, faced a dilemma: given the active anti-Semitism of some of its own members, could showing any compassion, however minimal, toward Jews victimized by the Nazis alienate the Poles who might win the nation's cause?[51] Karski would be confronted with this predicament in all of his missions: to say or do something for the Jews always carried the risk of seeming to transform the war being waged by the Poles, the British, the Americans, the free French, and the rest into a war for the Jews; this was the basis of the propaganda put out by the Nazis and the collaborationists in occupied Europe. George Orwell made this bitter observation in an article written in April 1945: "It so happens that the war has encouraged the growth of anti-Semitism and even, in the eyes of many ordinary people, given some justification for it. To begin with, the Jews are one people of whom it can be said with complete certainty that they will benefit by an Allied victory. Consequently, the theory that 'this is a Jewish war' has a certain plausibility, all the more so because the Jewish war effort seldom gets its fair share of recognition."[52]

In 1940, Karski's conclusion to his report was categorical: in the annexed zone, "Virtually all Poles are bitter and disappointed in relation to the Jews; the overwhelming majority (first among them of course the youth) literally look forward to an opportunity for 'repayment in blood.'"[53] Karski was, in a way, clairvoyant. There were some cases of Polish participation in extermination of Jews, starting with the massacre in Jedwabne, for which historian Jan Gross forged the concept of "neighbors."[54] This episode of "repayment by blood" took place on July 10, 1941, barely three weeks after the Nazis invaded the Soviet zone.

When Karski wrote his memoir in 1944, however, he made no mention of what he had so subtly perceived in 1939–40. Throughout his account of the birth of the underground, he talked only about the Soviets and the Polish resisters whom he had secretly encountered. The only Jews he mentioned were those fleeing Nazi-held territory with whom he sneaked across the border to Lvov. "I could see that there were many of all ages, old men and women, two women with babies in their arms, and a few young men and girls. They were all escaping Jews. It seemed as if they sensed what the future held in store for them, that soon the pitiless extermination of the Jews would start."[55]

By 1944, Karski knew just about everything about the extermination of Polish Jews by the Nazis. But those who reached the Soviet zone in 1939 could not have known. Couriers had a tendency to exaggerate their premonitions, even though the reports that reached the provisional government at the time confirmed Karski's observations about the Poles and the Nazis: "The Jews persecuted the Poles so horribly ... that at the first opportunity all the Poles—here, from old people to women and children—took a revenge so terrible upon the Jews that no anti-Semite would have thought it possible ... the choice was no longer between Zionism and the previous state of affairs; rather, it was between Zionism and extermination."[56]

This was why Lemkin was trying to flee not just Poland but also Europe.

New York, Emergency Committee in Aid of Displaced Foreign Scholars, Box 87, File 39, Raphael Lemkin: Rejected[57]

Lemkin wanted to keep working. His odyssey took him across Poland, Lithuania, and Latvia to Sweden, where he was hoping to obtain a visa for the United States through his prewar academic contacts. He and a law professor at Duke University, Malcolm McDermott, had in fact translated the 1932 Polish Criminal Code into English. McDermott responded to his appeal and contacted the Emergency Committee in Aid of Displaced Foreign Scholars. The letters, phone calls, and telegrams back and forth between the committee, located in New York, and McDermott, in South Carolina, and the appeals made to the National Refugee Service, also in New York, by Lemkin, immobilized in Sweden, are poignant. There were no fewer than twenty-four exchanges between May 27 and July 31, 1940. Those involved in the effort alternated between hope and despair, including Betty Drury, the Emergency Committee's secretary, who responded with the same cordiality to all demands and tried to find solutions; without a financial guarantee, no visa would be granted: "Mr. Henry Bane, attorney at law, tells us that according to Prof. McDermott, Dr. Lemkin is a most inspiring and brilliant man and would be a credit to any institution. McDermott is ready to take him into his own home, but a stipend will be needed" (June 4, 1940). Lemkin had naively assumed that his impressive curriculum vitae, his participation in numerous international judicial conferences, the list of his publications in multiple languages, and the assurance from Duke University that it would find a teaching position for him would easily swing open the doors to the United States.

Lemkin was not taking into account the drastic quotas and the extreme competition for visas by "displaced academics"—"displaced" being a euphemism for "fleeing, hunted, persecuted." It went without saying that although the word "Jew" was not used, it applied to most of the "displaced" people. Before the war, they had been Germans, Austrians, and Czechoslovaks; now they were Poles. After two months of correspondence, Lemkin became increasingly uneasy. He saw the war setting Europe ablaze: Belgium—where he had been promised a position—Holland, and France were defeated. He had spent two months stuck in Stockholm; soon it would no longer be possible to leave. But his American friends could not find the money necessary. At Duke, his application was rejected: "The financial limit here has been reached in the employment of refugee professors." McDermott, pressed by Lemkin, pressed the committee: "In a recent letter Dr. Lemkin informs me that after the month of June he would not be permitted to pass through Finland. He indicates that every day will make it more difficult for him to get out of Sweden. If your committee finds it possible to supply the necessary funds in aid of this brilliant Polish legal scholar, I suggest that you act promptly, for time is of the essence in this matter" (June 18, 1940). Lemkin also contacted Jewish organizations, but it was the fact that he was a lawyer that was emphasized: "I'm familiar with his scholarly work and with the remarkably high reputation for scholarship and general intellectual achievement which he enjoys with the world of learning and letters. I should like to express my own ardent hope that your esteemed committee will find it possible to contribute to the rescue of this brilliant and worthy man."[58]

Once again, letters, telegrams, and telephone calls followed until the decision—rejection—was made known: "The European crisis has brought so many urgent applications for funds and the C[ommittee] was obliged to try to stretch its limited resources to take care of as many scholars as possible. Preference was given to those scholars who were technically eligible for our support. As a former attorney, Dr. L[emkin's] case did not come within the scope of our work. . . . Then, too, the C[ommittee] preferred not to use its funds for scholars who were still in Europe."[59] This was the twenty-first letter. The committee knew all about Lemkin's double career as a lawyer and researcher and about his impressive bibliography. One can imagine his disappointment when he heard the news. And then, a dramatic turn of events: his persistence paid off as he found distant relatives living in New York who offered the required $1,200 to Duke; he could finally proceed with his visa application. Ms. Drury spread the news: "It is not very often that cases of this sort turn out so happily" (July 31, 1940).

"Okay, boy, you're in"[60]

Over nine months, Lemkin crossed the Soviet Union on the Trans-Siberian—it is difficult to understand how he was able to do this—reached Japan, then took a ship to Seattle. He was finally in the United States. He remembered his arrival, in April 1941, as if he were in a dream: the American customs agents, rude and punctilious, nevertheless seemed very friendly and welcoming to him. At least, that is how he reconstructed it later, out of his desire to portray himself as an exemplary future American citizen. He hurried to Duke to get to work, accomplish his mission, bring sight to the "blind world." Lemkin, a typical Central European intellectual, planned to fight against barbarism by putting his legal expertise to work to create new laws.[61] "I realized that the real issue at stake in the war was civilization not as a weapon of propaganda or a slogan but as a palpable reality."[62]

2

Karski Discovers the Annihilation of Lemkin's World

1941–42

The Germans are not trying to enslave us as they have other people; we are being systematically murdered. That is the difference. That is what people do not understand. That is what is so difficult to make clear. Over in London, Washington or New York, they undoubtedly believe that the Jews are exaggerating, that they're hysterical. . . . Our entire people will be destroyed. A few may be saved, perhaps, but three million Polish Jews are doomed. As well as others, brought from all over Europe.

—Karski reporting what his guide in the Warsaw ghetto said, summer 1942

"A crime without a name" (Winston Churchill)

After the defeat of France in June 1940, the Polish government in exile moved from Angers to London. In June 1941, the Nazi invasion of the Soviet Union opened a new phase of the war. Many members of the Polish underground state were tortured and murdered, particularly in the horrible Pawiak prison in Warsaw. Large numbers of Poles were deported to the concentration camp in Oswiecim (Auschwitz), including Marian Kozielewski, Jan Karski's brother, who was later released thanks to the intervention of his wife, a German-born Pole.[1] This, however, was no act of mercy. The Oswiecim concentration camp was being used as a site of terror against the Poles, and the few releases were employed mainly as a means of pressuring families.[2] Karski always kept in his archives a book translated into English from a 1943 Polish resistance booklet on the atrocities at Oswiecim, *The Camp of Disappearing Men.*[3] The book's protagonist is a fictional Christian resister,

Jan, who suffers many kinds of mistreatment: he must perform "gymnastics" in bare feet on sharp pebbles and is put to work exhuming the bodies of five hundred Soviet prisoners from a cave where they had just been tortured to death: "Jan discovered the secret of Purgatory and of five hundred dead Russians. He had a corpse by the arm and suddenly he stopped and stared into its face. 'My God!' he screamed. . . . Years ago—in 1917—he had seen that same spectral appearance when he came across a dead soldier in an abandoned trench. It was the mark of poison gas."[4] Jan, who has seen everything, borne everything—even the unbearable—finally throws himself against the electrified fencing. In a remarkable illustration by John Groth, the *Chicago Sun* war correspondent, the barbed wire forms a crown of thorns around his head; like so many Poles, Jan has met the "Golgotha of Oswiecim." There is no mention of Jews in the original Polish-language booklet; the American version contains a final note: "According to information from the Polish underground, up to July 1942 94,000 people were executed in Oswiecim. The death toll rose to 667,161 for the period between September 1942 and August 1943. According to a report by the Very Reverend Paul Vogt, of the Swiss refugee organization the Fluchtlingshilfe, the execution of Jews in Oswiecim amounted to 1,715,000 during the two years ended April 15, 1944, as reported in the *New York Times*, July 6, 1944."[5] The explicit listing of precise numbers of dead at Oswiecim was inversely proportional to the silence regarding the mass extermination still under way at Birkenau, the name of which wasn't even mentioned.

Executions of Polish Jews, and then Russian Jews, started in June 1941; most were shot by mobile killing teams until gas began to be used. In the former case, the murderers traveled to their victims; in the latter, the victims were transported to stationary death facilities. In 1940, Auschwitz had become the seventh concentration camp in the Reich's territory; in 1942, the sixth site for killing Jews was created at Birkenau—after Chelmno, Belzec, Sobibor, Treblinka, and Majdanek, all situated in the zone of the Polish Generalgouvernement.

The Nazis used trucks, then trains, to deport Polish Jews the short and medium distances from the ghettos and work camps to which they had been confined since October 1940; in 1942, the operation was extended throughout occupied Europe. The two forms of murder coexisted. Mobile killing teams operated up to the end of 1944, in parallel with the gas chambers at the largest extermination center, Birkenau, which received its first Jews on March 26–27, 1942, from Poprad, Slovakia, and from the Bourget-Drancy and Compiègne train stations, the origins of the first convoy from France. (My own great-uncle, Pierre Ignace, was in that convoy.)

But we must not let what we can reconstruct with some accuracy, eighty years later, hide the incredible chaos that was experienced in these places, and in the rest of the world, when the Nazis transitioned from active persecution of Jews to their extermination. On August 24, 1941, Winston Churchill, who had met with President Roosevelt on August 14—the United States was not yet in the war—gave an overview of the situation in Europe and Asia in a radio address:

> Since the Mongol invasions . . . there has never been methodical, merciless butchery on such a scale. . . . And this is but the beginning. Famine and pestilence have yet to follow in the bloody ruts of Hitler's tanks. . . . [The aggressor behaves with] the most frightful cruelties. As his armies advance, whole districts are being exterminated. . . . Literally scores of thousands of executions in cold blood are being perpetrated by the German police troops. . . . We are in the presence of a crime without a name.[6]

Did Raphael Lemkin, who had arrived in the United States in April 1941, listen to this address, broadcast around the globe, as he was already devoting himself to giving this crime a name? His relatives and friends in Poland were suffering through confinement in ghettos, forced labor, torture, and, finally, death. Churchill obviously had highly specific information on what Jews in Poland, the Baltic nations, Ukraine, and Belarus were living through, as the British had broken the Enigma Code in July 1941 and read the reports of killings carried out by the Einsatzgruppen. But he did not utter the word "Jew." As a politician and author, he chose his words carefully. He named all of Eastern Europe as the victim of these "frightful cruelties." The terms "execution" and "extermination" did not refer to a particular situation, and all the peoples under occupation were named one by one, except the Jews. In the summer of 1941, the mingling of war crimes and crimes against Jews was complete . . . or being maintained.

Of course, neither Churchill nor the governments in exile in London could have known what the Nazis had not anticipated. Although many Jews were killed as the troops passed, no general, global extermination plan had yet been established. During the winter of 1942, however, the increasingly detailed radio reports and information from couriers, including photographs, left no doubt: Jews were now the target of a massive, unprecedented extermination. While killings by shooting continued in the Soviet Union and in Lithuania and Latvia, which were very quickly rendered *Judenfrei*, the death centers were receiving more and more convoys. Most of the Jews in the Warsaw ghetto were murdered in Treblinka starting in summer 1942. It was at this time that Karski was brought into the ghetto as a resister, before leaving for London.

"A bestial policy of extermination, committed with sang-froid" (December 1942 memorandum addressed to President Roosevelt)

The information arriving in London was piecemeal and incoherent; it was often difficult to decipher, and what was known differed from what was believed or understood. The archives for the summer and fall of 1942, just before and during Karski's stay in London, offer a cruel demonstration of this. Day after day, documents arrived at the Foreign Office from occupied or neutral European countries and from Palestine. This information was cross-checked against that held by the Polish government in exile and by representatives of Polish Jewish organizations and the World Jewish Congress. Gerhart Riegner, a representative of the Congress in Switzerland, warned his counterparts in London in the summer of 1942 that 3.5 million European Jews were to be deported to the east and murdered with prussic acid. It was by this channel that Rabbi Steven Wise, president of the American Jewish Congress, directly received information that he agreed not to make public at the request of Secretary of State Sumner Welles. When Wise met with Karski several months later, he did not hear much that he did not already know.[7]

On December 8, 1942, the Americans—and, most significantly, President Roosevelt—received an extremely detailed nine-page memorandum on the extermination of the Jews, sent by a Polish resistance courier who had recently arrived in London: Karski.[8] By the time Roosevelt met with Karski six months later, in June 1943, he had read his report, along with dozens of others. Information was therefore circulating widely on both sides of the Atlantic. Proof of this is that the *New York Times* published, on the very day it was issued, the declaration regarding the "bestial policy of cold-blooded extermination" of Jews proclaimed jointly in London, Moscow, and Washington on December 17, 1942.[9]

Yet, far from being considered unique in the annals of war cruelties, the extermination of Jews was generally perceived as one atrocity among others. The information accumulated, but very few, including Jews, were capable of appreciating it—whence the despair of those who, through pessimism or lucidity, realized what was happening.

"Warning: Some images may cause distress"

One section in the British National Archives was titled "German Atrocities in Poland." It covered the entire country, and it contained much material. The rapacity had grown since the beginning of 1942: "It is clear that the terror campaign against the Poles in the annexed territories and the Gouvernementgeneral intensified in the period from January to March 1942; there have been more arrests and executions. It seems that the regime in the camp at Oswiecim has become even stricter in recent months. The Poles see this terror with their own eyes and suffer it in their own bodies"[10] No mention of Jews. On the other hand, the Polish point of view prevailed—a first draft of what the Allies would constantly repeat by rote: it was difficult, even impossible, to act at the moment, but once the war was won the German torturers would be punished.

Yet, in spring 1942, some interlocutors brought up the scope of the extermination. For instance, Ignacy Schwarzbart, one of the Jewish representatives (with Shmuel Zygielbojm, of the Bund) to the Polish National Council in London, wrote to the Foreign Office, "Please read this document with the greatest discretion: Statement on German Crimes Committed against the Jewish Population in Poland. These crimes form part of the atrocities committed against the population of Poland as a whole. The numbers speak for themselves."[11]

The specific aspect of the catastrophe of European Judaism lies in the fact that contemporary Germany under Hitler's leadership is aiming at the complete destruction and annihilation of Jewry, its biological destruction. . . . Hitler, the killer, is achieving this aim by converting areas of suffering Poland into mass graves for Jewry. . . . What is not accomplished by famine, disease, or natural death is organized by the murder of Polish Jews and Jews from other countries deported by Hitler to Poland . . . This surpasses the worst examples of barbarism in history. . . . All nations under Hitler's domination are experiencing terrible trials, but the Jewish nation is the greatest victim. We must do everything in our power to keep the population of Poland from being annihilated, especially the Jewish population, which is threatened with complete extermination, now. Only immediate action will keep Hitler from completing his criminal action.[12]

Words, numbers, photographs. Frank Savery, formerly the British consul in Warsaw and the Poland expert at the Foreign Office, complained about the reluctance of the cabinet of the Polish prime minister in exile, Stanislaw Mikolajczyk, to send him photographs that had been brought to England on microfilm by an underground courier in March 1942: "I had to remind him at least four times." Finally, the British had these thirty-eight photographs in their hands. The images were so dreadful that archivists attached a label to the file when they were declassified: "Warning: some images may cause distress."[13] By 1972, archivists and historians were well aware of the traumatic effects of images of the opening of concentration camps, of extermination sites, and of other Nazi and post-Nazi cruelties.

The photographs were in two series: Soviet prisoners of war in "occupied Poland" and "ghetto scenes." The diplomats called them "abominable" or "horrific." One of them wrote in the margin, "We don't want to see them again!" Is this why these pictures weren't distributed at the time? Or was there a more political reason? In the first series, prisoners of war have been killed "during escape attempts"—a body caught in barbed wire, a woman hanged—or "for guerrilla activity." In the second series, bodies of children and adults are seen in ghettos; these piles of skeletal corpses prove that civilians died of hunger or deprivation-induced disease. The diplomats were interested in the prisoners of war and wrote captions, in Polish and English, for these pictures. No explanatory details, however, were added to the ghetto pictures.

"No action seems necessary"
(Foreign Office memorandum, September 1942)

Were the "ghetto scenes" destined to remain hidden from the public? They were not; people in the British services were not the only ones to have seen them or to have read descriptions in the secret diplomatic telegrams and courier debriefings.[14] Representatives of Jewish organizations in London had received the same microfilm strips and published them in leaflets that were sold openly in order to make the public aware of the specific crimes against Jews. They also "illustrated" speeches given during public protests. On July 22, 1942, a first demonstration by Labour supporters was held to protest against the "Nazi atrocities in Poland and Czechoslovakia." It was known that liquidation of the Warsaw ghetto was in the process of being completed and that the trains had begun to roll from occupied Europe to the extermination centers. Shmuel Zygielbojm described things as follows:

> The Germans have chosen Poland for the place of execution of Jews of all the occupied countries, as well as Germany herself. . . . The fate of the remaining Jews in the ghettoes awaiting their doom, is much worse than the fate of those who have already been murdered. As a representative of those masses, I echo their outcry of pain and protest, and their appeal to mankind that means should be found to stop the greatest crime in history![15]

In London, meetings, declarations, and demonstrations succeeded each other throughout 1942. People spoke out constantly to keep the fate of the Jews in public view. For instance, General Władysław Sikorski, chief of the Polish armed forces and prime minister of the Polish government in exile, stated in a radio address, "The Jewish population of Poland is condemned to extermination in compliance with the principle that all Jews must be massacred, whatever the outcome of the war."[16] Nevertheless, in the six pages that he read into the microphone, Sikorski devoted only one short paragraph to the Jews and insisted that the "greatest crime" of the German Reich had been to force Poles to join its army.

Like Churchill and Roosevelt, Sikorski argued that, given that Goebbels and Nazi propaganda claimed that the war had been wanted and fomented by Jews, it would fit with their racist ideology to differentiate the suffering inflicted. As to the figure of seven hundred thousand exterminated, it was deemed highly unreliable. Even the idea that the Warsaw ghetto had been liquidated left diplomats skeptical. They attributed the suicide of the "mayor," Adam Czerniaków, and three other leaders of the Judenrat to their refusal to "see 100,000 Jews deported from the ghetto. . . . As regards the mass killings we have no very precise evidence although it seems likely that they have taken place on a large scale. *No action seems necessary,"* as a highly placed member of the Foreign Office put it.[17] Civil servants in the British government and the Polish government in exile were not the only ones to doubt the reality of the extermination; community leaders in the British Jewish community feared that publication of this information would sow panic among Jews with family in Eastern Europe.[18]

Conversely, the two Jewish members of the Polish National Council of London felt that it was crucial to point out what was happening to their people amid the catastrophes raining down on Europe.[19] In the leaflet *Stop Them Now: German Mass Murder of Jews in Poland*, Zygielbojm repeated the words of Nazi leaders—"Rid the world of the Jewish Pest . . . Exterminate the Jews"—and concluded, "It is evident that the policy of the Germans is to wipe out entirely, not only the Jews in Poland but the Jewish population of the whole of Europe."[20] "It *is* true," he insisted—and he repeated it over and over. Zygielbojm was well informed, but no more so than the authorities in London. Nevertheless, he quickly put words to the facts in the leaflet subtitles—"Mass murder by poison gas," "Gas chambers," "The dead desecrated"[21]—and publicized the testimonials of victims, such as a letter written by a woman to her sister, "one of the many thousands of letters travelling between the ghettoes of Poland": "'My dear, my hands shake so that I cannot write. It is very bad here. Our hours are numbered. God alone knows if we shall ever see one another again. I write and weep and my children are in despair. We want so much to live. We all take leave of you and kiss you. If you do not get another letter from me very soon, we shall be no more.'" Zygielbojm finishes her story: "The woman who wrote this letter and her children have since died. They were killed by poison gas."[22]

As desperate as he was, Zygielbojm wanted to continue to believe in his compatriots laboring in the resistance: "The walls of the ghetto have not really separated the Jewish population from the Poles. The Polish and the Jewish working masses continue to fight together for common aims, just as they have fought for so many years in the past."[23] Was this a fervent wish, an ideological conviction, or prudence on the part of this Bund member isolated in London? His family had remained in the Warsaw ghetto, and he opposed Zionists and other Bundists who did not share his views.

Zygielbojm pleaded stridently with his readers: "Will the world allow it? Will YOU allow it? Means must be found to prevent it. STOP THE GERMANS NOW"![24] Convinced that the disaster would have to be seen to be believed, he published three photographs from the Foreign Office series and captioned them. Under a pile of utterly emaciated bodies: "Not an illustration from Dante's 'Inferno,' but a real photograph of a mass grave of massacred Jews in Central Poland."[25] He may have thought that this was a ditch that the victims had dug together before being shot. In a reframing of the negatives, uniformed gravediggers can be seen, indicating that these were pictures taken, no doubt, in late 1941 or early 1942 at the Warsaw ghetto cemetery. These men, women, and children had died of hunger, deprivation, or ill treatment, as the captions make explicit. "Starvation" is the caption for the photograph of a man wearing a kippah who holds a horrifyingly thin dead child.[26] In a fourth picture, the bodies of four naked children have been tossed on the ground. The gravediggers, members of the Chevra Kadisha, are almost as thin as the people they are leading to their graves. Another picture is captioned "The tally of the dead": in front of the morgue door, a ghetto official fills out papers beside a small cart piled with corpses—human remains of bone and skin.[27] During his trip into the ghetto in the summer of 1942, Karski was stunned to see corpses lying in the streets. "'When a Jew dies,'" his guide told him, "'his family removes his clothing and throws his body in the street. If not, they have to pay the Germans to have the body buried. They have instituted a burial tax which practically no one here can afford. Besides, this saves clothing. Here, every rag counts.'"[28]

If Zygielbojm decided to publish these pictures, it was because he thought that they would allow people to see, and thus to "know," as much as—or even more than—the texts would tell them. Like many well-educated observers, he evoked Dante's imaginary "inferno,"[29] also used, later, by the Italian author Primo Levi. The author Marcel Cohen has remarked, however, that we always forget that Dante's inferno contained the guilty, not the innocent.[30]

Photographic evidence can be found, as we know, in the British National Archives, including the details of the liquidation *Aktion* in the Warsaw ghetto, which began on July 22, 1942. Although some information had arrived earlier, well before the summer, it had not been decrypted. Was this due to political calculation? Military choice? Indifference? Anti-Semitism? Because it was impossible to believe such aberrations? Or for all of these reasons?

Archival photograph sent to the Foreign Office and distributed in Shmuel Zygielbojm's leaflet *Stop Them Now: German Mass Murder of Jews in Poland*, p. 9, with the caption "The Tally of the Dead." In the BNA, photograph FO 371 31097. Kew National Archives.

Nevertheless, on June 26, 1942, Emanuel Ringelblum, the historian confined to the Warsaw ghetto, noted with relief the content broadcast in a BBC program:

> For long months we had been suffering because the world was deaf and dumb to our unparalleled tragedy. We complained about Polish public opinion, about the liaison men in contact with the Polish government-in-exile. Why weren't they reporting to the world the story of the slaughter of Polish Jewry? We accused the Polish liaison men of deliberately keeping our tragedy quiet, so that *their* tragedy might not be thrown into the shade. But now it seems that all our interventions have finally achieved their purpose. There have been regular broadcasts over the English radio the last few weeks, treating of the cruelties perpetrated on the Polish Jews: Belzec and the like. Today there was a broadcast summarizing the situation: 700,000 the number of Jews killed in Poland, was mentioned. At the same time, the broadcast vowed revenge, a final accounting for all these crimes. . . . Now for the first time we understood why they kept silent. London simply didn't know what was happening in detail; hence the silence. But another question [suggests itself]: Having their own radio station, how could the Polish government-in-exile not have known what was happening? Why did they know in London the very next day about 100 persons—political prisoners—executed in the Pawiak Street jail, but months passed before London found out about the hundreds of thousands of murdered Jews? This is a problem that no solution can satisfy.[31]

Ringelblum found it difficult to understand the time lag between the receipt of the information and its dissemination—between knowledge and action. He managed to persuade himself, however, that the message had finally gotten through. He even mentioned the "joy" that people in the ghetto felt when they realized that the world was better informed than they had presumed about the particular tragedy of the Jews within the tragedy of the war.

"For us, it was war and occupation.
For them, it was the end of the world." (Jan Karski)[32]

In his piece for the BBC on December 12, 1942, George Orwell cited part of the memorandum sent two days earlier by the Republic of Poland in Exile to governments at the United Nations:[33]

It is absolutely not propaganda and has been confirmed by various sources, starting with the statements by the Nazi leaders themselves. For example, in March, Himmler, head of the Gestapo, promulgated a decree requiring the "liquidation"—don't forget that in totalitarian language, liquidation is an elegant euphemism for murder—of 50 percent of the Polish Jews who survived the pogroms. . . . Out of slightly more than three million, one third, a million human beings, have been killed in cold blood or have died of hunger and physical misery. Many thousands of them, men, women, and children, were deported to Russia, crammed into cattle cars, without water or food, in which they traveled sometimes for weeks; by the time they reached their destination, half of the occupants of these cars had succumbed. If I mention this persecution of Jews, it is not solely to report atrocity stories; it is because this sort of cold and methodical cruelty, totally different from the violence that goes hand in hand with war, is proof of the true nature of the fascism against which we are fighting.[34]

Orwell acknowledged that "even after three years of war, during which sensibilities have been numbed, this news has provoked horror and deep emotion the world over." His faith was returning, especially because he believed that the Allies were finally ready to take action.[35]

Yet, although the suffering of the Jews was not glossed over, it continued to be generally thought of as confined to the occupation of Poland. This interpretation was perpetuated throughout the duration of the war, including in the French underground press. *Les Cahiers du Témoignage chrétien*, which devoted a full issue to Poland in early 1943, did not omit to mention the situation of the Jews—and in this respect it was unusual—but allotted it just a few lines, which was completely inadequate given the spectacular nature of the information:

Finally, it must be mentioned that the Gouvernementgeneral has become a ghetto in which all the Jews in Poland and Germany have been gathered and to which all Jews from all occupied countries are currently being brought. They are interned in ghettos established in large cities. Anyone who leaves the ghetto is shot. Exhaustion due to labor, hunger, cold, and disease deliver a rich harvest to death. Sometimes the Gestapo enters and conducts massacres. Mass shootings and gas poisonings are on the agenda. . . . *In total, more than seven hundred thousand Jews have been murdered in Poland, and there is no doubt concerning Hitler's plan to completely exterminate the Jews on the continent of Europe.*[36]

Both in official and public circles in England and in some underground press outlets in occupied countries, the specific situation of the Jews was indeed brought up. But what was the author of the piece in *Les Cahiers* thinking when he wrote, "There is no doubt concerning Hitler's plan to completely exterminate the Jews on the continent of Europe"? What did his readers make of this statement? *Completely exterminate*: words that were read, reread, repeated—words that made no sense, as they were senseless.

This was what so troubled the two activists who hoped to meet with Karski in Warsaw before he left for London. They were a Zionist and a Bundist—the same political configuration as that of the two Jewish members of the Polish government in exile, Schwarzbart and Zygielbojm. Karski, resister in the field, was now being asked to serve as eyewitness. His direct account would play the same role as photographs or reports, now so numerous that they had become illegible, incomprehensible. In fact, Leon Feiner, the underground Bundist called upon to guide Karski in the ghetto, had sent a first report on the massacres of Jews throughout Poland to London in May 1942 and a second one in late August. He also used the figure of seven hundred thousand exterminated, stated that at this pace there would soon remain not a single Jew in the country, and advocated for reprisals against German civilians. He wrote, furthermore, that the war had been started by Hitler to exterminate Jews; even if the Germans, in the end, were defeated, the primary goal—the only goal?—would have been achieved: "We are stunned and petrified at the scope of this murder, its massive nature, its cruel and sophisticated methods of killing."[37] Karski noted Feiner's extreme agitation and sense of absolute urgency. They no doubt met on August 31, 1942, just after Feiner sent this second missive.[38]

Feiner and his companion knew that the reports were reaching their addressees, that they would be published and debated but would remain incomprehensible, and so they once again described the senseless: "The Germans are not trying to enslave us as they have other people; we are being systematically murdered. That is the difference. That is what people do not understand. That is what is difficult to make clear. Over in London, Washington, or New York, they undoubtedly believe that the Jews are exaggerating, that they're hysterical. . . . Our entire people will be destroyed. A few may be saved, perhaps, but three million Polish Jews are doomed. As well as others, brought in from all over Europe."[39] Karski was now charged with their mission: "This was the solemn message I carried to the world. They impressed it upon me so that it could not be forgotten. They added to it, for they saw their position with the clarity of despair. At this time, more than 1,850,000 Jews had been murdered."[40] Although the constantly repeated figure of seven hundred thousand was one of the reasons for incredulity in 1942 and 1943, the figure put forward by Karski was much closer to reality—but a reality still not being heard in 1944, when he was writing his memoir.

Why Karski?

Given the information available in London when Karski arrived there in November 1942, why were the Polish Jews there, increasingly feeling abandoned, convinced of his specific importance, and how did the government in exile decide to send him to testify in the United States? The day after he met with Karski, on December 5, 1942, Ignacy Schwarzbart sent a telegram to the World Jewish Congress in New York: "Special envoy gentile . . . arrived here left capital this October saw Warsaw ghetto or last August and September witnessed mass murder of one transport six thousand Jews at Belzec . . . confirm all most horrible mass atrocities still living all remnants of Jews facing death. Brought desperate appeal of this remnant to world Jewry . . . details shortly."[41] Zygielbojm also returned to the subject in a telegram sent to Churchill several days after he spoke with Karski: "Last desperate appeal . . . the entire Jewish population of Poland, women, children, men, is disappearing."[42]

December 1942 was particularly crucial. Karski was far from the only one to testify to this. Abraham Stupp, a Galician who had studied in Lvov—as had Karski and Lemkin—and immigrated to Mandatory Palestine in 1939, sent a telegram from Tel Aviv to the World Jewish Congress on December 4, 1942:

> Some Polish with visas they report deportations started April after Himmlers visit first case Lublin 70000 deported out [of] those 7000 sent camps Majdany [Majdanek, several miles from Lublin] 63000 no trace left presumably murdered stop Krakow in May only 6000 Jews remained others deported unknown

direction presumably murdered Tarnow deported 10000 7000 shot railway station stop Warsaw deportations since 22 June 7000 daily once 20000 stop By October 36000 remained stop Deported carried Treblinka there everey [*sic*] day trainloads Jews arrive they are stripped naked clothes given tailors be cut through search jewellery heaps clothes lie about then Jews taken socalled bathhouse hermetically closed chamber air pumped away people suffocate other reports say Jews killed poison gas.[43]

Other reports arriving from Poland, the Yishuv, Sweden, and Switzerland were full of similar information during the fall and early winter of 1942. But Karski's words touched his interlocutors, at least, and ultimately those who knew already. His meeting with Zygielbojm was an example. All his life, Karski felt a form of guilt over Zygielbojm's suicide a few months later. He remembered it even during the shooting of *Shoah* in 1978, as the rushes show:

KARSKI: I saw in Zigelboim a man—with this kind of man I had no dealings, frankly, very much, either in my underground activities or before the war. . . . Very Jewish. . . . I had before me a proletarian.

CLAUDE LANZMANN: Did he have a Yiddish accent when he spoke Polish? . . . And he looked very Jewish?

K: He looked Jewish. He had rough hands, you know . . . nothing refined about Zigelboim. . . . Nervous. Agitated. . . . Most of the time he was pacing the room. . . . On numerous occasions I would stop. He said [Karski faces the camera and shouts], "Why don't you talk! Talk! You came here to talk!" From the very beginning we didn't start well. . . . He asked me in a rather sarcastic way Mr emissary I was told you want to see me. What do you want?[44]

Karski didn't realize—he had been in London for only a few days— how much information on the extermination had preceded him; at first, Zygielbojm "was not impressed." But when he realized that this non-Jew had actually entered the Warsaw ghetto—to which his own family was confined—and visited what they believed in 1942 was Belzec, Zygielbojm seemed increasingly desperate: "Aggressive, unfriendly . . . something like disintegrating." Karski reconstructed Zygielbojm's words:

к: He says: "So, what can I do! What can I do that I am not doing? I do everything! I do everything possible." So then I also half in anger at that time, I
gave it to him. I closed my eyes. [which Karski also does in this 1978 inter-
view] . . . "Jews are dying. There will be no Jews. What is the use of having
Jewish leaders? Let the Jews go to the most important officers, Allied officers. Let them demand. If they are refused, let them go out. Let them stay
outside. Let them refuse drink. Let them refuse food. Let them die. Let
them die a slow death. Let humanity see it. Perhaps it will move humanity."
And then he jumps [Karski, as Zygielbojm, jumps to his feet and spins in
the room]: "Madness! Madness! They are mad! The whole world is mad!
They do not understand anything! They will not let me die! They will send
two policemen, they will arrest me! They will take me to an asylum! . . .
Everybody is mad! So I have to do something? I don't know what!"

cl: Do you think he was already in complete desperation?

к: He is not mad, he is totally normal. I did not attempt any kind of what
today we call psychiatry. He was a leader, only he was lost in helplessness.[45]

Playing on the contradiction between his modesty and his heroic strength,
Karski was able to maintain his resister's image between 1942 and 1944, particularly by writing his memoir and giving a series of talks across the United
States. But the celebrity that he acquired in the 1980s should create no illu-
sions in retrospect, for his mission had concerned essentially the Polish
underground, not knowledge about extermination of the Jews. Why did his
different missions make him much more than a simple courier?

On the one hand, when he was arrested during one of his missions to
Poland, his courage while being tortured and his spectacular escape made
him a symbol of the resistance. On the other hand, the fact that he was a
practicing Catholic forestalled any suspicion that he had a special interest
in the Jewish cause, even though he was accused of exaggerating, spreading
rumors, or lying by those most determined to ignore the reality of the extermination. It was because he was not Jewish—he also undoubtedly evinced
a certain anti-Semitism that was unremarkable for Poland—that Karski
could speak of the fate of the Jews. But this was also true of other couriers,
such as Jan Nowak. When they went together to Westminster, they were
allotted only ten minutes to talk about the Polish resistance. Elsewhere,
both talked also about the Jews to people such as Anthony Eden.[46]

❡

In London and then in Washington, Karski was at the service above all of the Polish clandestine state, as the title chosen for his memoir, *Story of a Secret State*, makes clear.[47] There were "us," the Poles, and "them," the Jews. However, Karski forcefully explained during a BBC program broadcast in early 1943, during his stay in London, why it was his "duty" (a key word for him) to take an interest in the fate of the Jews.[48]

> I was a member of the Polish Underground Movement. It was my duty to keep in touch with all underground parties, including the "Bund." . . . Among my other duties, I collected matter on the Jewish mass-extermination. . . . I am not a Jew myself, and before the war I had very little contact with Jews; in fact, I knew practically nothing about them. But, at present, the extermination of the Jews has a special significance. The sufferings of my own Polish compatriots are terrible, and they are, of course, nearer to my heart; but the methods employed by the enemy against Poles and against Jews are different. Us, the Poles, they try to reduce to a mediaeval race of serfs. They want to deprive us of our cultural standards, of our traditions, of our education, and reduce us to a state of robots.[49]

Robots. Karski was appealing to history, in this complex dichotomy of Nazi anomie—or, rather, surnomie—between a return to barbarism and sophisticated modernity. Carel Capek coined the word "robot" in Czech in 1924 for his science-fiction play *Rossum's Universal Robots*. The word is derived from *robota*, "forced labor," "work party." Karski used it in this sense when he described the passing of a brigade of forced laborers, haggard with fatigue, in the Warsaw ghetto. Writing this word of Czech origin at a time when the Nazis were doing their best to make Slav cultures disappear was deliberately ironic. He continued, "But the policy towards the Jews is different. It is not a policy of subjugation and oppression, but of cold and systematic extermination. It is the first example in modern history that a whole nation (not 10, 20 or 30, but 100 percent of them) are meant to disappear from this earth." Karski emphasized both the historical continuity of the persecutions and the Nazi rupture: "I know history. I have learned a great deal about the evolution of nations, political systems, social doctrines, methods of conquest, persecution, and extermination, and I know, too, that never in the history of mankind, never anywhere in the realm of human relations did anything occur to compare with what was inflicted on the Jewish population of Poland."[50]

As a witness to the crime, Karski had to pass on what he had seen, but he was also entangled in the contradictory requirements of his sponsors. In late December 1943, knowing that he could no longer return to Poland because he had been too exposed, Karski submitted a report on the Polish underground state to the Ministry of Information in exile, written for the first time under his own resister's name. It would serve as the source for his memoir, published barely a year later, in which the paragraph titles would become chapter titles.[51] Yet, in this text, not a word on the Jews.

However, chapters 29 and 30 of the memoir were about his two "visits" into death zones: the Warsaw ghetto and "The final step" / "To die in agony," Belzec/Izbica. The Catholic resister deemed it necessary to combine in the last two chapters of his 1944 book the disaster experienced by Poles in general and that experienced by Polish and European Jews. In these passages, which represent less than 10 percent of his book, Karski returns to his previous accounts, including those that had been published by some underground newspapers in occupied countries. For instance, in September 1943 the French newspaper *Fraternité* translated from English what he had written in July; here we see the transfer of information from Polish to English, from English to French:

> I must, I think, explain why we were so interested in Jewish questions. I am
> not Jewish, and, before the war, I knew very little about Jews. I was even very
> ignorant about the subject. But at this time, the massacres of Jews are taking on special significance. . . . For them, it is a policy not of oppression and
> enslavement but simply of coldblooded and systematic extermination. It is
> the first time, in modern history, that an entire people . . . has been condemned in this way to disappear completely from the face of Earth.[52]

In 1942, depending on those he met with, Karski separated his accounts on the Poles and the Jews. In 1944, he added "Jewish" chapters to his final account, forming a sort of coda. Also in 1944, the *Polish Review* devoted much more space to the fate of Polish Jews. But, in 1944, there was no longer anyone to save. This was not the case in 1942, when Karski was preparing for his mission.

"The methods of this process are known to a certain extent, but the details are not"

Karski had seen. He gave details: "The method is, as you know, to collect the Jews from all over Europe, to dispatch them to the Ghettos of Warsaw, Lwev and Soon, where they stay for a certain time. From the ghettos they are 'taken East' as the official term goes, that is, to the extermination camps, of Belzec, Treblinka and Sobibor. In these camps they are killed in batches of 1,000 to 6,000, by various methods, including gas, burning by steam, mass electrocution, and finally, by the method of the so-called 'death train.'"[53] None of this information was new in London in fall 1942. It was also known that adjacent to the Oswiecim–Auschwitz concentration camp the Nazis had erected gas chambers at Birkenau to murder Jews swept up from throughout Europe. Those who were deported from France, Belgium, Slovakia, and Holland no longer transited through ghettos and work camps in the east. Starting in summer 1941, German and Czech Jews were deported to Riga, Krakow, Lublin, and smaller "transit" centers such as Izbica, from which they were deported again, to the first extermination sites.

The first stationary killing center, in Belzec, was designed and run by technical, medical, and police personnel, who had killed those who were supposedly mentally or physically handicapped and other "asocial" people in hospitals transformed into execution centers in Germany during *Aktion* T4. The code name came from the address of the Berlin headquarters for "euthanasia" operations, Tiergartenstrasse 4. It was ironic that this street was named after a zoo, as the Nazis were killing those whom they had condemned as bestial and monstrous.[54] Lorenz Hackenholt, driver and gravedigger at T4, played a major role in construction of the gas chamber at Belzec, under the leadership of Dr. Christian Wirth, one of the initiators of the T4 program. Wirth was made manager of Belzec, then inspector of the three main Reinhard *Aktion* killing centers, Reinhard Heydrich having been the supervisor of killings by the Einsatzgruppen since summer 1941.

Although most Jews were killed by blows or bullets, subjected to starvation and torture, or burned alive, some were temporarily kept alive for forced labor. Near the extermination centers, the inhabitants of small towns such as Volkovysk mingled with those who arrived by train from the huge ghettos in Poland, Lublin and Warsaw, and from Germany and Czechoslovakia.

Indeed, European Jews received differentiated "treatment." To the east, in occupied Poland and the occupied Soviet Union, the Nazis and their auxiliaries practiced cruelty over the long term: extermination by bullets or poison gas was preceded by weeks, months, or even years of confinement to ghettos, persecution, robberies, rapes, manhunts, arrests, forced labor, famine, torture, and the murder of sons and daughters, parents, spouses, cousins. Jews from Western Europe and, later, Hungary were destined for factory-style murder and killed much more quickly; from the roundup to the transit camp and the gas chamber took only a few days or weeks.

How Were the Jews of Volkovysk, Lemkin's Shtetl, Exterminated?

When Karski went to eastern Poland upon the request of two Jews he met in the Warsaw ghetto, he "saw" the destruction of Lemkin's family and the world of his youth. The "I" of the witness crossed paths with the "I" of the victim, now confronted with the death of his people—Jews killed because they were Jews. Indeed, Lemkin discovered, from the United States, the reality behind the concept that he had been trying to put forward since the 1920s:

> When I first conceived the idea of a law to make genocide illegal, how could I have imagined that I would be directly affected? During the war, forty-nine members of my family died in the genocide, including my parents. Suddenly I felt that the earth was crumbling before me, that the meaning of life was disappearing. . . . I decided to find strength in this law, to alleviate my sorrow by doing this work.[55]

It is very likely that Lemkin had read *The Volkovysk Memorial Book*, published in New York in Yiddish in 1949.[56] By adding the archives of the International Tracing Service and a few accounts by survivors, we can reconstruct the steps from the persecution to the extermination of the Jews of Volkovysk, his people.

Volkovysk had a population of seven thousand Jews out of a total of seventeen thousand in 1939. After the Soviet occupation started, about three thousand flowed in from the Nazi-occupied zone. The town was retaken by the Wehrmacht on June 28, 1941, six days after German troops entered Soviet-occupied Poland. Now, a descent into death began, in terror and abominable physical and mental suffering.

Ten thousand Jews were no doubt living in Volkovysk at the time, minus the approximately fifteen hundred killed in the Luftwaffe bombings during preceding days. They had to wear a yellow star on the front and back of their clothing, and their houses—or what remained of them—were marked with a yellow circle; they were forbidden to walk on the sidewalks and had to raise their hats when a German passed by; these were ordinary humiliations. Above all, the soldiers stole and killed. Then the members of the Einsatzkommando 8, seconded to Einsatzgruppe B, came to execute Jews who had been denounced by Polish informers for collaboration with the communists.

A cascade of guilty verdicts would attribute responsibility for these initiatives during postwar trials. Otto Bradfisch, leader of Einsatzkommando 8, testified in detail on the operations against "Communist subversion and looting" in the Bialystok region. Arthur Nebe, leader of Einsatzgruppe B, had not given the specific order to "annihilate the Jewish population of a town or area solely on the grounds of their racial identity," but in reality "every Jew was to be seen as a danger to combat troops and therefore liquidated."[57] In his turn, Nebe took shelter behind his hierarchy: he claimed that Himmler, visiting Bialystok on July 8, 1941, told him that "as a matter of principle any Jew was to be regarded as a partisan."[58] Nebe apparently interpreted his orders as "In some places and districts all Jews were to be exterminated irrespective of age or sex."[59] Battalion 322 of Einsatzgruppe B performed a "demonstration exercise" for Himmler that consisted of searching for partisans with the Wermacht, the police, and the Sicherheitsdienst (the information service of the SS) in attendance.[60] The partisans caught and killed were exclusively Jews, including women and children. After this conclusive exercise, all Jews "encountered" were killed, which explains the triumphant statistics of Einsatzkommando 8. From Himmler to Nebe, senior officials attended all of these *Aktionen*. In most cases, the massacres began with men; the extermination of women and children intensified only in September. Einsatzkommando 8, however, had anticipated Himmler's instructions: to empty the area of Jews. Volkovysk was situated in the unit's murderous path. At the same time, other SS units liquidated handicapped people in compliance with the T4 program; one of them was Hannah, a blind Jewish child in the village.

As chief of the Reich's criminal police, the Kripo, Nebe was involved with the T4 program and then became head of its Institute for Criminal Biology. The Reich's central security office did not take "biological" prevention and repression principles lightly. Nebe was very familiar with one of the techniques used since summer 1941 to kill mentally ill Poles in this region: gas canisters placed in trucks. Why not further simplify the procedure: route the exhaust pipe into the truck to make it into a transportable gas chamber? By early December, such trucks were in operation in the Soviet zone, and they were in Chelmno on December 8.

Although he did not know all of these details, Karski reported to his interlocutors in London on the scope of these killings and Himmler's role in the process. This information was reproduced in the note by the Polish government in exile on December 10, 1942, and in the joint declaration of the seventeenth.

In Volkovysk, the bombardments of June 1941 had been so violent that it was difficult to form a real ghetto in the ruins. In one photograph, a column of Jewish forced laborers crosses the village accompanied by guards—an armed Ukrainian (perhaps) and a member of the Judenrat recognizable by his armband—as non-Jewish people seem to go about their daily business, without glancing. Starting in spring 1942, hundreds of men and women were compelled to work for the municipal administration and the German Red Cross, erecting a rest center for the soldiers. The village, like Bialystok, the nearby large town, was within the borders of the Reich.

Some, such as "Lemkin's son, the blacksmith" (Raphael's cousin), joined the Soviet partisans. Doctors and radio technicians were tortured, then executed, for this, along with several hundred hostages. As usual, they were forced to dig their "trench grave," which was subsequently covered with earth and replanted so that the mass execution site would be hidden. According to one survivor, when they left the area, "the forced gravediggers suddenly saw the ground rise. They had to hit the ground until everything was still."[61]

Grueling labor, lack of food—much of it was rotten—and drinking water, heat or cold, and disease killed dozens, or even hundreds, of people. The living took possession of the clothing of the dead; some went mad beside the corpses of their loved ones. The guards sometimes shot randomly into crowds; bodies piled up, decomposing, or were carried to common trenches and thrown into them like animal carcasses.

The first "ghetto" liquidation *Aktion* took place on November 2, 1942. It was similar to the one that had taken place on October 5 in Dubno, the hometown of the Orthodox baker whom Lemkin had met on his exodus across Poland in fall 1939:

> The people who had got off the trucks, men, women, and children of all ages, had to undress upon the orders of an SS man, who carried a riding or dog whip. . . . Without screaming or crying, these people undressed, stood around by families, kissed each other, said farewells, and waited for the command of another SS man who stood near the excavation also with a whip in his hand. . . . At that moment the SS man at the excavation called something to his comrade. The latter counted off twenty persons, and instructed them to walk behind the earth mound. . . . I walked around the mound and stood in front of a tremendous grave; closely pressed together, the people were lying on top of each other so that only their heads were visible. The excavation was already two-thirds full; I estimated that it contained about a thousand people. . . . Now already the next group approached, descended into the excavation, lined themselves up against the previous victims and were shot.[62]

There were many Jews in Volkovysk, and the *Aktion* lasted a long time. The Nazis and their Polish and Ukrainian auxiliaries took sadistic pleasure in their unlimited power over life and death. They promised work farther east, saving a life—for two hours, or three days—for a fortune: a piece of moldy bread. Fathers were killed in front of their sons; children were torn from their mothers, who were executed in front of them. Lemkin's cousin was taken and killed as his parents watched.

The guards were insatiably corrupt. Indeed, one might wonder, given the general state of the town in 1942, what else could be found to offer in exchange for a life. On the slightest pretext, human beings were tortured, as Goldberg relates: "The Germans were beating Mr. Galin fiercefully, vehemently and without any mercy. . . . Then we heard two gunshots and the Germans left. We came out and found the body of Mr. Galin. He could not be recognized. It was a mass of bloody, contused and crushed meat. It was a terrible scene. It made a very depressing impression, even on us, who were accustomed to Nazi cruelty."[63]

From Einsatzkommando 8 to Treblinka

Now, the Jews of Volkovysk were confined and kept under guard, along with all those gathered from the region, including Bialystok. Volkovysk became the camp for this area, and no doubt twenty thousand people transited through the town on their way to the gas chambers at Treblinka. Vassili Grossman, war correspondent, gave an account of the arrival of Soviet troops in Treblinka:

> As a final way of tricking the people arriving from Europe, the bay platform itself at the death camp was made to look like a passenger station. At the platform, where the next twenty cars in line were being unloaded, they had erected a railway building with ticket offices, luggage storage, a restaurant with a dining area, and signs all over the place with arrows: "Board for Bialystok," "To Baranovichi," "Board for Wolkowysk," and so on. . . . There was something threatening and terrifying about this square, trampled on and leveled by millions of human feet. People's sharpened gazes quickly grasped the threatening details—on the ground, hastily swept probably just a few minutes before, discarded objects could be seen: a bundle of clothes, opened suitcases, shaving brushes, enamel pots. How did these items get there? And why did the railroad end immediately after the station platform, and beyond it there was only yellow grass and a three-meter fence? Where were the tracks to Bialystok, Siedlce, Warsaw, Wolkowysk?[64]

In the bunkers in Volkovysk, which had served as stalls for Polish army horses until 1939, several thousand people awaited transport toward what they were told were labor camps, but now, in late 1942, everybody knew better. Families were separated, with nothing or little to eat, in the cold, with the stenches and the diseases, including a violent typhus epidemic as well as tuberculosis, typhoid fever, and skin rashes:

> People walked around like shadows. They stopped talking to each other. What was the use? They died like flies. Every morning the ground in front of

the clinic was piled with dead people. Their bodies lying one near the other. Their faces seemed to be directed toward the skies and asking the eternal question, "Why, what did we do, to deserve such a miserable death." No answer! Quiet all around.[65]

The Judenrat was supposed to prepare lists for the "labor camps to the east." No one was fooled; everyone now knew how the story would end. Some preferred to die right away: mothers committed suicide, taking their children with them. Others were willing to do anything not to appear on the lists. Still others tried to flee: "If we're going to die, we'll die together." In the end, the lists were unnecessary: most of the Jews in Volkovysk were transported to Treblinka, where they were killed, between late November and December 1942.

Grossman continued his account:

The process of murdering in the chambers took from ten to twenty-five minutes. Initially, when the new chambers had just been put into operation and the executioners hadn't immediately figured out the gas supply and were conducting experiments to determine the dosage of various killing agents, the victims were subjected to terrible torments, taking two to three hours to die. In the first few days, the delivery and exhaust systems worked poorly, so the torments of the victims were prolonged, lasting for nine to ten hours. . . .

Residents of the village closest to Treblinka, Wólka, tell how sometimes the cries of the women being murdered were so awful that all the villagers, going out of their minds, ran into the distant forest just to get away from those earsplitting cries, cries that drill through logs, sky, and earth. Then the cries would suddenly stop, only to start up again later just as suddenly, the same awful, earsplitting cries, drilling through bones, skulls, souls. . . . This happened three or four times a day.

I asked S., one of the captured executioners, about these cries. He explained that the women cried out when the dogs were unleashed and the whole crowd of the condemned was herded into the house of death: "They saw death. Moreover, it was very crowded in there, and the *Wachmänner* beat them savagely, the dogs ripped at them."

The sudden silence descended when the gas chamber doors were closed. The cries of the women started up again when a new group was brought to the gas chamber. This happened two, three, four, sometimes even five times a day. The Treblinka slaughterhouse was no ordinary executioner's block. It was a conveyor belt of execution, organized in the flow method, borrowed from modern, large-scale industrial production.[66]

Were Lemkin's parents, Joseph and Bella, killed at Treblinka? As they were elderly, they may have been murdered by gas right in Volkovysk. The Nazis squeezed the last eighty ill and elderly people into an airtight cellar and pumped in sulfur dioxide. "The cellar was opened two days later and the bodies were found in all sorts of positions, distorted, the slow agony inscribed on the faces. The eyes of the dead were wide open, staring."[67]

The healthiest, who were still able to hide or to pay guards to escape Treblinka, were caught and sent to Birkenau; in both cases, they died in the gas chambers.

The hellish fire, extending its tongues like open arms, snatches the body. . . . The hair is the first to catch fire. The skin, immersed in flames, catches in a few seconds. Now the arms and legs begin to rise—expanding blood vessels cause this movement of the limbs. The entire body is now burning fiercely; the skin has been consumed and fat drips and hisses in the flames. One can no longer make out a corpse—only a room filled with hellish fire that holds something in its midst. The belly goes. Bowels and entrails are quickly consumed, and within minutes there is no trace of them. The head takes the longest to burn; two little blue flames flicker from the eyeholes—these are the eyes burning with the brain, while from the mouth the tongue also continues to burn. The entire process lasts twenty minutes—and a human being, a world, has been turned to ashes.[68]

In January 1943, Volkovysk and environs were finally declared "free of Jews," and neighboring regions also profited into the bargain. Karski had noted this in his 1939 report; Poles' hatred of Jews, particularly in the Soviet zone, did not escape survivors, who spoke of "pogromchiks," "organized anti-Semites,"[69] "Polish, Russian, or Ukrainian collaborators," denouncers of Jews, and partisans who "jeered" or "sneered" as they watched the forced marches of groups of deportees. During the winter of 1943, after the killings and the deportations to Treblinka and then Birkenau had come to an end, "the best items were sent to Germany for the 'German War Fund,' and the rest was sold to the local Polish population, which had long awaited the chance to do such good business."[70]

As of May 1945, seventy Jews in Volkovysk had survived six years of terror, committed mostly by Nazis but also, for those who had been sent to the gulag, by communists. Others, conversely—like Elias Lemkin, Raphael's brother—owed their survival to having gone over to the Soviet side while there was still time. What Raphael Lemkin discovered only between 1945 and 1949, Jan Karski, the non-Jew, had seen in 1942.

"The Spectacle of a People Dying": Karski in Warsaw and Izbica

"The cemetery is in Belzec in the exact same way as in Chelmno. . . . Chilling here is the same as in Chelmno. Our turn is approaching! . . . [It is] chilling the villages I mentioned in my letter."[71] In the winter of 1942, the historian of the Warsaw ghetto Emanuel Ringelblum was receiving letters like this, situating the Belzec extermination center near Zamosc and giving coded reports on the killings. He published these accounts of poisoning by carbon monoxide in Chelmno and by gas at Treblinka and Belzec in his underground archives, the Oyneg Shabes. This information, written in Yiddish, was also sent to all the underground Jewish and Polish broadsheets and reached the Polish government in exile in London.[72] In June 1942, the first real-time synthesis of the plan for total extermination of the Jews was published. "With the German attack on the Soviet Union a new, most horrible link has been added to the chain of unending Jewish suffering—Ausrottung, the physical extermination of the Jews, whom the Germans hold responsible for the outbreak of a war whose intensity has dwarfed all previous conflicts."[73] In the field, the different strata of murders could be easily grasped—the massacres by bullets in summer 1941, by gas in the fall—as the carnage by the killing squads continued. The liquidation of the Warsaw ghetto began in July 1942. This is where Karski's account begins.

To cover his tracks and protect himself and his informants, Karski said that he went to the Warsaw ghetto and to Belzec in July or September 1942. His account does not inform us of the number of daily killings. When he arrived in London, on November 25, 1942, it was more the way in which he reported the information than the information itself that would strike those who really wanted to hear him.

Karski had been able to observe the fate reserved for Jews in the Warsaw ghetto and in what he believed was Belzec. This location was in fact the transit station in Izbica-Lubelska, situated on the Lublin–Lvov railroad axis, near Zamosc, some fifty miles from Belzec. Izbica was the site of the final spoliation, where the fiction of deportation to a labor camp came to an end. Karski called it "some sort of transitional camp."[74] When there was congestion in Belzec, the trains were held at a stop until there was room in the gas chambers. In these few hours or days, the torture and killing took place in other ways.

In 1940, Karski had traveled with Jews passing through the Soviet occupation zone. He had left them on the way to accomplish his first resister's mission. After he saw the Warsaw ghetto and Izbica, his accounts differed radically from his 1940 report, that of a patriotic Catholic law student, little affected by the persecution and dispossession suffered by the Jewish minority. Now, he internalized the dehumanization that he beheld, as his ghetto guides had foreseen—and hoped: "They warned me that if I accepted their offer I would have to risk my life to carry it out. They told me, too, that as long as I lived I would be haunted by the memory of the ghastly scenes I would witness."[75]

Karski remained in the ghetto for only a few hours, however, and in Izbica for one day. In both cases, he disguised himself to pass unnoticed. In Warsaw, he was a Jew wearing a yellow star; in Izbica, he was a guard, in Latvian or Estonian uniform depending on the report version, but in reality he was dressed as a Ukrainian. And so, he passed as a victim in Warsaw, as an executioner in Izbica. The witness camouflaged himself to uncover the most extraordinary camouflage in history. In his accounts of late 1942, published in London and New York in 1943, and in his 1944 memoir, he wrote that the change in appearance gradually began to affect the witness's soul. He was no longer content with looking but began to engage more physically, with his senses.

Thus, Karski was adopting the strategy of his two Jewish guides who came and went under different identities and accoutrements on either side of the ghetto wall like performers in a laborious "farce." Their Judaism was literally stuck to their skin; their "Jewish features [were] difficult to . . . disguise."[76] And the moral spy serving the Polish cause, who was he?

"To pass that wall was to enter into a new world utterly unlike anything that had ever been imagined"

"Is it still necessary to describe the Warsaw ghetto? . . . There have been so many accounts by unimpeachable witnesses."[77] In his memoir, Karski minimized his personal testimony. Indeed, in 1944, one year after the revolt in the ghetto was quashed and the ghetto itself was destroyed, what he had seen in 1942 no longer existed. Nevertheless, he chose the chapter "My Visit to the Warsaw Ghetto" to be published in the magazine *The American Mercury* as he was correcting the proofs of his book.[78] This was the first time that he allowed his underground name to appear, and it would be his from then on.

In the Warsaw ghetto, Jan Kozielewski became Jan Karski. There, he discovered the annihilation of the Jewish people, the entire Jewish people. The first sign was those who were absent: old people, the first to die of deprivation and disease, the first to be transported to Treblinka to be gassed, had disappeared from the streets. As for the emaciated children, they were "play[ing] before they die[d]." The absent elderly, the children pretending to be children: "A cemetery? No, for these bodies were still moving. . . . They were still living people, if you could call them such. For apart from their skin, eyes and voice, there was nothing human left in these palpitating figures. Everywhere there was hunger, misery, the atrocious stench of decomposing bodies, the pitiful moans of dying children. . . . To pass that wall was to enter into a new world utterly unlike anything that had ever been imagined."[79] Karski described "shadows of what had once been men or women," a world in which the living were the dead, like animals with "their eyes blazing with some insane hunger or greed." Animals could be hunted, and that was the game played by two teenagers in Hitler Youth uniforms, who shot at human targets as if they were competing in a "sporting event."

When he arrived in Washington, DC, in the spring of 1943, Karski, as "Mr. B.,"[80] gave a long interview to the journalist George Creel, who published an extensive version in two articles in *Collier's Weekly* that fall:

Do you know why we are so desperately resolved to protect and train our youth, putting it against every other underground activity? It is because we see what evil teaching has done to young Nazis. . . . Thousands of German boys are schooled in Poland, barracked like soldiers. Believe me, sir, when I tell you that they are more cruel, more savage, than their elders. Governor General Frank has granted them the right to carry revolvers and rifles, and after school hours, it is their favorite sport to go into a ghetto and hunt the Jews as though they were rabbits in a warren. With my own eyes I have seen them shoot women down, and with my own ears I have heard them yell, "No, no, Hans, that one is mine. You had the last one."[81]

The "hunting" episode, featured in all of Karski's accounts from 1942 to 1945, was positioned as part of an exaltation of the Polish resistance, which educated its young people to protect them against "debauchery and defilement": "In every possible way, the Nazis try to deprave our youth. . . . A large percentage of the Germans in Poland are homosexuals. . . . In the cities, Black Shirts are under orders to abuse our boys, and the guards in concentration camps and labor camps, recruited from the slums of the Reich, practice perversions in every form on their young prisoners."[82] When, in early 1943, *Les Cahiers du Témoignage chrétien* devoted an issue to detailed descriptions of the tragedies of Catholic Poland, moral perversion was also emphasized: the "satanic depravity" of a population in which "alcohol and pornography flow freely."[83]

Karski expressed himself differently according to his perceived audience. Detailed accounts of cruelties against the Jews had to demonstrate the Nazis' sadism and justify the targeted killings by the Polish resistance—viewed very poorly in the United Kingdom and the United States. Karski glorified the Poles' moral, intellectual, and spiritual resistance with an ecumenism that included Protestants, an infinitesimal minority in Poland but not in the United States: "A whole people—Catholics, Protestants and Jews—have had a deepening of devotion. . . . I say this from my own experience." Naturally, he spoke at greater length about attacks against the Catholic religion. In Wilno archdiocese, hundreds of priests were being "murdered and imprisoned, and at Oswiecim, gray-haired prelates are cleaning latrines with their hands. . . . The revered head of the Polish Protestant Church, eighty-year-old Doctor Julius Bursch, was sent to the hellhole of Dachau, where the Gestapo beat the life out of his frail body." When it came to the Jews, he spoke only of material destruction: "Of all the stately synagogues, none remains for Jewish worship. Such as have not been burned are now stables and storehouses."[84]

Karski did not speculate who in Poland had availed themselves of these new stables for their animals, confining himself to demonstrating that the Nazi "swine" wanted to destroy all Poles: "It is spiritual resistance that calls for all of our courage—the desperate, unending fight to keep from being beaten down to animalism by systematic degradations. It is the soul of Poland that the Nazis mean to destroy [by reducing us to] hewers of wood and drawers of water for the Master Race."[85]

Karski tried to educate his American interlocutors—whom he sometimes viewed as almost childlike—by portraying the resistance "as a ruthlessly efficient organization, a combination of the F.B.I. and the Canadian Mounted." He did not hesitate to vaunt the Polish ingeniousness, comparing Poles to "Himmler and his thugs . . . a very stupid lot. . . . I doubt if your Mr. J. Edgar Hoover would give one of them a job." He further described them as "degenerate gangsters, a pack of wild beasts without even animal cunning."[86] Stupid, perhaps, but well trained for their tasks of torture: "There is nothing amateurish about the Gestapo. Everyone is a specialist in cruelty. When Heinrich Himmler came to Poland, one of his first acts was to set up a school in Poznan where men were trained in the art of torture just as you would train a mechanic. . . . Forcing lighted splinters under fingernails were little more than kindergarten lessons, for they went far beyond your Indians in fiendish ingenuity."[87]

The "Train of Death": Izbica

In late summer 1942, Karski's ghetto guides sent him to what he believed— or, at least, what he said—was Belzec. The first gassings took place there on March 17, 1942, in wooden barracks; production-line efficiency was achieved when six concrete gas chambers were built to exterminate 1,500 people at a time.[88] Between March and December 1942, 434,508 Jews—and more souls, with the Roma and Sinti—were killed there during Operation Reinhard. In reality, Karski had arrived in Izbica. This was where he passed into the world of an annihilated people; his descriptions became more detailed, as if the sensations he had had then were returning to haunt him.

In his early published accounts, Karski tried to distance himself by not giving his own name: "eyewitness" for the BBC; Mr. X, Mr. B, or "a Pole" for *Collier's Weekly*. It was not Jan Karski—even less Jan Kozielewski—who had seen these things but an anonymous person. This was because the prison-guard disguise that he used to enter the area surrounded by barbed wire and wooden palisades—in this case it cannot be called a camp—was a subterfuge that could not have happened had the resistance not paid a huge sum to obtain this favor, equivalent to what the corrupt guards stole from the Jews while claiming to save their lives before demanding even more money—or flesh in the form of rape—before finally leading them to their deaths.

Karski's conversation with a guard offered him a direct perspective on collaboration in the extermination enterprise by Ukrainians, Estonians, Lithuanians, Latvians, Belarusians, and Poles, of German origin or not:[89]

> "If he is willing to fork out plenty of hard cash, in advance, then I do what I can."
>
> "Have you saved many Jews so far?"
>
> "Not as many as I'd like, but a few, anyhow."
>
> "Are there many more good men like you there who are so willing to save the Jews?"
>
> "Save them? Say, who wants to save them? . . . But if they pay that's a different story." . . .
>
> I looked at his heavy, rather good-natured face and wondered how the war had come to develop such cruel habits in him. . . . Under the pressure of the Gestapo and the cajoleries of the Nazis, with everyone about him engaged in a greedy competition that knew no limits, he had been changed into a professional butcher of human beings. He had caught on to his trade and discussed its origins, used its professional jargon as coolly as a carpenter discussing his craft.[90]

Karski, though, was consumed by remorse: "I was in fact one of the enforcers. I believe that my action was justified. I could do nothing to stop what was happening, but by becoming a witness, I could give a firsthand report to the civilized world." The messenger had worn the uniform of barbarism; he did not give his name in order to respect the resistance and to hide what was unnamable in him.

Only the barbarian was named. The process of extermination was described through accusations against Friedrich-Wilhelm Krüger, charged by Odilo Globocnik's headquarters in Lublin with destruction of the Warsaw ghetto and the gassing operations in Belzec. This executioner's name was repeated a number of times by he who had no name: "It was Krueger who raised the number of concentration camps in his district from 22 to 41, and who started the practice of putting barefooted men, women and children into boxcars spread inches thick with wet quicklime. It was Krueger who set fire to synagogues after crowding them with Jews and who first conceived the idea of pumping poison gas into halls where human beings were packed like cattle."[91] A drawing portraying what Karski believed to be one of the highlights of the resistance illustrates the article: a successful attack by Poles disguised as Germans against the Nazi officer's car.[92]

The misnaming of Izbica was not Karski's only error—or omission. He traveled at night and arrived at a place that he was told was Belzec, and why wouldn't he believe it? Yet, he had been there previously, in December 1939, and had witnessed mistreatment of Jews on that visit. Because, at the time, the town of Belzec was on the border between the Soviet and German zones, the Nazis sent prisoners, mainly "Jewish families who illegally wanted to cross over to the Bolsheviks," there to dig antitank ditches on the line of demarcation and to build, first, a labor camp, then the facilities for the killing center. Karski's first report was very precise:

> Near Belzec . . . the Germans have created a camp of Jews. . . . An enormous proportion walked and slept under the open sky. Very many people [were] without proper clothing or other covering. While one group slept, the other waited its turn, so that outer garments could be lent one another. Those who waited jumped and ran around so as not to freeze. A few hundred people, among them children, women, and old people, run around for hours or jump in place, for if they stand still, they will freeze. After a few hours [the groups] change places. . . . All are frozen, in despair, unable to think, hungry. [They are] a herd of harassed beasts—not people. I watched this for a whole hour, riveted to my spot, frightened, confused. A nightmare—not real. Blue and red freaks—not people. I shall never forget it. Never in my life have I beheld anything more frightening. . . . The "Master Race" is really a nation of madmen, of brutal haters and heartless beings.[93]

The ice used for slow killing brings to mind a 1941 photograph with the legend "Execution of a Jew in an ice hole in the Belzec concentration camp."[94] The man had been thrown, alive, into a hole carved into the ice and had died of cold; in the picture he seems to be still alive, his bearded head fallen forward as if he was praying; his protruding ribs show his state of malnutrition before the final torture.

Why did Karski persist in saying that he had seen Belzec in 1942, when he had been taken to Izbica, and not talk about his actual visit to Belzec in 1939? Why did he never make the connection between the two times that he said he "would never forget," that would haunt him "as long as he lived": deaths by cold, by fire, and by gas (which he had not seen but reported on in his accounts) and the quicklime in the train, which became, once he arrived in London, his piece of "purple prose"? Indeed, it was because of what he termed "the death train" that Karski was an eyewitness to the German policy of extermination of the Jews.

"The camp is situated fifteen kilometers south of the town of Belzec," Karski wrote. "It is surrounded by a fence that runs along a train track about ten meters away. A narrow passageway, less than one meter wide, leads from the camp entrance to the train tracks. This passage is formed by two wooden fences."[95] Arriving in his guard's uniform, Karski discovered in a fairly small space, similar to a storage locker, a mass of people swept up during the *Aktionen* in the ghettos, left outside for three or four days, stripped of everything, with no food or water, not knowing if their relatives were already dead, gone mad with suffering and pain.[96]

The trains leaving Izbica, the planned gateway toward death, were headed for Belzec and its gas chambers. Karski, however, had seen another method devised to ease the crowding in the gas chambers. The trains were bringing too many bodies to kill, and the death machine was grinding to a halt; the prisoners had to be gotten rid of in another way, while training the guards in sadism. Samuel Golfard, who knew that his sister, taken before his eyes in the Przemyslany ghetto, had probably been killed in Belzec, hypothesized that electrocution was used—something Karski also spoke of: "We have been told that people are being put to death there on a suspension bridge charged with electricity, and then the victims are thrown into the abyss."[97] The unthinkable, even for those who saw it with their own eyes, had to follow a human logic: the trains, the electricity, and the suspension bridge belonged to a known form of industrialization, whereas these gas chambers were invented only to kill human beings.[98] And if it was impossible to imagine how they worked, it was because the technology used exclusively for death was no doubt unspeakable. The Polish underground newspaper *WRN*, translated in New York, stated, "The last Jews in Warsaw were systematically annihilated at Majdanek by suffocating gas cameras operated three times a week. As the crematorium is out of order, the bodies of murdered Jews are burned in huge piles."[99] The cameras took pictures of what could not—or should not—be seen; it was therefore said that they were used directly to kill.

The industrial and technical details of cruelty could not sanitize the suffering undergone by the victims: the smells, the screams. Karski placed himself at the heart of the *Hrbn*—the destruction, as Jews in the east said in their language, Yiddish; he offered his eyes and photographic memory as a means of transmission. For it was in fact in Izbica, through his sensory descriptions, that he most accurately conveyed the extermination of the Jews: "The air was full of stenches, odors, excrement, filth, and putrefaction. . . . We were forced to walk on the piled bodies. . . . Each time I walked on a body I was seized by nausea and stopped short, but my guide pressed me forward." The time came to "load" the boxcars headed for the fake labor camp; most knew that death awaited them. The only question was how:

> Around ten in the morning, a freight train stopped. . . . At the same time, the guards at the other end began to shoot into the air and ordered the Jews to get on the train. This way, they created panic among the prisoners to prevent any hesitation or resistance on their part. The Jews, pushed toward the narrow passageway that I have spoken of, rushed, shoving each other, into the first boxcar stopped at the end of the passageway. It was an ordinary car, the kind that indicate "6 horses or 36 men." . . . Three hundred people were pushed or thrown into this first car; I counted them myself. The doors were then closed and locked. The train pulled ahead a bit. The following car was then in place and the scene was repeated. I counted a total of fifty-one cars, into which were squeezed the six thousand prisoners in the camp. Only some thirty of them fell under the guards' bullets during the stampede into the train. Once the camp was empty and the cars full, the train began to move. I heard the end of the story from one of my so-called comrades, the camp's executioners who had been doing this work for several months, sending one or two trains a week.[100]

The Germans had simply issued orders to the effect that 120 to 130 Jews had to enter each car. . . . Alternately swinging and firing with their rifles, the policemen were forcing still more people into the two cars which were already overfull. . . . These unfortunates, crazed by what they had been through . . . then began to climb on the heads and shoulders of those in the trains. . . . [101] The bones cracked and the screams became insane. . . . It seemed impossible to squeeze more people into the boxcar, and yet at that moment the guards, helped by certain prisoners made half-mad with fear due to the gunfire behind them, began to throw people in. Thirty more were thus heaved onto the heads of those inside. Some women's necks were broken.[102]

From Quicklime to Exhaust Fumes

Karski described the extermination tool:

The floors of the car had been covered with a thick, white powder. It was quicklime. . . . Here, the lime served a double purpose in the Nazi economy of brutality. . . . The occupants of the cars would be literally burned to death before long, the flesh eaten from their bones. . . . In the now quiet camp the only sounds were the inhuman screams. . . . Then these, too, ceased. All that was now left was . . . a queer, sickening, acidulous odor which, I thought, may have come from the quantities of blood that had been left, and with which the ground was stained.[103]

The "death train" seemed to tremble from the effects of the quicklime on the bodies from before it left the camp until it stopped a few kilometers away, at which point everyone was dead. The impression of movement came also from the screams. Karski asked a question about the quicklime that is still being debated today, according to sources: was it used to clean, to kill, or both?[104] In April 1942, the Polish government in exile received details on Belzec in which the expression "death camp" was used for the first time; quicklime was delivered there.[105] In a memorandum submitted to President Roosevelt, on December 8, allusion was also made to murders by quicklime: "Masses of Jews were loaded into freight cars in batches of 150 when there was accommodation for less than one-third of that number. The floors are covered with a thick layer of lime or chlorine, sprinkled with water. The doors are sealed. When the trains reach their destination, half the occupants are dead from suffocation."[106] The long text published by the Polish government in exile on December 10, 1942, gave more or less the same description:

> The Jews were suffering for lack of air. The floors of the trucks were covered with quicklime and chlorine. As far as is known, the trains were despatched to three localities—Tremblinka [*sic*], Belzec and Sobibor, to what the reports describe as "extermination camps." The very method of transport was deliberately calculated to cause the largest possible number of casualties among the condemned Jews. It is reported that on arrival in camp the survivors were stripped naked and killed by various means, including poison gas and electrocution. The dead were interred in mass graves dug by machinery.[107]

All of these similar—almost identical—accounts came from a single source: Jan Karski, debriefed in London between late November and early December. When he met Roosevelt six months later, the president did not know that he already had Karski's reports in hand. But had he read them?

In his account for the BBC, Karski gave more technical details about extermination by gas outside a gas chamber: "The chloride of lime on the floor has the property of developing chlorine gas when coming into contact with humidity. The people jammed into the trucks for many hours are compelled, at some time, to urinate, and this (on the lime), instantaneously produces a chemical reaction. Death must in the end be welcome, for whilst they are dying by the chlorine gas their feet are being burned to the bone by the chemically active chloride."[108]

Other reports on the use of quicklime confirmed Karski's. As in Izbica on the way to Belzec, but much earlier—in October 1941—some of the Jews deported, particularly from Konin, were exterminated at Kazimierz-Biskupi, not far from Chelmno. The murderers, in their search for deadly productivity, tested methods that they hoped would be both more effective and less troublesome for the executioners than mass shootings:

> The Gestapo officers ordered the Jews to undress in front of the two trenches. At the bottom of the larger trench I saw a layer of unslaked lime chunks. They then ordered the naked people to jump into the larger trench. The screams and cries were indescribable. Some Jews jumped in themselves; others were

pushed. Some of the mothers jumped holding their babies; others pushed their children aside, while others still threw their children into the pit and then jumped in themselves. . . . Then a truck carrying four vats arrived in the clearing. The Germans hooked up a motor pump, then a pipe poured water into the trench. The Jews began to boil alive. The screaming was so horrific that those of us who were sitting near the clothing tore off pieces of material and put them in our ears.[109]

And so, trial and error by individuals and small groups paralleled the organization of the industrial complexes. A time when bodies and the soil bled. A time of another world, as epitomized by Auschwitz, where another formidable Polish witness, Witold Pilecki, was voluntarily imprisoned in order to organize the resistance: "In my recollections this was a point that marks the moment when I left behind everything I was familiar with 'on earth' and stepped into something beyond it. . . . All the notions we were accustomed to 'on earth' (the established order of things—the law) took a brutal kicking too."[110]

On August 5, 1942, *The Ghetto Speaks*[111] published a special issue on Chelmno, including the "first authentic report received from Poland on the execution of Jews by gas." They were transported to the changing rooms of fake public baths, where they were "appropriately" asked to undress and leave all their possessions; then, terror. The victims were herded onto trucks that the "SS driver-executioners" drove to trenches that had been dug in advance before activating the gas-feed mechanism. The Jewish gravediggers then did "their job. . . . [When the trucks were opened,] all the victims were . . . smeared with excrement—probably because of the effect of the gas and the horrible fear. . . . Two German civilians would again examine every corpse so as to rob the dead of their last belongings. They would fling off rings from the fingers, and lockets, too. With pliers, they would extract golden teeth from the mouths of the victims, and make certain that there were no hidden articles on the backs of the men, or in the sex organs of the women. The desecrated and robbed bodies would then be placed in rows in the grave under the direction of the SS man. . . . The head of one victim would be laid at the feet of another, and in the spare room which remained, children were placed. . . . In mid-January 1942, a precautionary measure went into effect: the layers were covered with chloride powder, so as to remove the nauseating odor."[112] In this account, like Karski's, there were no euphemisms. Everything that had been seen, felt, and heard was made available to secret services, diplomats, then British and American readers, as well as to Europeans via underground leaflets.

When Karski left the scene of horror and returned to the house where he had prepared himself, he quickly got undressed; he could not bear to wear his executioner's uniform for a single second longer than necessary. He washed himself to the point of splashing water all over the bathroom, but he could not rid his mind of the stenches and screams. The reek of death and of blood, excrement, and vomit, the racket of mad screams and gunshots echoed within him, and he vomited over and over. In the scene shot for the film *Shoah* during which he described Izbica, his mouth was twisted into strange grimaces. He tried to swallow, as if to purge his mouth, his ears, his nose of the horrible words, odors, cries that came out.[113] In 1942, he spoke of his nausea and his nightmares, as if he were possessed by the turmoil of death. Did his body, more than his words, express the ultimate truth? By vomiting, he returned to the state of human being, mingling his stench with those of all the others. At the same time, the reification was complete; he had to forget that he was human to be able to bear witness. He was no longer eyes and mouth, "not so to speak a human being, I was purely a camera, a recording machine."[114] And, he wrote, "I have no other proofs, no photographs. All I can say is that I saw it and that it is the truth."[115]

Can the body's language tell the truth? Karski's body already testified to his courage and heroism: arrested, tortured, he had slit his wrists to kill himself so that he would not talk. Taken to the hospital, liberated by the resistance, he would bear the scars of this incident all his life. During his time in the ghetto and at Izbica, his body was again assaulted—this time as a Jew's body; his soul, however, remained intact. As a fervent Catholic, he insisted on attending mass before leaving for London and on wearing the scapular that had been given to him, "the most beautiful of all gifts." Karski was not a priest, and it was a gift symbolizing the importance vested in him: "'I have been authorized . . . to present you, soldier of Poland, with Christ's Body to carry with you on your journey. . . . It will protect you from all evil and harm.'"[116]

In the ghetto, Karski had recognized Christ's suffering in certain victims he saw, *ecce homo*, but his guide spoke from the point of view of Jews: "'You other Poles are fortunate,' he began. 'You are suffering, too. Many of you will die, but at least your nation goes on living. . . . From this ocean of tears, pain, rage, and humiliation your country will emerge again but the Polish Jews will no longer exist. We will all be dead. Hitler will lose his war . . . but he will win his war against the Polish Jews. No—it will not be a victory; the Jewish people will be murdered.'"[117] Karski relayed these words in *Story of a Secret State*, but he gradually made them his own. Some of his interlocutors in London, starting with Arthur Koestler, were not fooled.

"Statistics don't bleed. Do you know what counts? The detail. Only the detail counts." (Arthur Koestler)[118]

By 1942, the Hungarian-born author Arthur Koestler had had much experience with wars and totalitarianism. An anti-Fascist in Spain, well informed on the Stalinist Moscow show trials, he was imprisoned as a "foreign enemy" in the Vernet internment camp in Ariège, France, from October 1939 to January 1940, an experience from which he drew material for a remarkable autobiographical essay, *Scum of the Earth*. When he went to England, he was imprisoned once again, as an "enemy alien." After he regained his freedom, as a refugee in London, Koestler collected everything published on the fate of the Jews. He met Karski, of course, and, in an ironic turn of events, he was charged by the MI5 counterespionage service with verifying his reliability. Very impressed by the "modest and aristocratic" Karski, he was then involved in creating the script for *Terror in Europe: The Jewish Mass Execution* for the BBC; in fact, he largely rewrote it, although he was "paralyzed by the feeling that the facts are so horrible that nobody will believe them."[119]

Koestler decided to incorporate Karski's account of Belzec into the novel that he was writing at the time. *Arrival and Departure* tells the story of Peter Slavek, an escapee from a central European country who reaches Portugal to enter service for the British: he arrives—*Arrival*—then hesitates, falls ill (the aftereffects of the trauma suffered in Nazi-occupied Europe?), hesitates a bit more as he has various romantic, medical, and political entanglements (the last with Nazi spies, perhaps), and finally decides to leave as a British agent—*Departure*. For the novel, Koestler borrowed from "details" that Karski provided for the BBC script, as well as other information that was circulating in London at the time. The choice of the word "detail" is not insignificant; in Karski's usage, details are flesh itself: they are destroyed souls. Koestler went even further: let us stop counting the suffering, the deaths, the injuries, let us stop treating this knowledge simply as bookkeeping figures; let us feel the indignation and the suffering. This leads to the hallucinogenic account by Peter—who could be named Jan—that takes up twelve pages of the novel. The fictional Peter, like Karski, provokes knowledge that has been taken for granted and shifts it to another level of awareness. In a section on the "mixed transport" trains, Koestler's blending of what we know today about extermination of the Jews, what was known in 1943, and fiction is truly stunning.

> "Nobody who has not been through it can understand it. Terror, atrocities, oppression—that's all words. Statistics don't bleed. Do you know what counts? The detail. Only the detail counts . . ."
>
> "I know."
>
> "No, you don't. You don't know the details. You haven't travelled in a Mixed Transport. You don't know what it is."
>
> "A mixed transport?"
>
> "Yes, that is a detail. There are trains which are scheduled on no time-table. But they run all over Europe. Ten or twenty closed cattle-trucks, locked from outside. . . . Few people see them because they start and arrive at night. I have travelled in one."[120]

"I," Peter, a political prisoner, discovers that the trains were called "mixed" because of the nature of the Jews being transported, who were placed in two groups:

> Two loads of Useful Jews . . . and five loads of Useless Jews, old and sickly ones, who were being taken to be killed. Then there were . . . two trucks with young women who were being taken to army brothels . . . and six trucks with people who were being taken to work in factories and labour camps. That's why it was called a Mixed Transport. . . . After an hour or so the train stopped at a station and they started shunting. One carriage with Politicals was detached from us and two more carriages with foreign labourers attached. . . . Two new carriages . . . contained the women and their children from a razed village where the men had been shot or taken away. At the next station we left

the Useful Jews behind and got instead two wagon-loads of gipsies who, they said, were being taken to be sterilized.[121]

The narrator offers a summary of Nazi persecutions, all categories of oppression combined: "At each station they started shunting us about again, as if playing general post; it seemed a favourite sport with them, perhaps because they enjoy organizing. They gave us nothing to eat or to drink, except for the women who were being taken to the brothels. . . . We had no ordure-bins in our trucks and were packed so tight that we could only sit, not lie. . . . We were treading all the time in heaps of dung."[122]

Koestler then describes in great detail the fate of the "Useless Jews": trucks arrived and parked near the train and men and women were made to get on them, their names and dates of birth ticked off on lists:

> When both vans were full . . . their doors were shut. . . . Both engines began to roar at full strength, but the vans didn't move. We watched the exhaust pipes and saw the pale blue gas stream out. . . . The engines went on roaring as before and the vans remained rooted to the spot, but the gas-jet from the exhaust pipes had disappeared. . . . Then a comrade in our carriage said he smelt gas and began to vomit. . . . After perhaps twenty minutes . . . the officer . . . peeped through what must have been a spy-hole. . . . The sound of the engines ebbed down to normal and the vans began to move. [They returned after half an hour.] They were empty, and their exhaust-pipes puffed merrily, like those of normal, healthy lorries. [The process began again.] After midnight the five trucks with Useless Jews were all empty.[123]

Koestler was combining what Karski had told him about the "death train" with other information available in London at the same time on the gas trucks in Chelmno. He powerfully evoked the fate of the Jews—the "useful" to forced labor, the "useless" to death—even though certain "details" would not stand up to analysis: for instance, the cars were hermetically sealed but gas could be smelled outside the train. Koestler understood the specificity of the "slaughter" of the Jews. He grasped well that Peter/Jan had shifted from eyewitness to moral witness, one who risked his life to speak out. When information was not disseminated with conviction, it disappeared.

Even though George Orwell felt that the novel was "not a satisfactory book" and was even "very thin"[124]—the political hesitations of the hero did not seem credible to him—he acknowledged that it contained "one of the most shocking descriptions of Nazi terrorism that have ever been written." Orwell placed Koestler in the category of authors who wrote in "the special class of literature that has arisen out of the European political struggle since the rise of Fascism": "They are trying to write contemporary history, but *unofficial* history, the kind that is ignored in textbooks and lied about in the newspapers."[125] Orwell would have appreciated the title of Lemkin's autobiography, *Totally Unofficial,* and probably its content.

In 1944, Orwell returned to both *Darkness at Noon,* which dealt with the Moscow show trials, and *Arrival and Departure*: "English disapproval of the Nazi outrages has also been an unreal thing, turned on and off like a tape according to political expediency. To understand such things one has to be able to imagine oneself as the victim, and for an Englishman to write *Darkness at Noon* would be as unlikely an accident as for a slave-trader to write *Uncle Tom's Cabin.*"[126]

Others did take the book seriously—in particular the chapter on extermination, which was also published separately. "We forget if we are not nailed to it," wrote the novelist Phyllis Bottome, "that Europe is a torture chamber a few miles away! . . . I also think it will decrease anti-Semitism except among the few determinedly mad."[127] A jibe by the critic Osbert Sitwell showed that even pessimists such as Koestler were far from the truth: "Is that rigmarole of Koestler's intended as fact or fiction?" Koestler's response, in the name of intellectual morality and ethics, was blistering:

> If I had published an article on Proust and mentioned his homosexuality, you would never have asked such a question, as you would "know," even though the proof of this particular fact is less obvious than that of the massacre of three million human beings. You would blush if you didn't know the name of a second-rate contemporary composer, painter, or author. . . . But you have the audacity to ask me if it is true that you are living in the time of the greatest massacre in history. . . . As long as you do not feel, against and independent of all reason, guilty about living while so many others are being put to death . . . you will remain what you are, guilty by omission.[128]

What was the origin of the denials by those who were "guilty by omission"—not only the British—as well as the denials of anti-Semitism and of the ongoing war with its unremitting cruelty? They were the product of a violent recent past, from World War I to the Spanish Civil War. Indeed, Sitwell added, contemptuously, "In ten years' time such information would be revealed as no more accurate than the lies manufactured to blacken the Germans in the First World War."[129] Sitwell, like so many others, remembered only the propaganda and myths of that conflict and had forgotten the true atrocities of the 1914 invasions, the specific violence against civilians, and the extermination of the Armenians. Koestler and Orwell, like Lemkin and Karski, or Varian Fry and Franz Werfel, were faced with the same barrier to memory. It had been only twenty-three years from 1918 to 1941: too many for complete forgetfulness, enough that the myths were still at work.

3

<hr />

Flashback

From Violence to Myth;
From One War, Another, 1942, 1914

What is happening in Europe is so horrible that the imagination refuses to picture it. . . . The sufferings of 1914–1918, and of much of the period between the two wars, led to a hardening of the hearts. The drain on sympathy began to be unbearable. We are in danger of becoming morally numb.

—Archbishop of Canterbury, 1942

In London in the fall of 1942, although the Nazi horrors were denounced in public demonstrations, things had not moved beyond the stage of moral indignation. The socially engaged author George Orwell reflected on one of the paradoxes of wars: their cruelties were always denounced as those of the other camp and barely analyzed on their own account—when they were not outright denied, as was the case after the Great War. "The truth, it is felt, becomes untruth when your enemy utters it." But, Orwell grumbled, "the truth about atrocities is far worse than that they are lied about and made into propaganda. The truth is that they happen. . . . These things really happened, that is the thing to keep one's eye on."[1] In the summer of 1940, Marc Bloch, a historian and a veteran of two wars, said just about the same thing, also condemning the media, public opinion, and military and political leaders: "They were thinking behind the times."[2]

Too many wars, too many atrocities—and too many rumors? These contemporaries were, indeed, still heavily steeped in the propaganda lies of World War I, which had ended less than twenty-five years before, not to mention the recent wars in Ethiopia and Spain.[3] Many were certain that German barbarism would last forever, including General de Gaulle:

The war on Germany began in 1914. The Treaty of Versailles in fact ended nothing. There was merely, from 1918 to 1936, a pause in the conflict, in the course of which the enemy rebuilt his forces of aggression. . . . In reality, therefore, the world is fighting a thirty-year war either for or against the universal domination of Germany. . . . As for the future, we will make our response. As long as free peoples, of which France was a leader in 1914, are able to liberate it, we answer that the war effort will not cease to grow until it becomes, no doubt, decisive.[4]

De Gaulle, Churchill, and many of their contemporaries who were veterans saw the horrors of the new war, at least until 1942—and some of them for longer—as a direct extension of those of the previous conflict. General Władysław Sikorski, leader of the Polish government in exile, was just as certain, although he added qualifications: "The Germans have always professed their faith in brute force, and their invasions have been marked by torrents of blood. They will refrain from overturning Hitler's regime, as it is the best fit for their national character, which liberates the dark forces of Germany. The year 1918 will therefore not be repeated this time."[5] In the view of Sikorski, a nationalist who had served in the Austro-Hungarian army from 1916 to 1918 and then distinguished himself in the Polish–Soviet War—the eastward extension of the world war—Germanism was certainly at work in Nazism. And yet Sikorksi, whom Karski idealized and who decorated him in London shortly before dying in a plane accident, also expressed the certainty that Nazism would overtake Germanism. How?

"Nazi War on Jews. The New Barbarism. Response of Civilized World."

On December 4, 1942, the *Times* of London blared, "Nazi war on Jews: Deliberate plan for extermination." The headline proved the acuity of its information; it quoted at length a "memorandum by the Polish resistance that has arrived in London"—Karski's. The article stated with certainty, "All other war aims of Nazism will fail in the end—and the defeat of German Fascism is inevitable—but this particular aim, a complete extermination of Jews, is already being enforced."[6] This was the *Times*, not a leaflet put out by the Bund.

The following day, the *Times* published a letter signed "William Cantuar, Lambeth Palace" and titled, "Nazi War on Jews. The New Barbarism. Response of Civilized World."[7] "Civilized world" against "barbarism"? Was the Archbishop of Canterbury seeing a repetition of 1914? In fact, in October

1914, ninety-three celebrated German intellectuals and artists had signed an "appeal to the civilized world" to defend their country, their *Kultur*, against the accusations of barbarism made during the early weeks of what was not yet being called the Great War. Using the anaphora "It is not true that," the ninety-three denied the German atrocities in Belgium in August and early September 1914. They attributed the invention of such accusations to propaganda and reflected them back on their Russian enemies and on wrongdoing by French and English colonial troops. "It is not true that our warfare pays no respect to international laws. It knows no undisciplined cruelty. But in the east, the earth is saturated with the blood of women and children unmercifully butchered by the wild Russian troops." The signatories rejected the accusations made against Germany and emphasized the British and French alliances with different of categories of patent "barbarians" such as the Russians, Serbians, and Mongols—the true Huns, the real Attilas; moreover, the British and French were bringing their colonial troops into line: "Those who have allied themselves with the Russians and Serbians, and present such a shameful scene to the world as that of inciting the Mongolians and Negroes against the white race, have no right whatever to call themselves upholders of European civilization."[8]

Between 1914 and 1918, racism was common to all of the belligerents. After all, the widespread belief that the Germans cut off the hands of Belgian children was born of a switch of images. In fact, in the Congo—the direct property of the Belgian king Leopold II—Victor-Léon Fiévez, leader of the equatorial district, had introduced the gathering of cut-off hands and excrement of the dead, not the living, even though rare cases of mutilation did exist. But this was in the context of staggeringly despicable forced labor, whence the birth of the myth within circles—still very small—of activists fighting against colonial abuses.[9] In the summer of 1914, Belgians, and then the whole world, *believed* that they had seen white hands, which they *had not wanted* or *been able* to see when the hands were black and in the Congo. These mythified hands took the place, in both cases, of real atrocities committed in the colonies since the nineteenth century and during the Great War and then were used as propaganda.[10]

The reader who wrote to the *Times* of London on December 5, 1942, knew one thing for certain: in 1914, true atrocities (atrocities, plural) had preceded the brainwashing. As for the present reality of World War II, it was revealed through a single "atrocity"—expressed in the singular—the horrifying Nazi extermination. And yet, most people, including the majority of those who debriefed couriers in London and Washington, thought exactly the contrary: all of this could not be true; these facts were, at best, gross exaggerations. They would not be deceived again, as they had been about the German atrocities of 1914. Indeed, how could the British and Americans, who were convinced that they had been tricked during the Great War, be persuaded that this time the events were of a different scope and scale than the "atrocities"—the scare quotes proving that they were largely hypothetical—of World War I? No, they would not be deceived again. Numerous members of the British Parliament, intellectuals such as H. G. Wells, and the most cultivated—and motivated—Americans reacted in this way.

It should have been no surprise. In 1978, when Karski was interviewed by Claude Lanzmann for what would become *Shoah*, he gave a detailed account of his meeting with Lord Selborne, chief of the Special Operation Executive,[11] in London in 1942:

> JAN KARSKI: I more or less told him the whole story [including his visits to the Warsaw ghetto and Belzec], and then, at a certain point, I finished. Lord Selborne, with typical English correctness, benevolence, tolerance, rationality, answers: "Mr. Karski, during the First World War we were propagandising that the German soldiers were crushing the heads of Belgian babies against the wall. I think we were doing a good job. We had to weaken German morale, we had to arouse hostility towards Germany. The war was a very bloody war. We knew it was untrue. Speak about your problem, your report. Try to arouse public opinion. I want you to know you do contribute to the Allied cause. We want this kind of report. Your mission is very important." He was clearly telling me, "Mr. Karski, you know and I know it isn't so."
> CLAUDE LANZMANN: "It's not true, but it's good for propaganda"?
> JK: Yes.
> CL: The same problem as in the First World War?
> JK: Yes.[12]

Lanzmann's questions and Karski's two affirmative responses prove that most historians until the 1990s also thought that the "German atrocities" of the Great War, such as the children's severed or crushed hands, were inventions or myths; they therefore kept them in scare quotes.[13] And yet, in 1921 Marc Bloch had transformed the "false news" of the war into a historical subject by reflecting on precisely this enigmatic episode:

> From the instant when the error made the blood flow, it was definitively established. . . . Even today, the majority of Germans are probably convinced that their soldiers fell victim to Belgian ambushes in great numbers. . . . It is easy to believe what we need to believe. A legend that has inspired momentous acts, and especially cruel actions, is very close to being indestructible. . . . False news always arises from collective representations that preexisted its birth; it is fortuitous only in appearance. False news is the mirror in which the "collective consciousness" contemplates its own features.[14]

In 1914, the German invaders of Belgium and northern France, under the impression that enemy civilians were snipers, felt that preventive attacks were necessary to protect themselves as the war began. This was the reason for their violent reprisals. Then, these real atrocities—civilians used as human shields, taken hostage and shot, women raped—were transformed with the creation of two myths: that of children's hands being cut off and that of enemies being crucified. These myths became so ingrained in memory that the caricaturist David Low attempted to use them, to doubtful humorous effect, in relation to the claimed mistreatment of German prisoners in 1942 by the British: "Reprisals for British atrocities. The hands of some prisoners were bound." "What, only the hands?"[15] On the severed hands, Bloch was once again very clear:

> The popular imagination always distorts. Whatever "atrocities"—alas, too real—were perpetrated by Germans on French soil, they became mingled with accounts that turned facts into the dregs of legends, such as the legend of the "severed hands." This would be . . . a good subject for study. . . . Would such work not be of use not only for clear history, but also for our propaganda, about which, since peace has come, there is still a useful task to accomplish—in Alsace-Lorraine, in friendly or allied countries, even in Germany? The truth loses its strength when it is mixed with falsehoods.[16]

Bloch was right to advocate research on the true atrocities at the same time as that on the acknowledged outrages that had succeeded each other since 1914. Each camp had used both the enemy's real actions and rumors in its propaganda and in order to prove how much its own society opposed the barbarism of the opposing side. Real atrocities and their mythification went hand in hand on the different invasion fronts and were extended into the territories occupied until 1918, and even until 1923 in the Russian civil war and the war between Greece and Turkey. The extermination of Armenians by the Ottoman empire under cover of war was their most extreme manifestation. Already people were seeing only what they wanted to see, even when it was right in front of their eyes.

"Corpse Factories" during World War I: From *Leim* (Glue) to Quicklime

In the 1920s, one of the great anti-German scandals of World War I reemerged in Great Britain and the United States: the use of the bodies of soldiers—including their own—for unspeakable purposes in "corpse factories." Although some explained—even in a stormy parliamentary debate in London on April 30, 1917—that only animal carcasses could possibly have been used, others remained convinced that the goal was to use human cadavers to extract fertilizers mixed with pig manure, the Germans being portrayed as lewd, repulsive pigs.[17]

Although in 1917 the "corpse factories" processed only animal fat into candles, glycerin, or glue,[18] words led to confusion, due to inaccurate translations, deliberate or not. The German word for glue is *leim*; its homonym in English is "lime" (in this case, short for quicklime), which was associated—until Karski reported on Izbica in 1942—with disinfection, including of bodies and cemeteries. The connection was quickly made:

> "Germans and their dead. A revolting treatment. Science and the barbarian spirit." . . . The trains arrive full of bare bodies, which are unloaded by the workers who live at the works. . . . They are equipped with long hooked poles, and push the bundle of bodies to an endless chain, which picks them up with big hooks. . . . The bodies are transported on this endless chain into a long, narrow compartment, where they pass through a bath which disinfects them. They then go through a drying chamber, and finally are automatically carried into a digester or great cauldron, in which they are dropped by an apparatus which detaches them from the chain. In the digester they remain from six to

eight hours, and are treated by steam, which breaks them up while they are slowly stirred by machinery.

From this treatment result several products. The fats are broken up into stearine, a form of tallow, and oils, which require to be redistilled before they can be used. The process of distillation is carried out by boiling the oil with carbonate of soda, and some part of the by-products resulting from this is used by German soapmakers. . . .

There is a laboratory, and in charge of the works is a chief chemist with two assistants and 78 men. All the employees are soldiers and are attached to the 8th Army Corps. . . . Under no pretext is a man permitted to leave them. They are guarded as prisoners at their appalling work.[19]

By denouncing the paradox of the Germans' science without a conscience in the industrialization of the process, the author wanted to prove that their technical superiority was leading them to commit even more crimes. The numerous caricatures—such as the one in *Punch* in which the Kaiser shows a terrified young recruit the "body factory" under his window with the caption "Know that I'll find a way to use you, living or dead"—proved that there was general awareness that this was the realm of propaganda. And yet, this idea of the processing of cadavers into soap was found in numerous personal diaries, as rumors were no doubt propagated once more, during the Great War, between battlefields and nearby civilians.[20]

The debate over the German word *Kadaver*—animal carcass or human cadaver?—was not settled then. It returned in 1925 when, during a speech in New York, the Briton Brigadier General John Charteris, former information officer for Major-General Douglas Haig, declared that he had invented the whole thing. He had apparently taken the caption for a photograph of dead horses being sent to the knacker and used it under another photograph showing bodies of soldiers being transported behind the front lines for burial. The world press seized on the photomontage. Ten years after the war, the use of images as propaganda was admitted by one of its protagonists; the British authorities, to their great consternation, were accused of manipulation. Debates in Parliament and a press campaign followed. Pacifists such as Bertrand Russell rejected all "German atrocities" wholesale: if some had been fabricated, why might others be real?[21] Had Charteris lied, or not? In 1917? In 1925? Was he a true forger of the false or a false forger of the true? People continued to believe what they wanted to believe.

Greuelpropaganda: Atrocity Propaganda

Such propaganda and counterpropaganda campaigns extended far and wide after World War I, particularly in Germany. In his *Mein Kampf*, Hitler noted that the British had proved to be far superior in spreading disinformation during the Great War: "The proof of this brilliant knowledge of the primitiveness of feeling of the great masses was to be found in the atrocity propaganda that had been adapted to this, thus ruthlessly and ingeniously securing moral steadfastness at the front, even during the greatest defeats."[22] Not only, said Hitler, had British morale been galvanized by the country's excellent propaganda, but the British had even managed to convince Germans of the truthfulness of their assertions, including those about the corpse factory. Thanks to this *Greuelpropaganda*, or atrocity propaganda, external enemies had enabled their domestic accomplices—socialists and, especially, Jews—to sharpen the daggers with which they would stab Germany in the back. The certainty that external and domestic conspirators had been created thanks to the false atrocities that spread during and after World War I would be found at the core of Nazism in 1933, as Victor Klemperer, an inspired observer of the language of the Third Reich, noted. Klemperer was not surprised that the same words, myths, and debates reappeared:

> Foreign Jews, particularly those from France, England and America, are today frequently referred to as "global Jews (*Weltjuden*)." . . . Does this mean that Jews are to be found everywhere on earth, except, that is, in Germany? And where are they within Germany itself? The global Jews disseminate "atrocity propaganda" and spread "horror stories" and if we report so much as a scrap of what happens here every day then we too are guilty of disseminating atrocity propaganda and are punished accordingly.[23]

In Nazi Germany, the myth of the snipers (*franc-tireurs*) was the first to resurface: it was now taken for granted that Belgian civilians had been involved in the war during the 1914 invasion and that the German army had simply defended itself. The *Manifesto of the Ninety-Three German Intellectuals*, written in 1914, makes this point: "It is not true that our troops treated

Louvain brutally. Furious inhabitants having treacherously fallen upon them in their quarters, our troops with aching hearts were obliged to fire a part of the town, as punishment." Starting in 1940, the Nazis did all they could—with archival research in Belgium, once again occupied—to prove that the Allied campaign on the atrocities of World War I was false, that the Kaiser's troops had only defended themselves against the combined assault of troops and civilians.

But the Third Reich was not a continuation of the Second Reich, particularly in the east, where even in 1940 there was no attempt to "correct" propaganda. At the time of the invasion of Poland, it was claimed that the civilians were barbarians, and Reinhard Heydrich proclaimed that the Jews were snipers and plunderers who had to be dealt with separately.

Among the Allies and resisters in occupied countries, the myths of the Great War were also brought back into service. "*Franc-tireur*" was given a positive gloss; it was—a random irony—the name of the resistance group to which Marc Bloch belonged.

Some of the most hackneyed rumors resurfaced in 1942, even in credible reports of the extermination of Jews. For instance, in the Foreign Office report of September 11, 1942, someone wrote on a typed text, "The facts are quite bad enough without the addition of such an old story such as the use of bodies for the manufacture of soap etc."[24] "Slain Polish Jews Put at a Million. One-third of number in whole country said to have been put to death by Nazis. Abattoir for deportees. Mass electrocutions, killing by injection of air bubbles described in reports."[25] The *New York Times* reported this British information on Belzec (the Karski effect), which had come to it through Rabbi Wise, and specified that human fat was being processed into fertilizer or soap. Those who thought that the victim numbers were greatly exaggerated raised an outcry. The detail—the soap factories—was used to deny the central information, the mass extermination. Similarly, up to 1945, *Christian Century*, a relatively moderate newspaper, returned to both the false figures and the false atrocities: "The use of corpses to produce fat and soap very unpleasantly reminds us of the lie of the 'corpse factory' that was one of the propaganda triumphs of World War I."[26]

And yet, a Canadian war correspondent in Poland in July 1945, Raymond Arthur Davies, reported on his visit to a "human soap factory . . . with

corpses from prisoner camps and concentration camps." He included photographs of decapitated heads with his account.[27] Experiments conducted
by Dr. Rudolf Spanner at the Danzig Anatomic Institute, mentioned by the
Soviets at Nuremberg, have been central since 1945 to the belief that the
Nazis produced soap with the bodies of their Polish, Russian, and Jewish
victims. Historians have recently established with certainty that this was
not the case, even though human fat in the process of being saponified was
in fact found in the abandoned laboratory.[28]

Karski kept a copy of Davies's book in his personal library, and even
today many are still convinced that the stories about soap factories are true.
This raises the question: why, during World War II, was there a general refusal to believe in the atrocities of World War I, still so fresh and reflected
in the moment, and then a return to the rumors afterward?

"Our skepticism has been fortified by our experience of 'atrocity stories' during the last war" (Varian Fry, "The Massacre of the Jews," 1942)

The denial of atrocities during the 1914 invasions became a central issue in
1942, at the very time when information on extermination of the Jews was
emerging with clarity. In a pamphlet published during the summer, *Rescue
the Perishing*, an activist member of Parliament, Eleanor Rathbone, pleaded
with Britons to take in more Jewish refugees, especially in Mandatory Palestine. She felt obliged to begin with a meaningful "appeal to the reader":
"These are not 'atrocity stories,' exaggerated for the purposes of propaganda.
They come from too many sources all of which are corroborated."

Whence the poignant appeals from Schmuel Zygielbojm to save the Jews
in Poland who were still alive in 1942 and from Victor Gollancz, another
of Karski's interlocutors in London: "Nothing is baser than 'atrocity mon-
gering' . . . for the sake of stirring up hatred against the enemy." A militant
pacifist, Gollancz was eager to distinguish hate-induced propaganda produced by both sides since the Great War from the reality of December 1942:
"*Unless something effective is done*, within a very few months these six million Jews will all be dead."[29]

Other men, as diverse as Cardinal Hinsley, Archbishop of Westminster,
and the philosopher Jacques Maritain, who had taken refuge at Princeton
University, made the same observation. Maritain wrote, "If we were tempted
to see the accounts that come to us as 'atrocity stories,' reverberating through

the echoes of horror, that would be enough for us to realize their plausibility."[30] And he returned to the facts, as did William Shirer in the *Washington Post*. In an opinion piece, "The Propaganda Front," Shirer reminded his readers that the Nazi authorities had used propaganda about the atrocities of World War I to mock and reject everything that came from England or the United States, as well as the joint Allied declaration on persecution of the Jews dated December 17, 1942; in this foreshadowing of Nuremberg and the United Nations, the British, Americans, Soviets, and governments in exile warned the world of the "bestial policy of cold-blooded extermination" and promised a verdict: "They reaffirm their solemn resolution to ensure that those responsible for these crimes shall not escape retribution, and to press on with the necessary practical measures to this end."[31]

Proclaiming justice, putting off all action until the end the war. To this, Gollancz responded, "Does it benefit the Jew, as he stands at the door of the execution chamber, that, after his body has begun to pass into the dust from which it came, his executioner also will be sent to the grave? . . . No, the proclamation of vengeance will bring back no single Jew from his nameless grave."[32]

The world had to be convinced not only that there was mass murder under way but also of the need to act quickly, not to put off until after the war the eventual punishment of the murderers. But the atrocity propaganda became entangled with this race against death. For instance, Shirer wrote that "the Nazis had always suppressed the slightest reference to the murder of the Jews" but that a certain number of Germans listened to foreign radio stations, which led to their counteroffensive regarding *Greuelpropaganda*: "The Allied governments had resumed their 'atrocity propaganda' against Germany. . . . It was a campaign similar to the last war, when the Allies claimed that Germans chopped off the hands of Belgian children."[33] In another article, "The Propaganda Front: No Atrocity Stories, Facts," Shirer reported on a survey taken in Detroit that revealed that the woman and man in the street did not "believe any of the stories about Nazi atrocities. . . . They were dead sure that the present reports about Nazi atrocities were similar to those we heard about the Germans in the First World War and therefore no more true." He therefore tried to find explanations for his compatriots' general skepticism after more than a year of engagement in the war. "In the two decades that followed the last Armistice, our vast disillusionment over the peace degenerated into a silly sort of super-cynicism and super-skepticism. We would believe nothing. In the weird process, we lost track of the true currents of contemporary history. The result was a terrible and costly confusion." Shirer was even more alarmed because he knew that "the Nazi themselves have admitted atrocities that have no parallel in the First World War. . . . The openly avowed aim of Nazi Germany is to destroy us. There is nothing secret about this aim. There is no earthly reason for us not to believe it."[34]

No reason, and yet every reason. If it was difficult, even in 1942 or 1943, to convince people that Jews specifically were being persecuted and that mass deportations were under way, then very few would be able to believe in the total extermination of the Jewish people. Gerhart Riegner, the secretary of the World Jewish Congress, who, in August 1942, sent the first telegram to the English and American diplomatic corps on the mass extermination, recalled this in his memoir. In a section titled "Why We Failed," he wrote, "The first reason . . . is that . . . there was no precedent for the Shoah." "A second factor, little known but extremely damaging," he went on, "was the precedent of reports on German atrocities during World War I, which after the war proved to be false. This caused us serious problems and we were always being told, 'That's all made up, just like during the First War.' We had to make enormous efforts to convince people of the veracity of our reports on the Shoah."[35] Although in 1998, when he wrote his book, Riegner was still confusing the real atrocities of 1914–18 with the consubstantial propaganda myths, he accurately reconstructed the climate of doubt in Great Britain and the United States, also confirmed by Raymond Aron for free France, where they "did not indulge in *Greuelpropaganda*, the expression the Germans had created in 1914 to denounce Allied propaganda accusing them of atrocities."[36] It was this doubt that Karski, Lemkin, and Varian Fry struggled with.

Fry, an American, had been expelled from Vichy in 1941. The Emergency Rescue Committee, which he had created in Marseille to save Jews who were being hunted, had been closed. In his own country, he was ignored, even spied on; he would never again have responsibilities matching those he had had in Europe. And so, he wrote a masterful article, "The Massacre of the Jews":

We are accustomed to horrors in the historical past, and accept them . . . as phenomena of ages less enlightened than our own. When such things occur in our times, like the Armenian massacres, we put them down to the account of still half-barbarous peoples. But that such things could be done by contemporary western Europeans, heirs of the humanist tradition, seems hardly possible.

Our skepticism has been fortified by our experience with "atrocity stories" during the last war. We were treated, during that war, to many accounts of German atrocities. We were told of the rape of nuns, the forced prostitution of young Belgian girls, of German soldiers spearing infants on their bayonets, or deliberately and wantonly cutting off their hands. Later . . . most of these atrocities were found to have been invented. The natural reaction was to label all atrocity stories "propaganda" and refuse to believe them.[37]

In 1939–40, Fry had been certain that most of the World War I atrocities were the product of rumor and propaganda; more specifically, he confused the myths born of the distortion of true atrocities with the actual atrocities. He admitted his own difficulty with "believing" the early Nazi cruelties perpetrated on the Jews in Germany. But by 1942, he was convinced: even if the Nazis lost the world war, they would have won the war in occupied Europe and murdered the Jews.

Fry then talked about a situation specific to World War I, that of the occupied territories in which harsh conditions and atrocities perpetrated during the 1914 invasion were extended in the form of requisitions, forced labor, and mass deportations and culminated during the 1918 retreat and the evacuation of these territories in the final destruction: "When we remember that, even after the war of 1914–18 was hopelessly lost and the German army was retreating in confusion on the Western Front, it still found time, and the will, wantonly to destroy the factories and flood the mines in the path, we may well believe that this time it will be even more thorough, go even more berserk."[38]

In the summer of 1942, before publishing this article, Fry sent a report to Eleanor Roosevelt; he was attempting through her to reach her husband, who was opposed to "fighting the war of the Jews." She asked Undersecretary of State Sumner Welles if she could mention it in her column as a form of protest.[39] Welles's response is not known, but Fry's exasperation with the procrastination was eloquent: it moved a man whom Fry did not yet know, Raphael Lemkin.

Lemkin, Legal Activist: Jews and Armenians before and after the Great War

Barely had he set foot in the United States, in 1941, when Lemkin was giving well-attended speeches on the sufferings of the Poles, in which he compared the horrors of the two world wars. But when it came to the destruction of entire peoples, he faced the systematic lies about the atrocities of World War I. "I found complete unawareness that the Axis planned destruction of the peoples under their control," he wrote. "Some answered that Washington would not believe it, and many still remembered the 'atrocity stories' told about Germans in the First World War. I thought: genocide is so easy to commit because people don't want to believe it until after it happens."[40]

In fact, in 1942 reports were coming from all over occupied Europe, but many thought they were highly embellished. Moreover, there was total confusion between Nazi atrocities in general and the specificity of the extermination of the Jews—what the historian Raul Hilberg, long after Lemkin, called "functional blindness." Indeed, many Americans—before Karski arrived in the United States, his reports having preceded him as Britons and Americans shared his data—invoked the lack of eyewitnesses and the doubts (many of them legitimate if one thinks of Katyn) about information coming from the Soviet Union.

Lemkin, however, knew that the real violence against civilians in 1914 had been both underestimated and mythologized, especially when one added the atrocities prolonged under different occupations—from Belgium and northern France to Serbia and Lithuania—and the extermination of the Armenians, the true scope of which had not yet been exposed. During his exodus and period of waiting in Sweden, he conducted a study comparing the occupation policies of the Nazis with those during World War I, and he collected the documents with which he would work in the United States to produce his master opus of 1944, *Axis Rule in Occupied Europe*, in which the word "genocide" appeared for the first time.[41]

In early 1942, the newly arrived Lemkin had reason to be bitter: he was simply a stand-in at Duke University despite the kindness of his colleagues. Almost no one understood the importance of his legal work in Poland and his participation in the great project of the League of Nations, the effort to unify criminal law.

Lemkin had realized very early, without expressing it clearly, that extermination wasn't an accidental cruelty but the essence of this type of war against civilians, the goal of which was to homogenize peoples and religions. In fact, this is what had happened during World War I in the processes of internal reconstruction of the Ottoman and Russian empires: population displacements took the form of social or ethnic reorganization, which included the extermination of Armenians and the deportation of "suspect" populations from Russia, starting with the Jews, the vast majority of whom in Europe were living in the residential zone that had been assigned to them in czarist times.

In his later writings, Lemkin placed less stress on his personal experience of pogroms before and after 1914 in his region under Russian rule than on the extermination of Armenians under the Ottoman Empire. As a Jew, he probably wanted to maintain his ideal of universality, so as not to be accused of taking a special interest in his own people. Although he was only six years old at the time of the Bialystok pogrom, in 1906, he would soon read the poems by Hayim Bialik describing the atrocities in Kishinev in 1903, including his elegy to the abominable, "City of the Killings":

Rise and go to the town of the killings and you'll come to the yards
and with your eyes and your own hand feel the fence
and on the trees and on the stones and plaster of the walls
the congealed blood and hardened brains of the dead.
And you'll come from there to the ruins and stop before the rents
and pass by the pierced walls and shattered ovens,
where the axe's head bit deep, to burst and deepen holes,
bearing the black stone and shears of brick all burned
and they'll look like the open mouths of black and mortal wounds
that have no remedy, that have no cure.[42]

As a student, Lemkin had been subjected to insults and beatings by his fellow students, who called him "Beilis," the name of a Jew wrongfully accused of a "ritual" murder of a Christian child killed near Kiev. Menahem Mendel Beilis was ultimately acquitted in 1913, but between the ages of eleven and thirteen Lemkin had lived with this tragedy, discussed every day by his family, and with the fear of an imminent pogrom.

In 1915, his hometown of Volkovysk—then in Russian territory—was caught up in the war. Although the Germans invaded and occupied it, putting its residents into forced labor, the town was at least spared the most brutal Russian decisions. For in the regions that it held, the Russian military conducted full-scale experiments to test its theories about "suspect populations": it imprisoned its nationals situated on the front line or expelled them to the interior, conducting "ethnic cleansing"[43] of Russian citizens of German origin, as well as Jews, on the pretext that their language, Yiddish, enabled them to conspire with the Germans. At least six hundred thousand Jews were deported, subjected to violence and pogroms, put into temporary camps, or forced to move farther east, taking nothing with them. The artist Abel Pann described and drew these war pogroms: civilians were chased into the forests and abandoned there in the snow, starving, or deported in cattle cars, their hands tied through the crooked floorboards; Cossacks on horseback pillaged, raped, and beat women, children, old people.

> In a few hours they were chased from their homes with unimaginable cruelty. The children were in front, it was all the others that were driven out as if they were the worst criminals. . . . They died there like flies; many lost their minds. . . . They opened the stomachs of pregnant women and filled them with feathers from torn pillows. . . . Jewish soldiers, mutilated, decorated for their bravery, returned to their hometowns and found nothing but corpses and destruction.[44]

The historian Simon Dubnow, whom Lemkin met in Riga in 1940, had witnessed these deportations in May 1915:

> An official campaign was openly conducted with the infernal intention of blaming the Jews for the military defeats. . . . I often think, where does such Judeophobia come from at such a time? Psychologically, it can be explained. In his way, the executioner fears his victim. The Judeophobes who have been tyrannizing the Jews for thirty years have their conscience suggest to them that the Jews would have to take revenge on their persecutors, and this likelihood,

in the executioners' minds, is transformed into something real. . . . The nightmare expands. Crazy and criminal things happen. In a single day several tens of thousands of Jews were expelled from Kovno and its province. In the army's chain of command, the talk was of their mass expulsion . . . and deportation. . . . The unfortunate exiles were shut into cattle cars. When they asked, "Where are we being taken," the answer was "Where we have been ordered to send you." . . . What is happening in Lithuania is beyond the imagination. There is talk of tens of thousands of exiles, who, on Shavuot, flowed into Vilna with babies in carriages.[45]

Since 1916, almanacs and war chronicles had been published to celebrate the resiliency of Jews in the east. These *Zalmbikner*—collections of details of daily life and personal diaries—were instrumental to Jews' becoming aware that they formed a people. Under attack specifically during that world war, they recorded the uniqueness of their lay lives, schools, sports clubs, and charity organizations. Facing them, however, was widespread anti-Semitic violence, which, long based on the idea of the idea of the Jew as "traitor," "infidel," "hoarder," and "speculator," was to grow with impunity thanks to the war: it was now permissible to "break the Yids." These were in fact "war crimes" committed by regular units, adding a new kind of mass violence to the old-style pogroms, and this was before 1917, the two revolutions and the civil war, the "turn to extermination."[46]

All memorial books for this region chronicle the extermination of Jews starting in 1941, dating back to the German, and then Russian, abuses of World War I, as the Jews' condition worsened during the Russian civil war.[47] Volkovysk was destroyed during the war between Russia and Poland in 1920, and Lemkin witnessed the anti-Jewish radicalization from 1918 to 1920 in these border regions between the new Poland at war with Russia, Ukraine, Belarus, and the former Austrian Galicia: from quasi-"extermination *Aktionen*" to the future Nazi sense of the word. In fact, those who were fighting against the Red Army took out their rage on the Jews, perceived as Judeo-Bolsheviks and impure organisms that were destroying the healthy (holy) body of Russia. In 1918, military confrontations between Poles and Ukrainians around the city of Lvov (formerly Lemberg, now the Ukrainian city of Lviv), where Lemkin went to university, ended, after the Polish victory, in a three-day pogrom that resulted in seventy dead and at least five hundred wounded. A *New York Times* headline read, "1,100 Jews Murdered in Lemberg Pogroms."[48]

In these regions, where the German, Austro-Hungarian, and Russian empires were disintegrating, the Great War was prolonged: more civilians than soldiers were mistreated, deported, or killed. The modernity of total war swept everything away between 1914 and the 1920s, and in these "lands of blood," Jews had already paid a higher price than the rest of the population: indeed, atavistic anti-Semitism was transformed into self-fulfilling prophecy when a number of Jews, like other minorities, were seduced by Lenin's promises of emancipation. We have seen, through Karski's eyes when he was in Poland in 1939–40, what happened in the zone occupied by the Soviets.

In 1919, other attacks against Jews took place not only in Galicia but across Poland. In article 93 of the Treaty of Versailles, the new country was ordered to protect its religious and linguistic minorities and to give Polish citizenship to everyone who came, in particular, from the Lvov region. After the pogroms, President Wilson established a commission of inquiry on the situation of Jewish Poles; the commission was chaired by Henry Morgenthau, former American ambassador to the Ottoman Empire, who had witnessed the partial extermination of Christian minorities in the crumbling empire, starting with the Armenians.

"When such things happen in our times, like the Armenian massacres, we put them down to the account of still half-barbarous peoples" (Varian Fry, 1942)

The "total extermination" of the Armenians was an attack that was literally inconceivable. The crimes of the Young Turks were well known and transmitted in public opinion in real time. However, these crimes were poorly understood because they were instrumentalized by the propaganda of the Entente: condemnation of them became a new war aim, a way to strike at the Central Powers through their Ottoman allies. As the deportations and massacres of Armenians were occurring, in 1915 and 1916, commissions of inquiry were publishing White Paper after White Paper on the atrocities committed against civilians in Belgium and Serbia in 1914. A 1916 caricature denounced the deportations from Lille during Easter of that year: *Boche* brutes are carrying away women and children as a soldier in a pointed helmet remarks,

"Accept them in memory of the last massacre of Christians." *L'Asino è il popolo: utile, paziente et bastonato*, Italian magazine published by Podrecca e Galantara, December 5, 1915.

"More tears!" The Sultan and William II cry crocodile tears contemplating their crimes: "One million Armenians are being exterminated." "I weep for Louvain and France." Drawing by Robert Carter, *New York Sun*, 1915.

ironically, "They complain. But what would they say if they were in Armenia?"[49] Although German atrocities in Belgium and northern France continued to be compared to the terror perpetrated against Armenians, some were already aware that something extraordinary was happening in the Ottoman Empire.

Talaat Pasha, a member of the triumvirate leading the Young Turks, described the deportations as the logical retribution for "traitors" bankrolled by the Russians. In the view of the Young Turks, the Armenian—pejoratively singular—was a potential traitor, an "irregular," "unwholesome." The domestic "enemy" was animalized, his ontological humanity denied. What remained was to "sideline" him, a euphemism for killing him.[50] Even in 1918, a French-language Turkish newspaper was denouncing the barbarism—of the Armenians:

> One trembles to see the scenes of atrocities that they have committed. . . . They have killed everyone they encounter, they have burned villages, slaughtered animals. . . . The Armenian organizations are systematically applying their plan to wipe out the Turkish race. . . . History will certainly pronounce itself one day on the actions of these civilized criminals. As for today, these madmen must know that their crimes will cost them dearly. It is not up to a handful of Armenians . . . to exterminate the Turkish race, which is so strong that it is guaranteed by nature and God Himself against obliteration. Furthermore, these crimes and atrocities will provoke unforgettable indignation in the world at large, stretching as far as the Chinese border, and as the Armenians are by God Himself condemned to live in the middle of this world, in whichever hands they find themselves, it will become hell for them. This can be the only outcome resulting from so many crimes![51]

In a mirror effect typical of mass murderers, the Turks attributed their own base acts to their victims and claimed to be defending themselves from these "civilized criminals," an oxymoron that defined the Turks themselves perfectly. It was the genocide-denial conviction of executioners who saw themselves as victims and manifested "apocalyptic racism" even as they exterminated Armenians by the thousands.[52] The Ottomans lost the war, but they won their battle: they obliterated the Armenians. Those who were not actually exterminated were destroyed in other ways. Rapes, conversions, forced marriages, and children kidnapped and raised as Muslims eradicated them as a people, as Christians, and their ancient culture was ravaged as churches and libraries were burned. And the seizure of their homes and belongings enabled the Turks to win the economic peace. Without Armenians.

"Crimes against humanity and civilization," "Murder of a nation": How Can the Extermination of the Armenians Be Defined?

In a telegram sent in May 1915, the French, English, and Russians called the "atrocities" committed against the Armenians "crimes against humanity and civilization." It was a vengeful observation, a paradigmatic case of war violence become "crime against humanity" and "genocide" before the legal concepts—and the terms—were invented. And it was difficult to agree on the words: "crimes against Christianity and civilization" or "crimes against humanity and civilization"?

This was a glaring semantic reversal. In the nineteenth century, the concept of "laws of humanity" was used in the positive sense, and actions were sometimes taken in the name of such laws. Now, there were "crimes against humanity." The Russian diplomats deemed the notion of "humanity" too vague and reintroduced "civilization." This represented *the* war aim of the Entente. One of the ironies of the May 1915 telegram is that it constituted verbal belligerence in response to the first Armenian massacres in winter 1915, which resembled the massacres of the past; it was, above all, a way to compensate for the lack of intervention during the massacres of 1894–97 and 1909. Jean Jaurès had thundered in 1896, "In the face of this violation of France's word and of human rights, not a single cry has left your lips, not a word from your consciences, and you have witnessed, mute and therefore complicit, the utter extermination."[53]

In April 1915, several months before the mass deportation of Armenians led to their extermination, the Allied declaration was based mainly on the world war underway, waged this time on Turkish soil. For years, the crimes against the Armenians were used to attack the Germans, the top enemy power and Ottoman ally. "The massacres of Armenia," wrote a historian at the time, "Turkey's work, Germany's method!"[54] But if the Turks were simply the puppets of the Germans, they were exonerated of their crimes.

A number of influential Americans, some of whom would meet twenty-five years later with Karski or Lemkin, took a position. In October 1915, Rabbi Wise denounced "inhumanity whether committed by Germans against Belgians, by Russians against Jews, or by Turks against Armenians."[55] But, in the name of strict neutrality, President Wilson wanted neither to seriously condemn the massacres nor to intervene in Turkey.[56] As for future president Franklin Delano Roosevelt, he had taken an interest in persecuted minorities—such as the Boers—as a student at Harvard and joined an organization called Near East Relief in 1921. Perhaps he had read the report sent from the Caucasus by one of his colleagues that mentioned "heaps of human bones and half-decomposed [Armenian] bodies representing the remains of 500 women and children killed in one spot."[57]

The prolongation of World War I in the modern state of Turkey at war with Greece, and in a Russia in the grip of revolution and then civil war, was to provide a further catalyst for these phenomena. Churchill, for example, wrote to the prime ministers of the Dominions about the "infernal orgy" of the sack of Smyrna by the Turks in September 1922, in which twelve thousand people perished in the flames in the Greek and Armenian parts of the city: "For a deliberately planned and methodically exercised atrocity Smyrna . . . must find few parallels in the history of human crime."[58]

"The bloodiest and most disturbing enigma in history" (Heinrich Vierbücher)

"The liberation and resurrection of Belgium and Serbia have been two of the most splendid outcomes of the World War, as the *debâcle* in Russia and the martyrdom of Armenia have been its greatest tragedies," opined *Punch*, almost tritely, in 1919.[59] Few observers at the time could get past the stage of describing the "tragedies," condemning them, and, above all, putting into words what had happened. Heinrich Vierbücher, a German who had served as translator for General Liman von Sanders in the Dardanelles, took an original view in 1930:

> The fifty long years of terror of the Great War found their climax not on the battlefields of Vaux and Douaumont but in the passes of the Caucasus, a Golgotha for the Armenians that went beyond all imagination of horror, beyond even the visions of Grünewald, Goya, and Bruegel. . . . Might the

greatest tragedy of the ordeal of humanity find one day a creator, an artist, a poet capable of capturing the gaze of men—for centuries to come—upon this time of madness, this evil Sabbath, that the self-satisfied, the cowards, and the idiots call the "world order"?

Not only did Vierbücher understand the extraordinary significance of this extermination but he also situated it within a series of massacres through history, as Lemkin would do later when he was refining the concept of genocide in the international debates of 1945–48:

> During the war, the Turks found the Germans just good enough to hold the curtain behind which they slaughtered more than a million innocents, men, women, and children. . . . The extermination of an entire people with the deliberate execution of women and children—this is a development for which the barbarous past was, no doubt, not "ready." One must think of the misdeeds of a Pizarro in Peru, the war of extermination of the red race by the whites, the manhunts by English "Christians" in Tasmania and New Zealand, the savagery of the Boer War, the extermination by thirst of the Hereros, for a simple glimpse of what happened near Kemah in 1915. Despite all the efforts at explanation and the addition of factors—pleasure of killing, rapacity, religious hate, despotism, stupidity—so many things remain incomprehensible that the tragedy of 1915 seems to us to be the bloodiest and most disturbing enigma of history. There will always remain an aspect that is unjustifiable and inexplicable, beyond all logic, and this vestige is unbearable.[60]

The reactions of witnesses who should have been the best informed, from 1894 to 1915 and from 1915 to 1942, are particularly incomprehensible. For instance, during the session of the House of Lords during which the Allied declaration of December 1942 was read, Viscount Samuel, "member of the Jewish community," took the floor: "The only events even remotely parallel to this were the Armenian massacres of fifty years ago, at the order of the Sultan Abdul Hamid, which were also carried into effect largely under the cloak of deportation. They aroused the outspoken indignation of the whole of civilized mankind, and they were one of the causes of the downfall of the Turkish Empire."[61] Except that the massacres of 1894–96, under the reign of the Bloody Sultan, were in no way comparable to the extermination of 1915 in terms of either how they took place or their scope. How could two episodes of the tragic saga of the Armenians be confused in this way?

"Why is a man punished when he kills another man, yet the killing of a million is a lesser crime than the killing of an individual?" (Raphael Lemkin)

The Lemkin family was affected by another consequence of the Great War: the Spanish flu. The global epidemic, which was responsible for more deaths than the war, claimed Samuel, Elias and Raphael's brother, in 1919. Raphael thus lived in a pivotal time, even though he reconstructed it in part in his successive accounts. When he studied linguistics and then law, he was passionately interested in crimes committed during World War I and the debates at the time. It was not by chance that he had first chosen to study philology. He was convinced that languages were key to understanding nations and their cultures. Influenced by the eighteenth-century philosopher Johann Gottfried Herder, Lemkin saw Herder's *Volksgeist* as a universal notion of national spirit, characterizing each national people. He deleted all references to other works, such as those by the Russian-born jurist André Mandelstam, who, like him, cross-referenced the tragedies suffered by the Jews of Russia and by the Armenians, and Lord Robert Cecil, who, in 1919, attempted to apply an international perspective to the persecution of peoples and religions. This allowed him to claim an immediate understanding of the facts that conferred a teleological slant on his autobiographical writings, even though some information, read in newspapers and discussed with friends or professors at the University of Lvov, had deeply touched him.[62]

And so, when the British government decided in 1921 to free 150 Turks who had been interned in Malta in 1919, Lemkin reacted: "I was shocked. A nation was killed and the guilty persons were set free. Why is a man punished when he kills another man, yet the killing of a million is a lesser crime than the killing of an individual?"[63] Seeking a legal and conceptual response to this quandary, Lemkin decided to change his orientation from philology to criminal law, which alone, he thought at the time, could be used to punish such specific criminals.

Also in 1921, Talaat Pasha, who had been exfiltrated to Berlin in 1919, was killed there by Soghomon Tehlirian. In Paris in 1926, an almost analogous act took place: Shalom Schwartzbard, a veteran serving in the French Foreign

Legion, executed Simon Petlioura, the general considered to be primarily responsible for the pogroms in Ukraine between 1918 and 1920. Lemkin followed both trials closely, noting that an Armenian and a Jew whose families had been victims of collective crime had taken justice into their own hands in the countries where the criminals had taken refuge, Germany and France. The societies in those countries could neither condemn nor acquit them; in both cases, they were held not responsible for their acts. Lemkin knew nothing about the real role of Schwartzbard, a communist and probably a GPU agent, in the "Jews' vengeance" or that of Tehlirian, an Armenian activist, in Operation Nemesis.[64]

What Lemkin wondered was why the Germans, who knew that Talaat was living in Berlin, had not arrested him. The legalistic answer, state sovereignty, disturbed the young legal scholar, even though it was implicated in the birth of the new Poland: "But sovereignty of states implies conducting an independent foreign and internal policy . . . [and] types of activity directed toward the welfare of the people. [Sovereignty] cannot be conceived as the right to kill millions of innocent people."[65] Lemkin took a moral point of view: the "crimes" of 1921 and 1926 bore a share of "goodness" because they had made it possible to expose the true criminals. This was also the position of the author Joseph Kessel, who attended Schwartzbard's trial:

> For me, his act was a sort of personal cause, as it was for all Jews who have blood running in their veins. . . . There's no doubt that I would never have committed his act, but simply because I lack the courage. . . . When it may be only to draw the attention of the civilized world to the awful tradition of the pogroms—and this could be done only in Paris, the most sensitive point of resonance, the most vibrant in the universe in this respect alone—Schwartzbard had to do what he did. . . . And that is why, whatever fate you reserve for him, I will ask him, when the debates are over, to do me the honor of shaking my hand.[66]

After Tehlirian's trial—he was acquitted in part thanks to testimony by Pastor Johannes Lepsius—Lemkin wrote an article in which he deplored the absence of any international law to standardize moral norms related to the destruction of national, racial, and religious groups.[67] In a 1949 interview for television, he returned to the roots of his work:

I became interested in the concept of genocide because it happened to the Armenians; and after[wards] the Armenians got a very rough deal at the Versailles Conference because their criminals were guilty of genocide and were not punished. . . . A man, [Soghomon] Tehlirian, whose mother was killed in the genocide, killed Talaat Pasha. And he told the court that he did it because his mother came in his sleep . . . many times. Here . . . the murder of your mother, you would do something about it! So he committed a crime. So, you see, as a lawyer, I thought that a crime should not be punished by the victims but should be punished by a court, by a national law.[68]

Lemkin turned from the moral and personal point of view—and it was even more poignant in 1949, for he now knew how his own mother had been exterminated—to that of a criminal lawyer. Weren't the laws written to judge individuals alone? It was a vicious circle. People could not take the law into their own hands no matter how just their cause, and so there was a need for an international statute: "In a rare moment of clarity that seething indignation instills, I further understood the concept of the crime that I was trying to establish."[69]

Contrary to what he stated, Lemkin was not the only one interested in the Armenians. The Germans, in particular, had closely followed the different testimonies and trials of the Weimar years.[70] But, starting in 1933, the memory of the extermination returned in force in Germany, both to the executioners—Hitler often used this example to prophesize the fate of the Jews and to jeer at his contemporaries' lack of memory—and to the Jews, who found analogies in the two situations. In 1933, Victor Klemperer, a cultured intellectual, made a play on words on the barbarian Germanic chieftain Arminius, who had defeated the Romans, and Armenia: "Instead of Germany, one should call it Arminia. This sounds more like Armenia."[71]

1933: Lemkin and the Invention of the "Crime of Barbarity" and the "Crime of Vandalism"

At the time of the Schwartzbard trial, Lemkin, an assistant professor in comparative criminal law, had just been appointed assistant public prosecutor for the district court of Warsaw. In fact, the First Conference for Unification of Criminal Law was held in the Polish capital in 1927 to address the question of global jurisdiction with regard to crimes against human rights.

The ambitious young lawyer, who lived in Warsaw, took advantage of this opportunity to become a contributor to these international conferences.

His name appeared on the conference's program for the first time in 1931, when it was held for the fourth time; he was tasked with reporting on "crimes that create a common danger." He was only thirty-one years old, but his work in collaboration with the most eminent Polish experts on the Polish, Russian, and Soviet criminal and tax codes had been noticed. We must not, however, subscribe to the retrospective intellectual logic that Lemkin asserted for understanding the genesis of his body of work, as experienced legal scholars had been working long and hard on "human rights" since the beginning of the century. During the congresses at The Hague in 1899 and 1907, there had been previous attempts to regulate war and invent peace. The Russian jurist Friedrich Martens, president of the Third Commission, on the laws and customs of warfare, became an advocate of the "Laws of Humanity," in a declaration—which became known as the Martens Clause—reproduced in the preamble to the 1899 Convention:

> Until a more complete code of the laws of war has been issued, the High Contracting Parties think it right to declare that, in cases not included in the Regulations adopted by them, populations and belligerents remain under the protection and empire of the principle of international law, as they result from the usages established between civilized peoples, from the laws of humanity, and the requirements of the public conscience.[72]

"Laws of humanity and requirements of the public conscience."[73] All of this had been largely swept away during the Great War, in particular with regard to invasions, occupations, pogroms, and even extermination when it came to the Armenians and Syriac Christians. New deliberations began under the auspices of the League of Nations. A personal report was commissioned from Lemkin for the Fifth Conference for Unification of Criminal Law, which was to be held in Madrid in 1933. Lemkin began to think about the possibility of a legal framing of crimes against the law of nations; his report was to be a decisive turning point, even though neither he nor his colleagues realized it yet. First, he situated himself with regard to previous conferences, in which the term "terrorism" had been used. In his view, "'Terrorism' does not constitute a legal concept; 'terrorism,' 'terrorists,' 'acts of terrorism' are expressions employed in the daily speech and the press to define a special state of mind among the perpetrators. . . . Neither 'public danger,' nor the political goal of the action, nor 'terrorization' of the population could constitute the main and exclusive criterion to formulate this crime as a crime against human rights." He concluded, "In this state of affairs, we are of the opinion that the creation of a new offence against the law of nations called terrorism would be useless and superfluous."[74] What should be done?

Lemkin's report now took an unprecedented direction. In effect, he proposed to turn the question around: because the problem involved the international nature of the crimes, the international aspects had to be dealt with first:

> The provocation of disasters in international communications, the vile destruction of works of art and culture, barbarous actions against a defenseless population, envisaged as crimes against human rights.
>
> a) Provocation of catastrophes in international communication
>
> b) Voluntary interruption of the exploitation of the telegraph, the telephone, post office, and T.S.F.[75]

To accommodate the modernity of the crimes, the law had to be modernized in order to resolve a paradox: communications were at the core of international life, and it was extremely easy to interrupt them. Lemkin was struck by train derailings: "What could be easier than placing on the railway, in a deserted place, stones or other obstacles? It is very difficult to apprehend the author and the consequences are expressed in the deaths of hundreds of innocent victims."[76]

"Innocent victims": Lemkin used the pleonasm as a commonplace. It was at this point that the report, intended to name specific crimes against human rights, struck out in an unprecedented direction with two terms: "vandalism" and "barbarity."

> c) The vile destruction of arts and cultural works (*vandalism*)
>
> The destruction of art and cultural works must be considered as the violation of international properties. The author of such a crime causes an irreversible damage, not only to the specific owner of the property and to the state

where the act is committed but also to the civilized world which is linked through numerous relations, and therefore benefits from the efforts of *all its citizens, the most industrious,* whose works appropriate everyone's culture and valorize it. . . . Such an act demonstrates not only a highly anti-social behavior, but also a specific *savagery* which puts its author outside the entire *civilized world.*[77]

Lemkin moved from crimes committed by individuals to their consequences for all of humanity. Citing the destruction of libraries as impeding all scholarly work, he proposed that "works of art and culture" be protected in wartime at the same level as Red Cross hospitals. The influence on him of the lexicon of World War I was obvious when he created a link between international humanitarian law based on the Geneva Convention and international criminal law, not without recognizing his debt to Nicholas Roerich, who advocated protection of cultural assets.[78] His debt to the Italian lawyer and professor Vespasian Pella was even greater: Pella had introduced, at the Criminal Conference in Palermo in early 1933, the term "crime of barbarity" and had worked to create an international criminal court.[79] This was Lemkin's fourth, and last, point.

d) *Barbarous* actions

Acts perpetrated against a defenseless population. These include *massacres, pogroms,* collective cruelties against women and children, treatment of humans in a way that *violates their dignity and humiliates them.* In the conception of such crimes, the following elements are considered: 1) the use of violence that proves the antisocial motivations and cruelty of its authors; 2) the systematic and organized action; 3) an action directed not against specific people, but rather against the population or a group of citizens, that is, an action not only collective in its nature but also an action directed against a certain collectivity; 4) the attacked collectivity is defenseless or is weak (in a contrary case, we would have equal or nearly equal chances); 5) the goal can be the intimidation of the population. . . . If these attacks and ferocities are executed in particularly cruel fashion and they manifest themselves in ways that can be characterized as savage, these acts evoke therefore a vivid reaction in conscience of the entire civilized world. The opinion of the entire world despises it and worries about the future of world culture. . . . The person who has participated in such barbarous actions in their country cannot be left in peace and go unpunished on the territory of another state; but the person must be pursued and punished wherever they are found.[80]

Lemkin's stroke of genius in 1933 was to link the two crimes, vandalism and barbarity; up to then, different criminal lawyers had been interested in these "evil acts."[81] What is more, when the proceedings were published, the order of the two crimes was inverted: the "acts of barbarity" went first.

The Acts of Barbarity
    . . . There are offences which combine these two elements. In particular these are attacks carried out against an individual as a member of a collectivity. The goal of the author [of the crime] is not only to harm an individual but, also to cause damage to the collectivity to which the latter belongs. Offenses of this type bring harm not only to human rights but also and most especially they undermine the fundamental basis of the social order. . . . Let us consider, first and foremost, acts of extermination directed against the ethnic, religious or social collectivities whatever the motive (political, religious, etc.); for example massacres, pogroms, actions undertaken to ruin the economic existence of the members of a collectivity, etc. . . . Taken as a whole, all the acts of this character constitute an offense against the law of nations which we will call by the name "*barbarity*." . . . The impact of acts like these usually exceed relations between individuals. They shake the very basis of harmony in social relations between particular collectivities.[82]

In his definitive publication, Lemkin passed from "acts of barbarity," to "acts of vandalism," and finally to acts of terrorism against international communications. He also added a fifth and final point, "propagation of human, animal or vegetable contagions."

Acts of Vandalism (Destruction of the culture and works of art)
    The art and cultural heritage in which the unique genius and achievement of a collectivity are revealed in fields of science, arts and literature. The contribution of any particular collectivity to world culture as a whole forms the wealth of all humanity, even while exhibiting unique characteristics. . . . It is also all humanity which experiences a loss by this act of vandalism.[83]

The combined emphasis on the religious and the national—aside from the pogroms explicitly mentioned—probably grew out of the episode of the Chaldo-Assyrians, then under threat in Iraq. In August 1933, two months before the Madrid conference, three thousand Chaldo-Assyrians, who had been unable to establish an autonomous territory in Syria under French mandate, were pushed back to the Simele District and massacred by Iraqi troops led by the Kurdish colonel Bakir Sidqi. Even as the Ottoman Empire disintegrated, the killings continued: the Chaldo-Assyrians exterminated in large numbers during World War I—today, it would be called genocide—were unable to find, any more than the Armenians, a state under the aegis of the great powers at the time of the "peace" treaties, or later at the League of Nations. They continued to be killed.

However, Lemkin was unable to go to Madrid to personally defend his arguments before his colleagues. A few months after Hitler came to power, the Polish government, drawing closer to Germany, could not accept arguments considered anti-German, and Polish anti-Semitic newspapers such as *Gazata Warszaka* quickly denounced Lemkin as working solely for his own Jewish interests. As Poland hardened its anti-Semitic laws, Lemkin was forced to resign from his official positions and turn to private law practice; he was also a Zionist activist alongside his brother Elias, who was hoping to move to Palestine (an idea that he later gave up on).

Lemkin was still participating in international criminal-law conferences, where his colleagues knew him as—or maintained that he was—a lawyer, not a Pole, and even less a Jew. Ironically, he was unable to attend the only conference at which his legal gravitas might have counted—the one in Madrid. Another irony: in 1934, Poland denounced the 1919 treaty on the rights of minorities, of which Jan Karski would be among the early historians, as he studied it for his dissertation, defended at Georgetown University—a Jesuit institution in Washington, DC—when he returned to his political science studies, interrupted by the war.[84]

In 1933, Lemkin went as far as he could down the path of a legal formula linking crimes against individuals who belong to certain collectivities and crimes against cultures. "Considering the contagious character of any social psychosis, actions of this kind . . . constitute a *general (transnational) danger.*

Similar to epidemics, they can pass from one country to another."[85] The medicalized vocabulary was typical of the 1930s, when the biologization of thought infected everything, even fierce opponents of the "Brown Plague." Like his contemporaries, Lemkin could not avoid these words even when he was trying to prevent attacks on individuals, including for the purpose of physical and cultural "triage." He was searching for the missing legal link that would make it possible to punish acts beyond the work initiated in The Hague at the beginning of the century. In vain.

No one, at the time, thought that this conceptual innovation should be pursued. Even Lemkin, though he was very active at the Copenhagen conference in 1935, fell back into line; there was a return to the expression "terrorism," discussed in the same terms as before. Yet, wounded by the lack of support for him in 1933, he returned to the subject in the 1950s, noting that the Nazi danger had not been comprehensible at the time. He often said that he had been uniquely prescient: "Many thought Hitler was just rhetoric. They tried to discourage me, they asked me not to continue to predict what seemed to be fantastical events and to formulate laws that were unnecessary, as this had almost never happened in history." Lemkin thought, on the contrary—as a Jew and a Pole—that this type of crime recurred "with almost biological regularity. We cannot close our eyes to it and hide our heads in the sand like ostriches."[86]

In 1944, the *Washington Post* was honest enough to credit Lemkin with the progress in Madrid: "If his proposal had been adopted then, Sir Cecil Hurst and his war crimes commission at the United Nations would not have found it so difficult to define the culpability of the Nazi oppressors."[87] Karski had testified in front of the same commission in 1943: "I told them what I had seen in the Warsaw ghetto and the Belzec death camp. My testimony was placed on record and I was told that it will be used as evidence in the United Nations' indictment against Germany."[88] When would Karski's testimony finally be heard, and why would it take so long? Delays, memory lapses, and camouflage obscured what World War I and World War II had in common.

One contradiction persisted: if the mental universe born of World War I had, in most cases, impeded comprehension of the destruction of the Jews in real time, conversely it contributed to the early clarity of certain observers and people smugglers in Great Britain and the United States, members of the British Parliament, Lemkin, Fry, and Werfel, as well as Rabbi Stephen Wise, a personal friend of President Roosevelt's, whom Karski met in Washington in the summer of 1943. In 1917, Wise wrote to his wife just after German bombs fell on London, where he was staying to attend meetings organized to provide assistance to Jews and Armenians, "What a noble deed the Germans yesterday wrought in London! Why are they bent upon plumbing the utter deeps of infamy? For centuries German will be synonymous with Hun, and worst of all the armor of their self-approval is impenetrable. I am yet to hear about the noon-day meeting for Armenia. If anything they are suffering even worse than the Jews. And I rejoice to think that I am helping them a little. But who can undo the evil done to them?"[89] In 1942, Wise wrote to his friend John Haynes Holmes, a Unitarian pastor who was a civil rights activist and a pacifist, about what was causing him great anguish at the time. "In addition to all your suffering over everything connected with the war, I have something more, namely the uniquely tragic fate of my people. You will be tempted at once to ask, why do I think of it as 'uniquely tragic'? Is it any worse than the fate of the Czechs, or Yugoslavs, or Poles?"[90] Wise went on to give a long description of the murderous *Aktionen* in the Warsaw ghetto.

At the same time, people who were trapped in the ghettos of Poland testified to this very culture rooted in the precedent of 1914–18. Calel Perechodnik related, with the vividness of desperation, that the *Greuelpropaganda* of the Great War had now been largely surpassed. The killing was real: his wife and child had really been loaded onto a train headed for Treblinka.[91] Franz Werfel's powerful novel on the extermination of the Armenians, *The Forty Days of Musa Dagh*, was also read in Poland. The historian Emanuel Ringelblum notes this in his description of the intensity of intellectual life in the ghetto and the frantic interest in World War I:

> Serious readers have a great interest in war literature. They read memoirs, such as Lloyd George's, great novels of the 1914–18 war, and so on. They savor pages dealing with 1918 and the German defeat. They seek comparisons with present times, they seek to prove that the defeat of the invincible German army is near. . . . For my part, I recently reread the great novel by Van der Meersch on the German occupation in France and Belgium. On each page, the comparison is obvious with the current epoch, which is even more terrible than that

of the preceding war. One thing is identical: the pillages and the pitiless, cold oppression of civilian populations in the occupied countries. The population was enslaved and subjected to forced labor, just as it is today. After reading this book, one must ask the question: What was done to forestall a new Hun power in Europe?[92]

The question posed by Ringelblum in the Warsaw ghetto in 1942 was raised again more than two years later in Washington: an important meeting was held at the White House to "discuss the problem of rescuing the Jews still living in Europe" just after the creation of the War Refugee Board, for which Henry Morgenthau Jr., secretary of the Treasury and increasingly critical of the State Department's inaction, had been an advocate. In fact, Morgenthau raised the first point, as he was "convinced that successful action could be taken, referring to the results of his father, Henry Morgenthau Sr., who, as ambassador to Turkey, had successfully gotten Armenians out of Turkey to save them."[93] A few days later, Randolph Paul, who had worked with Morgenthau to establish the Board, recalled that Morgenthau Sr. "had undertaken a similar operation when he was American ambassador to Turkey and had saved numerous Armenians."[94] Indeed, Morgenthau Sr. had done all he could on the ground in 1915–16 and, after he returned to the United States, from 1917 to 1919 to warn his compatriots about the massacres of Christians, Armenians, Greeks, and Syriac Christians. In June 1917, Felix Frankfurter had accompanied him on a US War Department secret mission to persuade the Ottomans to break away from the Central Powers. The mission also had another goal: to find ways to improve the lot of the Jewish community in Palestine, which was in the process of dying of hunger.[95]

We know how things went for the Armenians: there was more talk than action.

The Jews in Europe also had to wait. In March 1944, two months after the meeting in Washington, Ringelblum, who had found refuge in the Christian district of Warsaw, was shot by the Nazis, along with his family and the Poles who had taken them in.

4

Naming a Nameless Crime

Lemkin and Karski in the
United States, 1943–45

Germany will go down to utter defeat. But the Jews of Europe . . . have no assurance at present that a United Nations victory will come in time to save them from complete annihilation.

—Memorandum submitted to the President of the United States by a
delegation of representatives of Jewish organizations, December 8, 1942

A "Conspiracy of Silence"

Jan Karski arrived in the United States on June 16, 1943. With Polish ambassador Jan Ciechanowski as his guide, he was caught up in the political discord between those who, like him, supported the Polish government in exile and those who were already envisaging a "free," Sovietized Poland. In 1943, the Nazi occupiers made public that the Soviets had murdered Polish officers imprisoned in Katyn in 1940; yet, most of the Allies continued to claim that the massacre had been perpetrated by the Nazis. The Poles, however—and first among them Officer Karski, who had been taken prisoner by the Soviets and managed to escape to enter the resistance—had known the truth for a long time.

Karski could not get out of his mind what he had seen in the Warsaw ghetto and Izbica in the summer of 1942: although the Poles were enduring a horrible occupation, their suffering was not comparable to that of the Jews. The information in his possession had been sent to the United States by Great Britain. In June 1943, what revelations could he bring to a country where not only the leaders of Jewish organizations but the entire government, including

President Roosevelt, had been alerted to the situation in the spring of 1942? Stephen Wise, president of the American Jewish Congress, had been among the recipients of the Riegner telegram sent in August. On November 25, the *New York Times* summarized the report of the Polish government in exile on Belzec, Sobibor, and Treblinka under the headline "Himmler program kills Jewish Poles." On December 7, an encoded telegram labeled "This is of particular secrecy and should be received by the authorized recipient and not passed on" was sent by the British War Cabinet to the American State Department: "Massacres of Jews in Europe: While it is impossible to obtain confirmation of particular incidents or of allegations regarding the existence of a detailed plan for extermination of Jews, we have little doubt that a policy of gradual extermination of all Jews, except highly qualified workers, is being carried out by the German authorities."[1] And yet, the fate of the Jews did not move the Foreign Office except to the extent that "there is considerable public interest here and early action is advisable." No detail on the form of the killings was given.

In early December 1942, President Roosevelt received a long memorandum: twenty pages of details from every European country on the verified extermination of two million Jews by "caravans of Death, deportation . . . mass murder, organized famine, forced labor in disease-infested ghettos, slave-labor reservations . . . mass shootings in orgies of murder, deportation and extermination centers. . . . Germany will be defeated. But the Jews of Europe, whom Hitler has marked out to suffer utter extinction, have no assurance at present that a United Nations victory will come in time to save them from complete annihilation."[2]

And then Chaim Weizmann, president of the World Zionist Organization, declared bitterly in March 1943, "When a future historian assembles the sad history of our time, he will find two incredible things: first, the crime itself; second, the world's reaction to that crime. . . . He will be stunned at the apathy of the civilized world regarding this enormous and systematic massacre of human beings. . . . He will not understand why the world's conscience had to be stirred. Above all, he will not be able to understand why free nations, facing renewed and organized barbarism, had to be begged to grant asylum to the first and main victim of this barbarism. Two million Jews have already been exterminated. The world can no longer claim that these horrible facts are unknown or unconfirmed.... We are being destroyed by a conspiracy of silence."[3]

Did Karski, who had arrived in Washington three days before, accompany Ambassador Ciechanowski to a rally in New York on June 19, 1943, "in memory of the 35,000 Jews murdered in the Warsaw ghetto"? There, Shmuel Zygielbojm, the Bund representative for a free Poland based in London, explained that the past offered numerous examples of "black records of violence and persecution" but that "never in the whole history of mankind have its chronicles registered so continuous, so methodical, so iniquitous, so barbarous, so inhuman a system of cruelty and mass extermination."[4] Adolph Held, president of the Jewish Labor Committee, denounced the tragedies and lauded the sacrifices, including Zygielbojm's. The telegram that Zygielbojm had sent to Churchill in December 1942 was poignant but futile. "I address to you and to your government this last appeal of despair.... As [a] man who directly represents the unfortunate Jewish population of Poland I convey to you ... this last appeal for help."[5] A few months later, he committed suicide, as did so many Jewish leaders in Europe. He sent his last will and testament to General Sikorski:

> The latest news that has reached us from Poland makes it clear beyond any doubt that the Germans are now murdering the last remnants of the Jews in Poland with unbridled cruelty.... I cannot continue to live and to be silent.... My comrades in the Warsaw ghetto fell with arms in their hands in the last heroic battle. I was not permitted to fall like them, together with them, but I belong with them, to their mass grave.
>
> By my death, I wish to give expression to my most profound protest against the inaction in which the world watches and permits the destruction of the Jewish people.
>
> I know that there is no great value to the life of a man, especially today. But since I did not succeed in achieving it in my lifetime, perhaps I shall be able by my death to contribute to the arousing from lethargy of those who could and must act in order that even now, perhaps at the last moment, the handful of Polish Jews who are still alive can still be saved from certain destruction.
>
> My life belongs to the Jewish people of Poland, and therefore I hand it over to them now.[6]

He who had been treated with contempt during his lifetime and considered, including by the Bund, a poor choice for a representative became one
of the heroes of the Jewish uprising, celebrated alongside the ghetto fighters. From Poland to London, and in Washington, DC, those who were collecting archives and telling the story were fighting the same battle. The
heroic Jewish discourse that would become that of the first remembrance of
extermination emerged in real time: "The Jews who died in Warsaw fought
the same cause as allied soldiers in Africa and that their feat would 'be resurrected on the pages of future civilized historians."[7]

Jan Karski in Washington: Bearing Witness
Deep in the "most powerful nation in the world"

Karski was seen as a "civilized" witness. He "looked as if he had gone through
great suffering and hunger and his burning eyes reflect[ed] keen intelligence
coupled with childish candor," a "tall, dark young man, of striking appearance,"[8] and he spared no effort to continue what he had started in London.
He gave interviews to the press—he was Mr. B in *Collier's*—and met with
everyone deemed influential in Washington. Although he knew that he had
nothing new to reveal in June, July, and August 1943, he willingly engaged
in a new round of meetings. But did seeing, hearing, or reading him mean
understanding him? As he had in London, Karski spoke mostly about the resistance and his mission. Yet, his words were not heard except to the extent
that they served the purpose of his interlocutors.

For instance, on July 10, 1943, Assistant Secretary of State Breckinridge
Long returned from a requiem mass for General Sikorski, who was revered
by Karski and who had made sure that he was sent to the United States—
and who had just died in a plane crash (an assassination?). Sikorski had been
the guest of the Americans; his farewell speech in New York in early 1943
showed that he was hoping—or was it wishful thinking?—for an American–
Soviet victory that would not damage democratic Poland, which he envisaged as a member of a "Central European Federation." Sikorski referred
once more to 1914–19: "After the victory, we will be faced with the problem
of organizing a just, democratic peace, a peace more durable than that of
1919. . . . Under the guidance of President Roosevelt and Prime Minister
Churchill the American and British peoples have realized the meaning of
these last two world wars. The first one which started in Belgrade in 1914,

and the present one launched by an attack of German bombers on Warsaw in 1939. These two world conflicts have proved that it is no such thing as isolation from common dangers and suffering and that real peace is indivisible and touches the world over."[9]

After Sikorski's death, the Americans became increasingly concerned about the abominable relations between the Poles and the Russians, which were the subject of Long's memorandum: "Sikorski's death settles nothing. He was the only one who could heal the rifts among Poles and keep them together as a nation. No one can replace him. The elites are dying by the hundreds in the German concentration camps. Unfortunately, we have obvious proof: the account by resister Jan Karski that the ambassador told us about yesterday evening leaves no doubt of this."[10] Long, notoriously indifferent to the fate of the Jews, was struck only by the fate of the Polish elites.

On July 28, Lieutenant Karski and Polish ambassador Ciechanowski met with the president of the United States in his office. "This was the very citadel of power. I was to meet the most powerful man in the most powerful nation of the world." All this "power" accounted for twenty-one lines in his memoir and fifteen words about the Jews: "He asked me to verify the stories told about the German practices against the Jews."[11] As a refugee in the United States, Karski was cautious. Ciechanowski, however, reported the interview in 1947, when all was lost for the free Poland that they had envisaged. He had resigned so as not to represent a government in communist hands, whence the title of his book, *Defeat in Victory*, in which he made Karski one of his spokespeople in the cold war that was underway. Eleven pages were devoted to the meeting with Roosevelt, which dealt mainly with the organization of the Polish resistance, the future free Poland without a Danzig Corridor, and the negotiations with Stalin on territorial compensation for eastern Prussia. In the rushes for *Shoah*, Karski recounts that the ambassador had given him detailed instructions: "'Now you be careful. You are going to see the most powerful man on this globe. This man evidently is busy. He thinks in terms of the war, of humanity. . . . He thinks after this war the human race will be organised in such a way: no more wars, and he will play a key role in this arrangement. So, again, be brief, be concise.'"[12]

Karski was clear: the Jewish question was only a secondary problem for the president of the United States. Karski saw things the same way at the time, even though he felt some guilt later, especially when Claude Lanzmann pressed him on the extermination of the Jews: "You realize that throughout my entire mission, for me the Jewish problem was not the only problem. For me the key problem was Poland, the Curzon Line, Soviet demands, Communists in the underground movement, fear of the Polish nation. What is going to happen to Poland? This was the emphasis."[13]

Roosevelt, who had read so many reports, wanted to hear a single voice. Karski talked—but less than Roosevelt, who asked questions about the Polish economy and assured him that a solution would be found for eastern Prussia. Karski did not manage to say one word about the Jews; finally, just before the interview ended, he raised the issue. Roosevelt simply made a gesture. "What was the significance of this gesture? Was it a gesture, or was it an expression of good will of the centre of power, who does not deal with particular problems? I still don't know until today."[14]

Roosevelt knew. He didn't need Karski's information. He also knew that he had a war to wage, advisers and ministers with strongly opposed opinions, and Jewish friends, including Supreme Court justice Felix Frankfurter, who were recalcitrant regarding any specific policy for their people. On the other hand, he had a list prepared for Karski of important Jewish figures to meet, including the justice. Neither in Frankfurter's published memoir nor in his handwritten notes is there any mention of his meeting with Karski.[15] Frankfurter was very well informed; he read the same reports as did the president, as well as the news reports, and he was a long-standing friend of Rabbi Stephen Wise, who had informed him of the gassings in September 1942.

Even in 1978 Karski had not forgotten the stereotypes of his childhood when he described Frankfurter: "A little man. He did emanate brilliance. Very alert, his eyes. Unimpressive physically, a little man, Jewish-looking. Very friendly, smiling, towards me all the time friendly."[16]

"No! No!" Frankfurter, who knew, could not "believe" what Karski had seen and was telling him.

AMBASSADOR CZIKANOWSKI: Felix! . . . [Karski's account] was checked and rechecked ten times . . . He is not lying.

FRANKFURTER: I did not say that he is lying. I said that I don't believe him. These are different things. My mind, my heart, they are made in such a way that I cannot accept it. No! No![17]

Karski was not discouraged. On August 9, 1943, he addressed the representatives of Polish Jews in the offices of the World Jewish Congress. These men had been fighting the State Department for months—as their British counterparts had been fighting the Foreign Office—for action, finally, to save European Jews. Two avenues were proposed: to attempt actions in Nazi-occupied Europe and to authorize refugees to move to temporary refugee camps in southern Italy or liberated North Africa.

Karski presented himself as an apostle of truth, an "envoy" in an almost-religious sense of the term:

> I have been asked by the leaders of Polish Jewry to tell you of Jewish sufferings and to inform public opinion of the plight of the Jews in Poland—so that at some later date no one may arise and claim that the world was not aware of the tragedy of the Polish Jewry. I can give you my personal guarantee that everything I report to you now is authentic and true. I speak from personal knowledge as well as from well-authenticated reports given to me. I am ready to testify to the veracity of everything I say under oath.[18]

The messenger repeated the accounts he had given in London: "I have given a report of the Jewish situation in Poland to leaders of the British government as well as to the British Labor movement. . . . They can make no pretense of ignorance of the true state of affairs." He dissected the system of "terror, starvation, ghettos, deportation, extermination," the reports by executioners, victims, and neighbors, and the information that had reached the British and Americans. He went into more personal detail, recounting how he had saved an old friend, a Jewish officer in the Polish army, from the Otwock ghetto; asserting that the Polish were active on the black market; and defending Jewish councils in the ghettos against accusations that they had sent their own people to their death by saying that it was impossible for them to do otherwise. He recalled that many of them—including Zygielbojm[19]—had committed suicide in response to the tragedy.

As a Polish resister, Karski also wanted to preserve the honor of his homeland. Too much so? "Poland has no traitors. We have no Quislings. The Poles know that their country lives and will live on and that only the Polish Government is qualified as the mouthpiece of the Polish People."[20]

One of his interlocutors in London, Ignacy Schwarzbart, would say in 1945 that he had lost all trust in the resistance couriers, "for in none of them, even in Karski, did I feel a heart for the Jews."[21] Yet, Karski remained very clear on the mediocre assistance provided by the Poles to the Jews. If the resistance conducted reprisals against informers, that was because there were in fact informers. "I do not mean to say by this that all Poles have changed their attitude against the Jews, but I can testify that all are opposed to the tortures they are enduring."[22]

Karski noted that Poles who helped Jews risked the death penalty. But he went further than this constantly repeated argument. Yes, Poles were put into forced labor, undernourished, subjected to terror and cruelty, but "they are not murdered outright by the Nazis as are the Jews. . . . At the time when I left Poland, the German terror was still raging. The Jews feel that the situation will become even worse. The Poles are now afraid that Hitler will turn against them and will murder them as he did the Jews. But the Nazis were determined to wipe out the Jews, as a people and as individuals. It was their intention to exterminate them as a race, systematically, without exception. The massacres of Jews that were committed were therefore without historical precedent. It was mass murder, pure and simple."[23]

"It was the murder of the truth: suppression of the notice of murder" (Raphael Lemkin, 1943)

And yet. In Washington in 1943 the same phenomenon occurred as had occurred in London a year earlier. The British, starting with the Foreign Secretary, Anthony Eden, had questioned Karski in order to corroborate their information on the Polish resistance. On both sides of the Atlantic, some thought that all this, which would lead to rescuing the Jews—even if they truly realized that the Jews were the Nazis' main, if not only, target—might compromise the main war effort. It took almost the entire duration of the conflict for this wait-and-see attitude, or even denial, to end—two more long years, during which almost all the Jews in Europe would perish.

Although Karski had accomplished his mission, he had the impression that words remained just words, that neither the Americans nor the British were taking—or wanted to take—the true measure of the crimes. It was for this reason that he decided to write his memoir, *Story of a Secret State*, the main subject of which was his Poland and its resistance. But it was when he was describing the fate of the Jews that he used the words "annihilate," "wipe out," "exterminate," "massacre," and "mass murder."

In his personal archives are pamphlets that he referred to while writing his memoir, all of which speak first of the fate of Catholic Poles. One is *Oswiecim Camp of Death*, published in Polish in 1942 and translated into English in February 1944. After forty pages devoted to the fate of the Poles in the main concentration camp, Oswiecim, an appendix gives a mapped typology of the hundred concentration camps scattered around Poland; it shows "camp districts," "temporary concentration camps," and "general concentration camps," including the largest one, Oswiecim, "recently greatly expanded by . . . [a] '*camp of death*'" (emphasis added; though not named, this was Birkenau), as well as camps situated in Germany (Dachau, Mathausen, Ravensbrück, and others) in which Poles were imprisoned. Also listed were "forced labor camps," "concentration camps for clergy," "camps for 'improvement of the race,'" "camps for 'correction of youth,'" and "concentration camp for children, so-called 'educational institutes.'" Between the camps for clergy and those for "improvement of the race" appears the category "Concentration Camps for Jews":

> These camps have been established in conjunction with the Nazi campaign to liquidate the European Jews. Some of them are simply places of execution where Jews from Poland and the rest of Europe are asphyxiated, electrocuted, and machine-gunned. The most notorious of these are:
> Belzec
> Sobibor, near Wlodawa
> Tremblinka [*sic*] III
> Six other camps for Jews are located in:
> Starogard II
> Potulice III
> Kosow Podlaski
> Trawniki
> Pomiechowek II
> Between Chelm and Wlodava (the name could not be ascertained)
> In these camps, too, the Jews are murdered, but mostly by starvation, disease, torture, and forced labor.[24]

The information was detailed, and the distinctions were well described. But there was a concept missing, a word that did not yet exist, a word that Raphael Lemkin was looking for at exactly the same moment.

In fall 1943, Karski was cited by leaders in the Treasury Department who were in favor of taking action against the "timorousness"—an understatement—of the State Department. Indeed, the small group working around Treasury Secretary Henry Morgenthau Jr. to establish the War Refugee Board was devastated: "Mr. Cox: . . . In the first place this is a problem which we have gotten facts on. It covers all of occupied Europe. . . . German policy has been clearly one of extermination of the Jews, complete and final, and we have talked to people from the Polish underground, who also, incidentally, have talked to the president about that firsthand observation. . . . Unless you get effective action . . . many of these people are turned back. . . . It means certain death as far as the Germans are concerned. . . . Now, the President has heard that fellow, Karski, who came out of the Polish underground. He knows what is happening there."[25] This verbatim account underlines that President Roosevelt was affected by what Karski had had to say, even though he did not decide to renounce his wait-and-see approach.

The British, who did not want to put undue stress on their strategy in Mandatory Palestine, blocked Jewish emigration as of 1939. Morgenthau and his advisers could not have criticized this move more harshly—to the point that they were comparing the British policy to that of the Nazis.

> Mr. Paul: I said that there isn't any difference between the British position, as you have described it there, and the German position. If anything, the Germans are somewhat more merciful. They proceed much more rapidly. How can we ever accuse the Germans of cruelty to these Jews in Europe when we decree the same sort of death, or a more lingering death for them?
>
> Mr. Dubois: . . . There is a group of Jews the Germans are not killing, and that is the group who have visas for Palestine. They are specifically setting them aside in camps so after the war, they can say that the United Nations were just as much to blame as Germany: "Here is a group of Jews who had visas for Palestine whom we were willing to let out, and they would not let them come out."[26]

A plan formulated by the World Jewish Congress was considered: find the financial means to help neutral countries that would take in exfiltrated Jews by making payments to the Nazis. "Extraordinary measures to take to save the Jews of Hungary," deported in 1944, were now sought. Karski's testimony was evoked once again:

> He expressed his conviction that it would be possible to gain agreement from the German government to release a considerable number of Jews:
> a) If a certain number of countries declared themselves prepared to receive them;
> b) If a large ransom were paid to the German authorities. The catastrophe that is befalling the Hungarian Jews pushes us to resort to methods as extraordinary as those suggested by Mr. Karski and the Jewish leaders in Slovakia.[27]

Karski was well aware of the appalling corruption of the Nazis and their henchmen in Poland. But the State Department was not planning to offer extra visas or to become involved in the corruption of rescue for ransom. Giving money to the enemy seemed neither politically nor morally acceptable.

Could large-scale immigration to Turkey or Iran be organized, with the Jews returning when "Europe was purged of Hitler"?[28] But how, after the war, would survivors be able to return to their countries purged of Jews? Or should transit camps be opened in zones where the Americans had landed: North Africa—which the French and de Gaulle were blocking—Sicily, southern Italy, Sardinia? All these proposed solutions came to naught.

It was then that two of the most senior executives at the US Treasury Department, Randolph Paul and John Pehle, seriously challenged the State Department and Assistant Secretary Breckinridge Long. In their *Report to the Secretary on the Acquiescence of this Government in the Murder of the Jews*, they wrote, "Since the time when this Government knew that the [European] Jews were being murdered [summer 1942], our State Department has failed to take any positive steps reasonably calculated to save any of these people."[29]

The Treasury Department moved from observation to attack: those who did not act were guilty of complicity in murder. The executives at the State Department had, in effect, falsified the statistics on immigration to the

United States: "The most glaring example of the use of the machinery of this Government to *actually prevent the rescue of Jews* is the administrative restrictions which have been placed upon the granting of visas to the United States."[30] The tenacious Long had continually lied about the number of Jewish refugees accepted into the country in order to make the president believe that the country was concerned with their fate.[31]

The highly detailed report of errors since 1942 was unusually forceful: "If men of the temperament and philosophy of Long continue in control of immigration administration, we may as well take down that plaque from the Statue of Liberty and black out the 'lamp beside the golden door.'"[32] The Secretary of the Treasury, Henry Morgenthau, sent another secret report. The pressure became too great: on January 22, 1944, the War Refugee Board was created. The very name is striking: even though it was known that Jews were the refugees involved, it was only war refugees in general that were mentioned.

More than a year after Karski's visit to the White House and six months after the creation of the War Refugee Board, President Roosevelt reaffirmed the principles proclaimed by the Allies since the signature of the Atlantic Charter: win the war, punish its instigators: "Please express to those gathered at the meeting to protest the *deportations and cruelties* visited upon the *remaining Jewish community* of Europe my feelings of abhorrence of these desperate acts of the enemy. I repeat to all concerned my earlier warning that those who participate in *these acts of savagery* shall not go unpunished."[33] This message proves once more the president's cynicism—or realism?—with regard to the specificity of the war being waged against the Jews. He knew; he knew everything: "the remaining Jewish community of Europe," "deportations and cruelties," "acts of savagery." But he did not say the word "extermination." At what point did silence, restraint, and prudence become complicity? This was what Lemkin was wondering, too.[34]

Lemkin Confronting Denial: Finding the Words

"Data compiled by Dr. Raphael Lemkin when he was on the faculty in Stockholm, Sweden and at Duke University, North Carolina, then as consultant for the Board of Economic Warfare."[35] When Lemkin arrived in Washington, his experience of occupied Europe was validated, but his 1933 conceptualization, "crimes of barbarity and vandalism," was not. He felt totally abandoned: not only were the Jewish people in the process of "disappearing from Earth," as Hitler had prophesized, but the Allies were participating indirectly in the crime by their procrastination.

Lemkin was absolutely determined to meet with President Roosevelt, who he felt was lacking information. To his dismay, he was allowed only a brief memorandum: "How could I compress the pain of millions, the fear of nations, the hope for salvation from death onto one page?"[36] Then, it was weeks before advisers responded that he had to be patient. Mortified that neither President Roosevelt nor Vice President Wallace, for whom he was working directly, had perceived the urgency of the situation, his sense of foreboding grew: "'Patience' is a good word for when one expects an appointment, a budgetary allocation, or the building of a road. But when the rope is already around the neck of the victim and strangulation is imminent, isn't the word 'patience' an insult to reason and nature?"[37] He was shattered to discover that "this was a conflict not between the Jewish people and the German, but between the world and itself":

> The impression of a tremendous conspiracy of silence poisoned the air. There was no escape from this feeling. . . . A double murder was taking place. One committed by the Nazis and the other by the Allies. Were the Allies refusing to make it known that the execution of nations and races had already begun? . . . The silence of murder started the day the first reports of mass executions reached London from Warsaw late in 1942. It lasted until December 1944, almost two years. No acknowledgment was made of the death of a nation that had given the world the belief in one God, whose Bible was still read every day in the Allies' churches. It was the murder of the truth: suppression of the notice of murder.[38]

"A dog run over by a car upsets our emotional balance and digestion; three million Jews killed in Poland cause but a moderate uneasiness. Statistics don't bleed; it is the detail which counts." (Arthur Koestler)

Lemkin and Karski were not the only ones to express the idea that the complicity of silence also meant complicity in murder. For instance, Samuel Golfard said, shortly before he was murdered in a Polish ghetto, "The Germans are not alone guilty of our tragic fate. The English and the Americans who tolerated the acts of the German nation are also guilty. They fattened Hitler and nurtured the present regime in Germany."[39] Once the war was over, in 1948, Isaac Schneersohn—the French Emanuel Ringelblum, founder in April 1943 of the Centre de documentation juive contemporaine, secret at the time, in Grenoble—expressed the same despair in his recollections:

> The nations that were to defeat Germany did nothing to top its barbaric madness against the Jews. They allowed it; they stayed quiet. They did not use reprisals. They later feigned that they had been unaware of the excesses of these crimes. An unacceptable excuse when one thinks of the sources of information of all sorts that the wartime secret services were providing to them. . . . The Allies opposed nothing. When the political assault against Europe became an assault against the essential principles of modern humanity, they undertook no counterattack. They never thought to make good use of their advantages, as their victory advanced and the Germans began to weaken, to break the only front on which the latter continued to win and to persevere even more desperately: the Jewish front.[40]

On February 7, 1943, an article of rare invective appeared in the *New York Times*, written by an author who had been living in the United States for a long time, Sholem Asch. If the unusual length of the article did not catch the reader's eye, the drawing of a swastika crushing a landscape empty of people but populated by scavenging crows in flight certainly would.

"In the Valley of Death. That valley is the scene of Hitler's mass murder." Asch described Polish ghettos and extermination camps, "dumping ground and a clearing house"; the Jews of Europe were transported there in "sealed, unventilated, lime freight cars which are death traps" (Asch had read Karski). "Those that survive become as human waste to be thrown into mass-slaughter houses which the Nazis had created for all Jews. These houses of death consist of gas chambers and blood-poisoning stations. . . . Regardless of origin, age, or sex, all are being killed." Following were accounts of the extermination of children and adults in three health-care and charitable institutions that Asch had visited before the war in Warsaw, including Dr. Korczak's orphanage. Asch not only described the killing of all the Jews by the Nazis; he also searched for their friends and excluded no member of the human community:

When I think of the state to which Hitler has brought humanity, I am disturbed by one thought: after all, Hitler belongs to the human race and so do
the other Nazis. They were accepted as a part of us, I daresay a part of the
system in which we are living. They are not a cause, they are the results of our
behavior, of our psychology. . . . Never would Hitler have dared to select a
people for annihilation had not the way been prepared for him by all kinds
and degrees of anti-Semites. A person's constitutional rights are secure only
when his social standing in a community is secure. If a people is singled out
for hatred, as a group, if the fact of just belonging to this group is considered
enough to count as a crime, that people loses, in the eyes of its persecutor, the
dignity and mysticism in the eyes of a human being. . . . All who have prepared this ground of hatred toward the Jews and other races are exactly as
responsible for the bestial slaughter of the Jews in Poland and others as Hitler
and his clique. . . . Hitler only gathers the fruits of their well-planted seeds.[41]

In January 1944, Arthur Koestler, also infuriated, published an article in
the English and American press, illustrated in the *New York Times* with a
drawing of Hitler and Himmler calmly conversing in front of a scene of
hanged people and piles of cadavers: "It is the greatest mass-killing in
recorded history; and it goes on daily, hourly, as regularly as the ticking of
your watch." Increasingly desperate, Koestler returned to what he had said
in 1942. He set the number of deaths at three million—and yet he was far
from the actual count—as he contemplated a double-sided nightmare: on
the one side the reality of the atrocities and on the other side the refusal of
the English and the Americans to see it. Koestler placed himself among the
"screamers," those who yelled as they unveiled photographs, films, books,
witnesses—nothing was missing, and yet nothing changed, despite the insane
risks taken by the "resisters who came from Poland." Then, "Nine out of
ten average American citizens, when asked whether they believed that the
Nazis commit atrocities, answered that it was all propaganda lies, and that
they didn't believe a word of it! . . . [It is the same in England.] They don't
believe in concentration camps. They don't believe in the starved children
of Greece, in the shot hostages of France, in the mass graves of Poland;
they have never heard of Lidice, Treblinka, or Belzec." Were the screamer-
messengers as certain that they would lose the game as the "prophets of the
Old Testament" or "Cassandra"?[42]

Koestler offered an explanation: "In reality both 'knowing' and 'believing' have varying degrees of intensity." It is easier to believe what is close in time and space and what one is capable of integrating.[43] Faced with the absoluteness of Nazi crimes, people remained speechless. "A dog run over by a car upsets our emotional balance and digestion; three million Jews killed in Poland cause but a moderate uneasiness. Statistics don't bleed; it is the detail which counts. [This sentence was taken from the mouth of his protagonist, fashioned after Karski, in his 1943 novel *Arrival and Departure*.] We are unable to embrace the total process with our awareness; we can only focus only on little lumps of reality. . . . When we approach the sphere of the Absolute, our reaction ceases to be a matter of degrees."[44] What to do? Think specifically about the murders. Koestler took the example of a British lecturer—the publisher Victor Gollancz, who had been so upset by his meeting with Karski in 1942—who imagined what the victims had suffered: "One day he tried to feel what it was like to be suffocated by chloride gas in a death-train; another day he had to dig his grave with two hundred others and then face a machine gun."[45] Koestler recommended that newspaper readers undertake such an exercise for two minutes every morning to break through their oblivious normalcy.

As some accurately described the mass murder of European Jews by the Nazis and accused the Allies of inaction and public opinion of being complicit in the silence, others sought the underlying causes, starting with anti-Semitism. Raphael Lemkin chose to take both paths to try to tear the Jews away from their executioners. He directly addressed the American people—and, beyond them, the world—to break the "conspiracy of silence" in a book, *Axis Rule in Occupied Europe: Laws of Occupation, Analysis of Government, Proposals for Redress*. He reported on the sacking of all of Europe and the exterminatory exactions, proposed concepts to explain them, and expressed his wish for a quick turn to action. Lemkin sought words, the word, to describe this form of violence that was both "ancient" and so contemporary.

"How strange that I was among both the mourners and the dead" (Raphael Lemkin, 1943): Toward the "Genocide Pact"

Since the 1920s, and especially since the advent of the paired "crime of barbarity"/"crime of vandalism" in 1933, Lemkin had become an activist—

a soldier for his cause—in the debate that had raged since the invention of his concept: what is a genocide? Or, rather, what are genocides? For the plural was obvious to him, but because the word was coined by a Polish Jew in 1943, it was quickly assimilated with the Genocide (with a capital G) of the Jews. This is a mistake, if one analyzes his writings. Lemkin blurred comprehension of his work by predating his invention, referring only to the legal concept even as he made himself the historian of his own life. He was Jewish, a member of a national minority that the League of Nations, for which he had worked so hard to standardize international criminal law, had not been able to protect. He had become a victim of the concept that he had theorized. Although he probably created the word "genocide" in the name of dead Jews—his own—he was convinced that he could mourn as an individual only on behalf of all humanity. And so, he reconstructed his final days in Poland with his family and other inhabitants of the shtetls, which he described in his autobiography: "It was like going to their funeral while they were still alive. The best of me was dying with the full cruelty of consciousness."[46]

> During the war, forty-nine members of my family perished from genocide, including my parents. . . . Suddenly I felt that the earth is receding under from under my feet and the sense of living is disappearing. I transformed my personal disaster into a powerful moral force. . . . Was it not the best form of gratitude for my mother, who had awakened me to the idea of these persecutions, to engrave "genocide pact" as an epitaph on her symbolic gravestone to ensure that she and millions of others had not died in vain? I decided to make this law my strength, and to make my work a respite from my sorrow.[47]

Horrified by his own apocalyptic visions, Lemkin told many morbid stories in which he depicted himself, traumatized, in the place of all victims: "I myself am living in a procession of the afflicted, following the bodies of dead nations. Strange that I was among both the mourners and the dead. Strange to feel my living body as my soul was taking to its grave. . . . All over Europe the Nazis were writing the book of death with the blood of my brethren."[48] In his papers was a profession of faith, *This I Believe*, in which he proclaimed his faith in a law opposing inhumanity in almost mystical terms. Although he used the word "genocide" in this essay, indicating that it was written after 1943, he dated this description of his flight across Poland to 1939–40:

In the forest, I pronounced to the dead and to the living that if I survive I will devote the rest of my life exclusively to outlawing genocide. I reviewed my history through memories of my eyes. I believe that memory stimulates conscience. Looking at the stars, I asked myself . . . The same sun shone . . . over the [illegible] of the Huguenots before the night of St. Bartholomew's, shone on the Catholics in Japan in the seventeenth century, and shone over Warsaw, where neighbors from the frontier came to kill my people. Sameness, oneness, but yet no recognition of the place of the component parts in mankind. . . . The words of love must be spoken, although it fills the heart with serene silence. . . . [Doing] constructive work while bombs [are] destroying the forests fully and dying trees crying over groaning of man. Two beliefs from forest: 1) Realization of parts to be allotted by law so they may not be destroyed. 2) Belief in ultimate victory of constructiveness over the destructiveness. The lesson of the arts.[49]

Lemkin, the intellectual, kept his impulses to himself, even though he knew how to transition in his public writings from the personal to the universal, in both present and past: "History provides us with other examples of destruction of national, ethnic, and religious groups. The destruction of Carthage; those of religious groups during Islamic wars and during the Crusades; the massacres of the Albigensians and the Waldensians."[50] But, he also affirmed, genocide is "a modern crime," and he reduced his field of application to the twentieth century and the two genocides that had taken place during his lifetime: those of the Armenians and the Jews, to whom he added the Gypsies. For the rest of his life, he would be faced with this quandary: whether to make genocide a spatially and temporally universal concept or to limit it to the contemporary. If the latter, the "crime of crimes" would be punished in the present in the name of the recent past and prevented in the future thanks to the "law of laws," in parallel with the humanitarian and legislative progress of the nineteenth and twentieth centuries.

The concept gestated over an extensive time and space, the 1920s and 1930s in Europe, but was invented specifically in the United States in 1943, when Lemkin wrote chapter 9 of his *Axis Rule*, titled "Genocide." Once the book was published, in 1944, the concept passed into the public domain: it was commented on, critiqued, and escaped its inventor, who undertook an international lobbying effort for its recognition at the Nuremberg court—in vain—then for its legitimization by the United Nations: committees, commissions, amendments, votes, rejection. Although both the concept and its inventor were growing in influence, Lemkin was also dispossessed of his initial project. It was therefore difficult to establish who thought what about genocide, including Lemkin himself.

For Lemkin was acting with a tenacity approaching obsession, capitalizing on his credentials as a legal scholar and his participation in the prewar sessions on the standardization of international criminal law. To better attract and convince his interlocutors, he presented himself as Polish, Jewish, a Polish Jew, an American, an immigrant, or a friend of Armenians and thus of Christians. At the very time when he was inventing his concept, his beloved mother was murdered. "Genocide hit his family home."[51] His accounts always began with his mother, who made him read Henryk Sienkiewicz's *Quo Vadis* when he was very young.[52] That book would serve the cause that Lemkin opportunistically reconstructed in the 1950s: his extremely precocious invention of the concept leading to the word "genocide." Sienkiewicz was Polish, and he described the fate of Christians "collectively sentenced to death for no reason except that they believed in Christ. And no one could help them."[53] He received the international recognition of the Nobel Prize for Literature in 1905, and the blockbuster movie adaptation premiered around the world in 1951.

The Creation of a Barbarism: Genocide

Lemkin built the argument of *Axis Rule* around an analysis of "German techniques of occupation," culminating with the chapter "Genocide." His compilation of European laws under Nazi domination was particularly remarkable given that he was working in Sweden until 1941 and then in the United States. This did not keep him from reading everything about what was happening, as the war never cut off the flow of information, notably via the neutral powers.

If the table of contents, from chapter 1, "Administration," to chapter 7, "Labor," seemed banal for the study of the occupation, chapter 8, "The Legal Status of the Jews," singled out in four pages their fate deriving from the statute adopted in Nuremberg in 1935: "The treatment of the Jews in the occupied countries is one of the most flagrant violations of international law, not only of specific articles of the Hague Regulations, but also of the principles of the law of nations as they emerged from usage among civilized nations, from the laws of humanity, and from the dictates of the public con-science."⁵⁴ The last sentence of chapter 8, introducing chapter 9, noted, "The Jews being one of the main objects of German genocide policy, their par-ticular situation in occupied Europe has been additionally treated in the chapter on genocide."⁵⁵

At the moment when the word "genocide" was offered to the world for the first time, there was no ambiguity: it referred to Jews. Or, more exactly, to Jews as a group. Lemkin brought together the different forms of belong-ing to Judaism—paradoxically, in the way envisaged both by the Nazis, to better hunt down and exterminate them, and by Jews themselves, particu-larly Zionists, for whom this group constituted a people. Yet, after singling out Jews as specific victims of the Germans, Lemkin combined them with other European peoples under Nazi tyranny, group by group.

> *New conceptions* require new terms. By "genocide" we mean the *destruction of a nation or of an ethnic group*. . . . Generally speaking, genocide does not mean the immediate destruction of a nation, except when accomplished by *mass killings* of all members of a nation. It is intended rather to signify a *coordi-nated plan* of different actions aiming at the destruction of essential founda-tions of the life of national groups, with the aim of annihilating the groups themselves. The objectives of such a plan would be *disintegration of the politi-cal and social institutions, of culture, language, national feelings, religion, and the economic existence of national groups, and the destruction of personal secu-rity, liberty, health, dignity, and even the lives* of persons belonging to such groups.⁵⁶

Lemkin reflected on the targeted groups and the individuals who com-posed them, and on those who targeted them; such a plan could be "coordi-nated" only at the national level. This violence, flowing from a deliberate policy, presumed intention and preparation and was identified with differ-ent acts of persecution and destruction that ultimately formed a whole: genocide. The word was composed of two parts: the people or ethnic com-munity targeted, *genos*, and that which kills, *occidere*. By combining a Greek and a Latin root, Lemkin, an excellent linguist, deliberately built a semantic monster, a barbarism, to express the barbarity of barbarities, the "crime of crimes." In fact, it was no longer possible for him to use the German term *Völkermord*, as he had for the extermination of the Hereros and Armenians, for German was the language of the annihilators of his parents, their culture, and their language, Yiddish. However, the adoption of his invention in Polish, *ludobojtwo* (murder of a people), in a note by the government in exile, must have gone straight to the patriot's heart.

Some of the documentation presented in *Axis Rule* in 1944 was dated, however, as Lemkin had begun to think about the texts he had gathered before he left Sweden in 1941. He said so clearly when he sent his work to the War Refugee Board on April 14: progress on the book was already quite advanced, and he thought that it would be useful to the committee created several months before. However, it was his 1942 compilation of laws that he sent,[57] not his list for the book, although the two had some texts in common, and so the word "genocide" did not appear in it. Were these documents from 1941 and 1942 useful to the War Refugee Board in its frantic struggle to avoid the massive deportation of Hungarian Jews in 1944?

Lemkin also collected laws and declarations on the separation and "legal" persecution of Jews, published in the form of posters or leaflets aimed at occupied populations. Nothing that was secret—the trial and error and experiments with extermination—appeared in his compilation, because this was in fact not a legal matter.[58]

Here is an example of the laws collected by Lemkin for the case of Yugoslavia:

Anti-Jewish Legislation

AN ORDER concerning Sheltering of Jews, of December 24, 1941. (Verordnungsblatt des Militärbefehlshabers in Serbien, No. 27, 1941, p. 196.) . . .

Section 1—Any person who

a) shelters or hides Jews

b) accepts (from Jews) for safekeeping objects of value of any description, furniture, and money, or acquires them by way of purchase, barter, or any other transaction shall be punished by death.[59]

If Lemkin was working in this way, through accumulation, it was because he wanted to start on the basis of occupation laws and thus on what still formed, in appearance at least, the undergirding of a "law of war": the Hague Conventions, the idea of law of nations, the Geneva Convention for International Humanitarian Law. But the Nazi war aimed to transform European demography as a whole—to Germanize it—while destroying or enslaving other peoples. What was acquired through prolonged occupation would be perpetuated whatever the outcome of the war: "Their general plan consisted of *winning the peace*, even if the war was lost, and this goal could be obtained by permanently reversing the European political and demographic balance in favor of Germany. . . . They were very close to achieving their goal in terms of extermination of Jews and Gypsies in Europe."[60]

"Winning the peace": that is what the Young Turks had done by wiping out the Armenians in their Anatolian homeland and replacing them with Turks. The Nazis, for their part, exterminated the Polish Jews and their world, the *Yiddishkeit*. Lemkin's "winning the peace" dovetailed with two categories established by today's genocide researchers: that of the "frenzy of the victors" in 1941–42 during the murders by gunfire in the Soviet Union and that of the "triumph of the defeated" when, as the war was about to be lost, the Nazis made the killing system even more efficient—for instance, exterminating four hundred thousand Hungarian Jews at Birkenau in summer 1944—even as the older methods continued to be used until May 1945.[61]

But—and this was behind the ambiguities of the concept—Lemkin did not reserve the term specifically for Jews. The Poles, the national and religious majority, were also described as victims of genocide. Lemkin contradicted himself twice: he based his concept on all the crimes of mass murder in history even as he said it was a "modern" crime, and he universalized it even as he dwelled upon the primary victims, the Jews.

Lemkin's Campaign: From 1944–45 to 1914–18

"Dr. Raphael Lemkin, distinguished Polish jurist, economist, authority on international law, author and traveler, will tell of his experiences of World War I and II tonight at the Woman's National Democratic Club."[62]

In the United States, Lemkin explained the coherence of the "thirty-year war": in his country-by-country analysis of the occupation of Europe, he took his readers to the occupied territories of World War I—the deportations, the forced labor, particularly in Belgium. Indeed, he had been informed of the situation of civilians in these countries by his Belgian friends and colleagues encountered during international conferences. In 1939, he had thought of moving there; by 1940, this had become impossible.

The Nazi desire in 1940 to repair the consequences of World War I provided Lemkin with a link between the occupation policies instituted during the two conflicts. The 1914–18 precedent was central to his demonstration—particularly the case of Belgium, where an order was issued for the "restitution of the rights of persons persecuted . . . because of their collaboration with the German Army of Occupation during the war of 1914–18."[63] In effect, the Nazis wanted to wipe clean the legal slate of those who had collaborated between 1914 and 1918 and were sentenced in the 1920s. Whence the annulment—in the name of German honor—of legal decisions made by the Belgian state to punish acts of collaboration—deemed uncivil—after 1918. The Nazis ruled that "Wrong demands restitution. In the war of 1914–1918, inhabitants of this country tried to adopt a loyal attitude toward the German Army of Occupation and to obey its rules. For this they were persecuted by the state and certain sections of the population. They suffered penalties of death, hard labor, and imprisonment. . . . At that time, as today, these regulations had to be enforced just as did the Belgian laws. And so the persecuted people were acting in a way that was by no means unlawful."[64] As the new rulers of Belgium, Lemkin opined, they wanted to go even further, "[trying] to disintegrate Belgium by creating and exaggerating differences between the Belgians and the Flemings [*sic*], and the latter collaborating with Germany were given special privileges."[65]

Lemkin had access to the works of American legal scholars such as James Garner, who concluded from the Belgian archives that in 1917 the United States had joined the "good camp," that of the law, in this war of laws. Conversely, in 1914 the Germans had begun a war of atrocities, counter to the values of humanity and international law; the deportations of civilians from the occupied country proved it:

> By tearing away from nearly every humble home in the land a husband and a father or a son and brother, they have lighted a fire of hatred that will never go out. . . . [It] will impress its horror indelibly on the memory of three generations, a realization of what German methods mean, not, as with the early atrocities, in the heat of passion and the first lust of war, but by one of those deeds that make one despair of the future of the human race, a deed coldly

planned, studiously matured, and deliberately and systematically executed, a
deed so cruel that German soldiers are said to have wept in its execution, and
so monstrous that even German officers are now said to be ashamed.[66]

The forced labor imposed twice on the occupied populations of Belgium
and northern France were of particular interest to Lemkin. In chapter 7 of
Axis Rule, titled "Labor," he quoted General Erich Ludendorff in 1917 to
explain the Nazis' choices in 1942:

> "The existence of a large mass of unemployed labor is a danger to public
> safety. With a view to averting that danger, men may be sent compulsorily to
> any place where they are needed; whether at home or abroad is immaterial."[67]
> ... By deporting millions of able-bodied men and women from the occupied
> countries, Germany moreover hopes to disrupt centers of political resistance
> ... and ... by separating families and keeping the men far away from their
> homes, a policy of depopulation is being pursued.[68]

The 1914–18 period was used as an argument. At that time, the laws of war
and occupation were violated—the Germans were not the only ones to do
so—and, especially, the innovation of which World War II was the extreme
consequence was introduced. The battle was waged not only on men wearing uniforms who might be protected by international humanitarian law
when they were out of combat, wounded, or taken prisoner. Civilians were
at the center of the conflict, physically, in reality, and in propaganda. And
yet, international humanitarian law did not cover them. Not yet. Lemkin
differentiated between groups "selected" for who they were and "collateral
victims," who found themselves in the wrong place at the wrong time:

> When, in 1918, a German shell fell on Église Saint-Gervais in Paris, a large
> number of people belonging to a specific religious group were destroyed. Yet
> although this was a war crime (because civilians were killed), it did not con-
> stitute an act of genocide, as it did not involve the destruction of a specific
> category of civilians; there was no selection of the victims.[69]

Departing in an original way from his contemporaries, Lemkin wanted
both to invalidate the propaganda and rumors of the Great War and to

observe the new forms of violence. Although numerous doubts subsisted regarding the "German atrocities," the occupations and forced labor in Belgium and northern France, the pogroms against the Jews in Russia and Poland, and the extermination of the Armenians had actually taken place, even in the opinion of the most skeptical.

Yet, paradoxically, Lemkin put aside the extreme violence against civilians that he knew the best, that against the Jews of Eastern Europe and the Armenians of the Ottoman Empire, at the very moment when he launched his campaign for recognition of the word "genocide," between 1944 and 1946. He retained only the military and occupation violence of 1914–18, returning in a classic way to the Great War.

In 1945, Lemkin wrote to Robert Jackson, who had just been appointed prosecutor of the Nuremberg Trials, to offer his services to the Americans in two ways: participating in the prosecution and judgment of Nazi criminals and making his new concept central to the court. He was in fact engaged as an expert by the American team, but he went to Nuremberg only occasionally, as he was confined to Washington, DC, most of the time to prepare documentation for the Office of Strategic Services (the forerunner of the CIA) and its War Crimes Office. Although he knew a number of influential figures, few of them considered him, whether for good reasons—he was very individualistic, sharing little with the team—or, above all, for bad ones: the highest-profile lawyers at the time were thinking mainly in terms of war crimes until Hersch Lauterpacht's "crimes against humanity" concept was adopted, and not in terms of genocide. Yet, Lemkin was strongly committed to his concept. He wrote to Jackson, "I am taking the liberty of sending you my article 'Genocide.' This article contains a statement by the recently captured Marshal von Rundstedt . . . that points to the particular responsibility of this man as a major war criminal."[70]

Why was Lemkin so interested in von Rundstedt? Because at the time he was charged only with "criminality of groups and criminal organizations." Lemkin wanted to see him charged differently, for the archives left no doubt about his participation in the "crime of genocide." Indeed, he had "approved and transmitted to his troops" a document by Walter von Reichenau, on October 10, 1941: "The most essential aim of war against the Jewish bolshevistic system is a complete destruction of their means of power and the elimination of Asian influence from the European culture. . . . The soldier in the eastern territories is not merely a fighter according to the rules of war but also a bearer of ruthless national ideology. . . . Therefore the soldier must have full understanding for the necessity of a severe but just revenge on subhuman Jewry."[71]

Lemkin returned yet again to World War I in his description of von Rundstedt "aping the Fuhrer": "'One of the great mistakes of 1918 was to spare the civil life of the enemy countries, for it is necessary for us Germans to always be at least double the numbers of the peoples of the contiguous countries. We are therefore obliged to destroy at least a third of their inhabitants. The only means is organized underfeeding, which in this case is better than machine guns.'"[72]

Lemkin presented the Nazis as capable of conceptualizing depopulation through the indirect extermination brought about by hunger or murder because of their experience in World War I, their heritage, their mental universe. "Hitler was right. The crime of the Reich in wantonly and deliberately wiping out whole peoples is not utterly new in the world. It is new only in the civilized world as we have come to think of it. It is so new in the traditions of civilized man that he has no name for it. It is for this reason that I took the liberty of inventing the word 'genocide.'"[73]

Lemkin had an encyclopedic knowledge of Nazi Germany that was very valuable to the prosecutors. This was why, in 1942, he was hired by the Board of Economic Warfare, an extension of the War Trade Board formed during World War I. Vice President Wallace, who led the board, was also convinced that the new world after 1918 had not been well understood, and he might have supported Lemkin. But he came into permanent conflict with the State Department, and Lemkin may have been the victim of this conflict. When Lemkin asked Wallace to promote his book, Wallace answered coldly, in keeping with his political calculations: "Thanks so much for delivering a copy of your book. It seems to me to be an extraordinarily competent job in a very complicated field. . . . PS: I am returning the literature that you were kind enough to leave with my Secretary."[74]

Lemkin "alerts the world to genocide"[75]

Wallace had Lemkin pegged: "extraordinarily competent job in a very complicated field." In contrast to the image of the solitary researcher that he—or certain of his later sycophants—cultivated, Lemkin was now well established in Washington and knew how to slip in everywhere, from newspaper pages to commissions of experts, from London to continental Europe. He published his book, to favorable criticism, and wrote short articles that he had translated into various languages. The "genocide" chapter had been written between 1943 and early 1944, and the book came out in November. On December 3, 1944, the *Washington Post* published the first article with the word in the title, directly inspired—even dictated—by Lemkin, who knew the newspaper's editor well. Reprinted widely in the American and British press and then in all other countries with a free press, the editorial informed hundreds of thousands of readers about the contents of the enormous tome that they would never read, with its precise facts and obscure definitions.

The editorial was introduced by the War Refugee Board's report of the preceding week: to the "shock" and "shame" of having to write about such "atrocities" one could contrast the response of the new concept:

> In Birkenau, between April 1942 and April 1944, approximately 1,765,000 Jews were put to death in ingeniously constructed chambers; their bodies were then burned in specially designed furnaces; their ashes were distributed as fertilizer. . . . It is a mistake, perhaps, to call these killings "atrocities." An atrocity is a wanton brutality. There were unspeakable atrocities at Auschwitz and Birkenau. But the point about these killings is that they were systematic and purposeful. The gas chambers and furnaces were not improvisations; they were scientifically designed instruments for the extermination of an entire ethnic group. On the scale practiced by the Germans, this is something new. And it is this purpose that human beings find it difficult to believe or understand. Yet it is a purpose that Hitler has openly avowed.
>
> We have never even had a word for it until now. But one has been recently coined by a noted Polish scholar and attorney. Professor Raphael Lemkin . . . has devised the term "genocide."

The author emphasized the unique extermination of the Jews, yet closely associated them with other Europeans:

> Thus Jews were gassed at Birkenau and Aryan Poles and Russians and Slovenes were otherwise butchered, not for any crime or any resistance to Axis

authority but because the Nazis wished to terminate the ethnic groups to which they belonged. . . . The Germans have committed genocide in virtually all the countries of Europe that they occupied. They have struck deliberately at the culture, language, religion, political institutions, and economic existence of the peoples they conquered—all with a view to undermining their national identity and weakening them, physically and morally, so that they would become subservient to German rule.[76]

The concept was broadened to include all national groups that had been victims of Nazism; it also explained the hundreds of pages of *Axis Rule* devoted to exactions, including forced labor. This does not seem to have caused many problems, and would not do so for some time, as could be seen in the Jewish press itself. For instance, the *Palestine Post* printed the following: "The nature of this crime, which was practiced against the Poles as well as against the Jews, is a systematic attack on the different aspects of life of captive people."[77] Then, *The Polish Review* devoted an article to Lemkin and Karski: the thinker and the soldier did not know each other, but they were brought together in the Polish patriots' newspaper.

It is easy to see Lemkin's hand behind the *Washington Post* article, which referred to his 1933 proposals in Madrid for "crime of barbarity and of vandalism," predating the term in a rather dishonest way: "As long ago as 1933, Professor Lemkin proposed the recognition of genocide as a crime under international law."

So that American readers in 1944 would come to the desired conclusion, they had to be convinced that an international law was essential to the indictment, judging, and sentencing of those who were found guilty of crimes throughout the conflict, and particularly the crime of genocide. This way, the sovereignty of nations and morals would be respected. But the contradictions led to criticisms. To a *Post* correspondent who asserted that the Hague Conventions would suffice for the War Crimes Commission to act, Lemkin pointed out the shortcomings of the 1907 convention, according to which decisions reached under its provisions would apply only to the treatment of populations under military occupation; in fact, in Madrid he had proposed that war criminals be arrested and tried in the countries that may have given them asylum. He had in mind the Turkish killers exfiltrated to Germany in 1919.

In 1944, Lemkin's response was based on the idea of the general guilt of those whom he would soon call "genocidists." To judge them, a new international law was needed here and now:

> If we treat the mass murders of Birkenau and Oswiecim as simple murders, only the comparatively few who were directly involved could be prosecuted. For the murder of several million people, only some hundreds of officials and subordinates could be directly accused. As I have defined genocide for the purpose of an international treaty, all persons who incited the population to committing and approving this crime and who provided the legal bases and machinery for its commission should be considered accessories to the crime. Thus, Goebbels and his many associates would be equally responsible for Birkenau, although they may not have given the direct orders to kill. . . . We should not fail to create a more readily enforceable machinery . . . for the fight against the onslaught of barbarism.[78]

Lemkin's definition of genocide remained vague at this stage: this was why he cited both Birkenau, referring to the gassing of Jews, and Oswiecim, the Polish name of which pointed to the martyrdom of Poland as a whole.

Nazi Guilt, German Guilt?

In late December 1944, the literary critic for the *Washington Post*, in his turn, urged "all intelligent Americans" to read Lemkin "on trial and punishment for international gangsters. . . . Unfortunately, millions of Americans do not believe that the Germans have systematically practiced 'genocide,' the calculated extermination of national and racial groups." The writer scathingly derided the "smug individuals . . . the party of those who know nothing," who he felt represented the majority of his compatriots, those who "want a soft peace." He counted upon the lawyers to inflict a "hard peace," one that was definitive, on their enemies; otherwise, the war would return to haunt their own grandchildren. Like Lemkin, he established a continuity among all Germans: "No mercy should be shown a nation that has made national heroes of aggressive tyrants, that has fed its youth upon Clausewitz, von Treitschke, Nietzsche, Bernhardi, and the paranoic vapors of Adolf Hitler."[79]

The *New York Times*, for its part, assigned its senior critic to open the book section with a review of *Axis Rule*, a rare honor. But beyond the praise for the intellectual performance that exposed the skeleton of the "twentieth-century Moloch," Nazism, the critic wondered whether the accusation made against all Germans as a perverted race was not counterproductive; he even posited that Lemkin, as a Pole, "would not want to be held personally responsible for all the acts of the Pilsudski regime."[80]

A *Washington Post* reader also noted that genocide, founded on a biological argument, was "dangerously close to Nazi theories. One only has to translate genocide as '*Völkermord*' and one finds oneself with a classic Nazi slogan: it's even incredible that the Nazis haven't thought of this themselves." These critics did not understand not only that Nazism was a crime against humanity—I use this nonlegal wording here deliberately to expose the various hesitations—but that genocide also defined something else, despite its gaps and ambiguities: "Nazism is a crime against the spirit and not against a biological notion, and if we need a new international crime, why not call it simply Nazism, instead of trying to incorporate by a Greco-Latin word what we have been fighting against during the last few years. If we don't find the spirit of man worthy of protection, the biological notion of nation does certainly not seem to be worthy of protection either."[81] Another stated with dark irony that the Czech government in exile, which was preparing to require a million Sudeten Germans to adopt the Czech language and culture, would be guilty of a "perfect genocide."[82]

"A cry of horror from the abyss"[83]

Lemkin had written a relentless book, but so full of statistics, texts of statutes, decrees, and contradictions that it is difficult to follow. Meanwhile, Jan Kozielewski set out to write his memoir while working at the Polish embassy under his resister's name, which was now his. His clandestine identity had been discovered by the Nazis, who accused him on the airwaves of "spreading lies about the Third Reich." The war had turned him into a different man, with a different name, Jan Karski. Published in fall 1944, *Story of a Secret State* became a Book of the Month Club selection the following December and January. The publisher advertised heavily in most American newspapers, including in Chicago, the city with the largest Polish immigrant population in the United States. The intense campaign bore some resemblance to that which had preceded the publication of Erich Maria Remarque's *All Quiet on the Western Front* in 1928. Remarque, who had barely seen the front, had nevertheless written a novel that was taken as the reality of the Great War. Karski's autobiography was presented, conversely, as a thriller, a spy novel: "Jan Karski has emerged from the Polish underground to reveal how his countrymen built a whole secret government under the Nazis' noses";[84] "Spine-Curling Saga of the Polish Underground."[85] The book garnered numerous reviews, promoting both Karski's incredible courage and the various miracles by which he had escaped the "Nazi Gehenna." "Here is the Jeremiad of western civilization, realistic, appalling."[86]

The handsome young Pole had to get Americans to understand what was playing out in Europe. During this time, when newsreels and news photographs were essential, many organizations put together exhibitions and conferences on propaganda. Karski went to the exhibition in New York glorifying Polish heroism, inaugurated in September 1944 by his host, Ambassador Jan Ciechanowski: "If ever a nation has won its right to freedom, then surely Poland's record in this total world war has won her that right. . . . Her people have uninterruptedly fought and suffered. . . . They have been ruthlessly decimated by methodical extermination, and yet they have never faltered."[87] Playing on his charming modesty despite his heroic aura, Karski posed across the country in front of posters for the exhibition *The Secret Polish State* taken from pages of his book. The images vaunted the entire Polish nation, standing up against the Nazi evil, denouncing forced labor and the enslavement of an entire people. Everywhere, children exalted the renaissance. In Los Angeles, they waved Polish and American flags in front of a poster: "Poland: First to Fight." Front and center were the soul of the Poles and the attacks against their culture, such as the destruction of sculptures of Chopin: "The conquerors were not able to break the Polish spirit of resistance, so now they want to erase their culture."[88] At the New York Public Library, an exhibition of old Polish books pointed out how important the collection could be in helping with the cultural reconstruction of the devastated country. The final display was organized around Karski's book; in just a few weeks he had become the paradigmatic Pole—he who had suffered, resisted, and who would make it possible for his country to be revived, as it had been in 1918. A photograph often reproduced shows an inscription of the resistance in Warsaw: "*Deutschland Kaputt*, 1918–1943."[89]

"Jan Karski bridges the all but unbridgeable gap between American civilians who have suffered virtually nothing in this war and the harassed, starving, mortally wounded masses of conquered Poland. If anyone can pierce the elephantine skin of the callow noncombatant, Karski can."[90] A gentle caricature by a compatriot portrays him in front of his book, his finger pointed as if on a military propaganda poster, issuing an invitation to astounded American visitors: "Poland's Heroic Spirit."[91]

And the Polish Jews? Although they weren't forgotten, they were simply an adjunct to their nation's suffering. The major exhibition held at Freedom House in New York, inaugurated by such eminent American and Allied figures as Eleanor Roosevelt and the Czech diplomat Jan Masaryk, drew a parallel between the resistance in Warsaw in 1944 and that in the ghetto in 1943. The Jews were not hidden away, but their specific fate was marginalized: given the terrible suffering of the Polish people in general, how could extermination be classified? The article that announced the Book of the Month award for Karski was, however, divided into two equal parts, one on the fate of Poland in general and one on the two chapters describing the Warsaw ghetto and "Belzec"; the author of the review slip, Clifton Fadiman, considered these chapters the most important and quoted Karski: "I know history. I have learned a great deal about the evolution of nations, political systems, social doctrines, methods of conquest, persecution, and extermination, and I know, too, that never in the history of mankind, never anywhere in the realm of human relations did anything occur to compare with what was inflicted on the Jewish population of Poland."[92] Fadiman wrote that Karski "record[ed] the kind of facts about the Germans which, for some mysterious reason, the American people all through this war have not been particularly encouraged to learn. The basic truth about this particular aspect of the conduct of the German people is that, as Karski *proves*, 1,800,000 Jews have been murdered. Not killed in battle. Not even executed for 'crimes.' But murdered, sometimes quickly, sometimes slowly, but murdered. Murdered by Germans, tens of thousands of Germans (many of them not 'nazis'), and murdered with every appearance of alacrity, not to say profound pleasure."[93]

These sentences were published in December 1944. Majdanek had been "opened"[94] by the Soviets in July; the abandonment of Auschwitz-Birkenau was underway, and its survivors were being forced into wintertime death marches.[95]

"The nightmare that is a reality"[96]

Yet, as the American and British troops discovered for themselves the horrors of the camps (although never specifying exactly which "camps"), the debate over belief and nonbelief resumed. It was the Soviets who discovered the extermination sites such as Treblinka, and in 1943 they established their commissions of inquiry; on January 27, 1945, they entered Auschwitz-Birkenau.[97] The Americans and British, in the west, liberated concentration camps—including Dachau and Buchenwald—where survivors of the death marches, deported from Birkenau, were imprisoned.[98] This furthered the incomprehension, the difficulty with creating a hierarchy of horrors: it was hard to know which was which. For instance, how could people interpret the photograph, taken on April 16, 1945, by soldier H. Miller, in which skeletal people, their bulging eyes overwhelming their entire faces, are squeezed four by four onto cots? The *New York Times* published the picture on May 6, 1945, with the caption "Crowded Bunks in the Prison Camp at Buchenwald." Today, we recognize long-term deportees at Buchenwald, as well as the young Elie Wiesel and other Jews from Hungary who had survived the death marches and had recently arrived from Auschwitz-Birkenau.[99]

The United States was much quicker—due to anti-Japanese racism and national pride following the Pearl Harbor attack[100]—to denounce the atrocities by the Japanese than those by the Nazis, as Paul Winkler noted: "The cruelties committed by the Germans are at least as great as those of the Japanese. Members of the various European undergrounds go to great risks to smuggle out reports on these matters, but they get pitifully little hearing in the United States."[101]

Once more, it was the cartoonists, with their talent for immediacy, who brought to light the confusion that arose from the geographic and mental distance between the American people at war and devastated Europe. A young mother proudly shows her toddler in a playpen surrounded by barbed wire to her friend who has come for tea: "We want him to be better prepared to meet the facts of life than we were," she says.[102] A reader returns two books to the library, saying, "I don't think I can stand another concentration camp." Or "I thought the whole thing was terribly dated. Nobody ever murders with prussic acid any more."[103] And a reader besotted with Karski tells him that the passage in his book where the Gestapo begins to torture him is so beautiful.

"We want him to be better prepared to meet the facts of life than we were"

Cartoon by Garner Rea published in *Colliers*, February 19, 1944.

"I don't think I can stand another concentration camp."

Cartoon by Helen Hokinson published in *The New Yorker*, May 20, 1944.

"*I thought the whole thing was terribly dated. Nobody ever commits murder with prussic acid any more.*"

Cartoon by Helen Hokinson published in *The New Yorker*, May 13, 1944.

The critic at *The New Yorker* tried to figure out why the eyewitness accounts were so limited: the Pole, Karski, had written the "best book" on the resistance in Europe, and yet it was not possible for him, who had fought, who had seen, "by writing books, to catch up with the terrible reality." Why?

The events of the present war . . . have burst the barometer of human response. The demands made upon our emotions so exceed our ordinary capacity for either sympathy or excitement that we almost cease to feel at all and simply begin to things for granted. The feverish exploitation of glory by the jingo, still so much in evidence for the last war, has become almost as impossible as the indignant humanitarianism of the liberal and the socialist. . . . Books and articles . . . all alike seem fatally inadequate to make us realize either the dimensions or the profound effects of what is going on.[104]

Inadequate—truly fatally inadequate? And all of this because it was impossible to believe in old rumors, traces of World War I? Late in 1944, however, the Gallup polling firm, surveying Americans again on the "atrocity stories," reported that 76 percent of them believed that the Germans had murdered "many people" in the concentration camps, 12 percent weren't sure, and 12 percent did not believe it at all. But among those who said "many people," all underestimated the number, and only 12 percent thought that the reports had assessed it at more than two million. The *Washington Post* headline emphasized this underestimation, as the report by the War Refugee Board, which situated the number of dead at 1,765,000 for the Auschwitz camp alone, had just been published, but the author acknowledged, "Regardless of the numbers involved, the American people are fully prepared to believe atrocities have taken place."[105]

This poll was published in the *Washington Post* on the same day as the editorial titled "Genocide," the first time that the word appeared in the press. Readers did not necessarily make the connection between the two, and they continued to mix all the atrocities together, from one war to the other. How could it be otherwise?

When the American soldiers arrived, in their turn, in the concentration camps, they finally became aware, at least, of the reality of the exactions. For instance, when Ohrdruf was opened, "The *Post* correspondent, who had been a skeptic ever since the last war when men argued about Edith Cavell and the Belgian babies who were supposed to have had their hands cut off, drove all the way to Ohrdruf to join in the grim procession. The thing we had heard about was right before our eyes in the yard of the concentration camp. . . . A soldier of one of Patton's Infantry divisions . . . murmured, 'Good Lord' [then] 'This is hard to believe when you read about it . . . but there it is.'"[106]

"The casting into doubt of atrocity stories after World War I is probably partly responsible for the current rejection of the World War II stories. But this time, the skepticism is not justified," stated Shirer.[107] Again on May 6, 1945, a *Washington Post* reader recalled "Lord Bryce's committee on the supposed German atrocities in 1915 and the prison camp in Wittenberg. Today, our forces occupy Wittenberg. During World War I it was as terrible as Buchenwald today. . . . We have forgotten Wittenberg. For how long will we remember Buchenwald and Dachau?"[108]

By invoking the burden of the rejection of World War I atrocities, Lemkin had perceived very early what many discovered in 1945, including *The Christian Century*, which finally made an honorable amend: "We have found it hard to believe that the reports from the nazi concentration camps could be true. . . . Or perhaps they were just more atrocity-mongering, like the cadaver factory story of the last war."[109]

Concentration camps, extermination sites—the confusion was at its height, including among those ready to accept the word "genocide." It was still very far from Marcel Cohen's clear response: "I knew, very young, the unfathomable distance between slavery and mass slaughter, between what one could still attempt to express and the silence of the factories. One of my aunts was selected for labor. . . . Speaking of the laborers, she said 'us.' About those, in another line, on the ramp at Birkenau, who were going to their death, she bowed her head and was silent."[110]

5

∽∽∽

The War Is Over

Weep for the Dead, Find the Living,
Judge the Criminals

Throughout the ages, the victims of genocide have filled history with their pain to the point that humanity can no longer avoid identification of the consequences and its own moral responsibility.[1]

—Lemkin

"All wiped out. No more family."

Devastated, in shock, Raphael Lemkin gradually learned about the abominable conditions under which the Volkovysk ghetto was destroyed and his parents were murdered. Might he really have thought that the sufferings of Jews were intermingled with those of others in the disaster of Europe, or had he wept for them in private, even as he was pushing forward his universal conception of genocide?

In 1946, the "crime of genocide" began to be integrated into certain proclamations, as it was into the UN resolution of December 11 of that year: "Genocide is a denial of the right of existence of entire human groups, as homicide is the denial of the right to live of individual human beings."[2] But 1946 was also the year of the Kielce pogrom, on July 4: forty dead, more than eighty wounded. Everywhere in Poland, Jews who had survived ghettos, labor camps, and concentration camps or who had returned from the Soviet Union were either killed or so worried that they preferred to flee again. Their former neighbors had taken their belongings or, finally freed of their "Jewish problem," were not keen to see them come back, even though barely three hundred thousand out of the three million had survived.[3]

As Lemkin was visiting displaced persons camps, he was unaware that his older brother, Elias, with his wife and two children, was at Neu-Freimann in Bavaria, not far from Nuremberg. The two brothers were among the *lebensgeblibenen*, Yiddish for "Jews who stayed alive." Raphael was more of a *survivant*—he had escaped in time—whereas Elias was more of a *rescapé*.[4] But these considerable semantic differences in French do not exist in the English language, which uses a single word, *survivor*.

In 1944, the Allied General Staff created the status of "displaced persons," a provisional and imprecise term. Among the eleven million people moving through the Western zone, at least eight million transited through Germany. It was a paradoxical situation: although the country responsible for the tragedy was in utter ruins and occupied, it was where displaced persons found a temporary safe harbor—including 250,000 Jews, most of them from Poland.[5]

At first, the Allies didn't separate the Jews from the other refugees; the idea was to create a contrast with Nazi ideology. However, they ran into specific difficulties, as reported disapprovingly by Earl Harrison, President Truman's envoy to these camps: "The Jewish refugees . . . are in need of attention and help. Up to this point they have been 'liberated' more in a military sense than actually. . . . They feel that they, who were in so many ways the first and worst victims of Nazism, are being neglected by their liberators."[6] Indeed, certain Baltic, Polish, and Ukrainian refugees repeatedly harassed Jews gathered in the same locations. Harrison also deplored the fact that some former concentration camps, such as Dachau, were serving as displaced persons "camps." Finally, he was surprised that the desire of most Jews to immigrate to Palestine was not being taken into account. His report ultimately had a broader scope, as it made it possible to identify Jews as a people and thus, indirectly, to better apprehend Zionism.

And so, separate camps for Jews were organized and managed by the American Joint Distribution Committee. The Joint, as it was known, had been created in November 1914 to assist Jewish populations in Central and Eastern Europe and in the Middle East, notably those in Palestine under Ottoman domination, who were suffering from a terrible famine. Henry Morgenthau Sr., American ambassador to the Ottoman Empire and father of Treasury Secretary Henry Morgenthau, had been active in the Joint. In yet another way, one world war was extended into the next.

An amateur film shot in fall 1946 shows General Dwight Eisenhower visiting the Neu-Freimann camp. School, synagogue, warehouse: the common buildings were labeled in English and Yiddish. Crowds—Elias Lemkin's family among them, perhaps—pressed forward to welcome a relaxed Eisenhower.[7] The conquering general, who, staggered, had declared at the Ohrdruf camp in 1945 that now American soldiers knew why they were fighting, could never comprehend the unprecedented tragedies that these people had just gone through. For instance, in the extended Lemkin family, the survivors wept for some fifty dead.

The files of the Red Cross are overflowing with both details and poignant gaps: "Elias born in 1895, his wife, Lea Winograzka, in 1899, their two sons Sholom and Samuel in 1928 and 1935. Jews from Wolkowysk, Poland." Elias was a "farmer" and "office employee" until 1941; the family were then "*Statenlos*" [sic], stateless, and wished to immigrate to Canada or the United States, because they thought they had relatives there. In 1945, Elias tried to reach his brother, Raphael, through an American journalist he met in Moscow, as he thought he recognized him in a photograph taken in Nuremberg: "Your brother, his wife, and their two sons are looking for you, they have a decision to make that will affect their entire life. . . . Your parents and the rest of the family stayed in Volkovysk and we have never heard anything about them. The only thing they know is that all the Jews were deported by the Germans and no doubt perished with the millions of other victims of the Nazis."[8]

Elias did in fact still have a brother, but Raphael never received the letter. A sister also reached Palestine, but in those years, when millions of refugees were on the move, it was impossible to find her. Also, to the question "Do you want to return to your home country?" Elias answered "*Nein.*" If no, why not? "*Alles vernichtet. Keine Verwandete.*"[9]

The forms left little room to describe how the Lemkin, Pomeranz, and Winograzky families had been "wiped out" or how some had survived. It was mentioned that Elias, his wife, and their two sons lived in Volkovysk, near Bialystok, from 1936 to 1939; then, starting in 1941, they were "wearing the Jewish star" and "living illegally"; they were "liberated by the Russians in 1944." They did not figure on the "legal" (in the Nazi sense) lists of deportations and camps. They hid—they therefore encountered saviors during their ordeal—then reached the Soviet Union.

The salvation of the Polish and Baltic Jews who fled east is sometimes minimized, even though we must not forget those who were deported, transported, or killed. In fact, without intending it, the Stalinist USSR saved hundreds of thousands of Jews. Soviet citizens of Jewish origin who were deported (most of whom survived the conditions of forced labor and transportation) or evacuated and those who fled were the only ones to escape the Nazi genocide in Eastern Europe. About 10 percent of the five hundred thousand deported from the "new territories" (including eastern Poland) after 1939–40 were Jewish, as were 40 percent of the seventeen million evacuees. Of course, many thousands of them would not live to see the end of the conflict: the mortality rate in the nonoccupied USSR during the war, and especially in the camps, exile zones, and refugee zones, was two to three times higher than the average during peacetime. Nevertheless, a huge number of "evacuees" and "forced settlers" escaped the certain death reserved for them by the Nazis.[10] Late in 1943, several American senior government officials summed things up: "The Soviets did more for the Jewish refugees than any other state in the world."[11] They remembered that in 1942, when they had tried, from Washington, to set up refugee camps in North Africa or liberated southern Italy, their own hierarchy and their allies—from the British to the free French—had barred them from doing so.[12] After the war, however, these Jews did not want to stay in the Soviet Union, which is why they traveled west, among them Elias's branch of the Lemkin family.

Elias's family managed to obtain Canadian identification papers. They tried to get their hands on some reparation compensation and persisted in the search for the rest of their family. "All wiped out. No more family"; at each stage of their journey, the same words were repeated. They kept quiet about their hunt, however, and about the places where they had hidden throughout Poland after 1941, their arrival in Moscow, their survival thanks to the Anti-Fascist Committee, their return via Bialystok, the desolate void of a Volkovysk in which not a single Jew still lived, their departure for Berlin, and finally their transit through the displaced persons camp at Neu-Freimann before reaching Canada.

One of their cousins, Daniel, born in 1919, the son of Raphael and Elias's uncle, Benjamin Lemkin, reached the Bamberg displaced persons camp in Bavaria. He lived there until late 1950 and then left for the United States via Bremen after an incredible voyage that is recounted in his papers. On the

Red Cross forms, the list of the main camps was printed in advance; the camp or—more often—camps that had been "visited" could be simply ticked off: "1.8.41–15.8.43, forced laborer Bialystok; 18.8.43 KZ Maidanek; 28.12.43, KZ Blizics; 15.10.44 KZ Auschwitz ZaL Kirchhof; 18.11.44–11.4.45, KZ Buchenwald, liberated."[13] After his liberation in 1945 and before his arrival in Bamberg, in 1947, Daniel returned to Volkovysk. Did he meet his cousins there; did they discover together their town empty of Jews? He then wandered for two years before reaching a camp of another type, free but having become destitute. Almost three more years of steps followed before he could emigrate. Between the beginning of the war in 1939 and his arrival in the United States in late 1950, Daniel, a typographer and bookbinder, suffered eleven years of the worst mistreatment in forced labor camps and in extermination camps where all of his relatives died and then wandered through a totally destroyed Poland and Germany, where he was classified as a "stateless Jew." Surviving. But living?

Could even a man such as Raphael Lemkin feel what his family members had experienced, displaced in the Soviet Union or confronted with mistreatment and death? He had experienced the beginning of the war, the difficulties of immigrating to the United States, the long voyage across the USSR, Japan, and the Pacific Ocean. But that was nothing in comparison with what they had gone through. By escaping, he was able to bring the world a new concept: genocide.

A Mitigated Victory: The Term "Genocide," 1945 to 1948

Two days before May 8, 1945, under the title "Retribution," the *Washington Post* ran an anonymous article explaining Germany's defeat as due to its immorality and its total lack of honor and humanity. Its punishment had to be proportionate to the catastrophe it had wreaked upon the world: "Death, sorrow, degradation, hunger prowl through Germany . . . because the world did not allow the completion of the pitiless plan for the entire destruction of other peoples that was to satisfy Nazi ambitions. . . . Their weakness was not military. It was their total absence of morality and respect for human rights."[14]

In fact, Lemkin had written the article. He was aware of the difficulty of importing the new concept into the great trial that was being prepared, because laws could not be applied retroactively. The Nazis had practiced "genocide" before the concept was invented and defined by international bodies. Therefore, he stressed, Hitler and the Nazis were common-law criminals. He raised the problem both of the German population and of collaborators in Poland, France, Norway, and other countries. "When one man is murdered, it is murder. We cannot accept the proposition that organizing the murder of millions is less than murder."[15] This was exactly what he had said about the Turks between 1919 and 1933. In 1944–45, however, Lemkin put his research on the Armenians aside. It was not until 1946 that his lobbying in favor of calling a vote on a convention against the crime of genocide caused him to return to the Armenians and then to what he called victims of all genocides through history.

The small American legal team led by General Taylor was far from operational when it was formed in May 1945 to prepare for the Nuremberg trials: "The first question a prosecuting attorney asks in such a situation is 'Where's the evidence?' The blunt fact was that, despite what 'everybody knew' about the Nazi leaders, virtually no judicially admissible evidence was at hand. . . . In fact, the OSS [Office of Strategic Services] included a number of able and learned experts on the Third Reich [Franz Neumann[16] and Raphael Lemkin were specifically mentioned in a footnote here]."[17] Although Neumann (the main representative of the Frankfurt school in New York) and Lemkin offered avenues "valuable as background information," this was "neither documentary nor testimonial evidence suitable for court use."[18] Taylor's team used the word "genocide" in relation to "the extermination of racial and national groups . . . particularly Jews and Poles and gypsies and others,"[19] but without a legal definition genocide simply did not exist, even if Sir Maxwell Fyfe, the British prosecutor, included it in some of his cross-examinations; it was therefore just a descriptive term.

Hersch Lauterpacht, a British lawyer who also worked on preparations for the Nuremberg trials, recommended that the extermination of the Jews be called a "crime against humanity." In an extraordinary coincidence, Lauterpacht was born in Lvov, where he studied law, like Lemkin; he then went on to Cambridge, where he became a professor in the late 1920s. Simultaneously promoting the introduction into the international legal arsenal of the concepts of crime against humanity and genocide were two Jews who had studied in Lvov. The city has been known, successively, by four names—

Lwow, Lemberg, Lvov, and Lviv (the Polish, German [Austrian], Ukrainian, and Russian versions)—symbolizing the upheavals in European boundaries.

Lemkin, not taken seriously, having heart problems, often hospitalized, tried—not without difficulty—to carve out a place for himself at Nuremberg, where he believed he could make his concept known to the entire world. But Lauterpacht was ahead of him. Celebrated in Great Britain, he had given lectures in the United States and knew Robert Jackson, the American prosecutor.[20] However, Lauterpacht disapproved of the concept of genocide and was fiercely opposed to the book by Lemkin, whom he called a "pale lawyer." In his view, both criminals and victims were individuals: justice was rendered against the former; for the latter, there was no group that applied—neither Nazis, nor Germans, nor Jews, nor Poles.

Lemkin thought exactly the contrary: in his view, groups and their members, not individuals, were the targets: "Genocide is the crime of destruction of human groups, just as homicide is the crime of destruction of individuals."[21] But he convinced no one. He and his concept were relegated to the sidelines when it came to settlement of the conflict. Some of his self-important colleagues on the United Nations War Crimes Commission went so far as to question his skill as a linguist because he had mixed Greek and Latin in his neologism. *Le Monde* did the same in its editorial of December 11, 1945, in which the term "genocide" was used in French for the first time one year before the UN declaration was issued:

> Now we have been enriched by a monster. Of course, the man who, according to Professor Lemkin's definition, committed the "genocide" is himself a monstrous person. But was it necessary to coin, to designate his crime, one of those barbarous words made of the coupling of a Greek and a Latin root? The Latin *gens* would have done just as well as the Greek word *genos* to say what he wanted to say, and the analogy with homicide, fratricide, regicide, etc., for example, would have been complete. But we wager that, in a time when words get used up so fast, this one will cause an uproar for one or two seasons: by synecdoche—or else by catachresis—it will be used in disputes to express the highest degree of contempt.[22]

At the same moment, Dr. Leo Alexander, a physician and an expert witness at Nuremberg who described the Nazi doctors' "quest for the ecstatic pleasure of death," was searching for a term including *thanatos* (death) as the medical equivalent of "genocide." He questioned Lemkin, who confirmed that the Nazis' medical "experiments" had been conducted for a single purpose, to develop the "science of murder,"[23] and proposed two variants for the "techniques" of murder and of sterilizations or castrations: *ktenotechnics* (from *ktenos*, "murder') and *sterotechnics* (from *steirosis*, "infertility"). Alexander approved, and he coined "ktenology as a scientific technique of genocide." The term was not widely adopted, but the episode proved Lemkin's mastery of Greek, as he had deliberately opted for a loaded linguistic barbarism to define the barbarity of barbarities.[24]

At the War Crimes Commission, Lemkin compiled thick bibliographies on the three indictments finally chosen for prosecution at Nuremberg: crimes against peace, war crimes, crimes against humanity. Did he know the role played by Lauterpacht in the attempt to unite Americans, British, French, and Soviets around "his" crime against humanity? Lemkin, who never gave up trying to convince, added paragraphs to his previous texts, including chapter 9 of *Axis Rule*:

> The concept of genocide gives a formula for covering not only the destruction of the Jews but also of other peoples, like the Russians, Czechs, Poles, Yugoslavs, Frenchmen. If one should stress only the Jewish aspect of the crime of destroying peoples and races, it would invite further attempts on the side of the defendants and their supporters to use the court for antisemitic propaganda. However, if the broader concept of genocide would be used more prominently the defendants would have to declare themselves as enemies of all other nations to justify their actions. Therefore, the use of the term genocide in any further proceedings is also important from the point of view of trial strategy.[25]

Lemkin was never short of ideas. When the films of Nazi atrocities were screened—for the first time ever—at the international court, he came up with the idea of the International Film for Discovery of War Criminals: to use films not only as clues to crimes but also to hunt down perpetrators. He proposed that the defendants be filmed and that the films be shown to survivors in displaced person camps, as well as "in countries where a number of victims may be found, such as New York, Palestine, Sweden, Portugal, and

Shanghai."[26] To modern criminality, a modern response; to global crimes, a global response. Once more, Lemkin was innovating. Later, he made a film strip from still images called *Le Génocide, le plus grand des crimes* (Genocide: The Greatest of Crimes): "The first part presented an imaginary group, the Extabians, who were persecuted by their government, not allowed to marry; sent to a labor camp, and eventually died there."[27]

"The guilty should be punished like common criminals and the world protected from the Crime of Genocide"

At Nuremberg, the word "genocide" was used more often than Lemkin acknowledged; he was annoyed that it wasn't mentioned in the indictment or the conviction statement. The day the trial opened, French lawyer Pierre Mounier spoke the word for the first time in a court of law, under the heading of "war crimes." He was followed by the Soviet lawyer, who situated it within "crimes against humanity," also a first in a courtroom, after attempts to invent the term during World War I in relation to the extermination of the Armenians. As we recall, at that time, it was a term of revenge against the enemies of the Turks, not a legal charge. Lemkin, left behind in Washington, was disappointed: the trial continued, day after day, without his concept being cited again, but only "crimes against humanity." Why had this term, which hadn't existed in international law before Nuremberg any more than "genocide" had, received the court's favor when it was just as retrospective?

Bitter, Lemkin insisted, "The inclusion of the word genocide in the verdict would help to create an atmosphere likely to prevent the repetition of such acts of barbarism." The "crime of barbarity" dated from 1933; it had now become "genocide." Thirty years of intellectual battles, a second world war, and yet a legal void persisted that the concept of genocide alone would be able to fill, whether it was physical, biological, or cultural: "We cannot continue to speak to the world in interminable sentences: 'Do not assassinate members of national, racial, or religious groups; do not sterilize them; do not steal their children.'"[28]

Lemkin was convinced that the Allies were being too timid because the Nuremberg trials were military tribunals, and war crimes or crimes against humanity were linked to combatants. The crime of genocide, however, concerned civilians, whose fate the military forces were incapable of envisaging.

But he was wrong; although crimes against humanity were not yet totally detached from the notion of "armed conflict," their defenders were using the term to account for the fact that civilian populations had suffered more from the war than had soldiers.

During this period of intellectual gestation, "crimes against humanity" referred to the question of protection of civilians and genocide to the protection of minorities. This was in fact how Sir Hartley Shawcross, prosecutor for the United Kingdom, understood it when he included the word "genocide" in his closing argument devoted to "crimes against peace." Benjamin Ferencz, the young American prosecutor at Nuremberg who tried the "subsequent" cases in the American occupation zone, was the first to truly distinguish "war crimes" from "crimes against humanity" in his indictment opening the trial against the Einsatzgruppen in 1947. He was thus the first to slip genocide into the category of crimes against humanity, whereas at Nuremberg it had remained an act underlying war crimes. Yet, he could not have spoken more harshly of Lemkin in 1945: the team around Jackson had no time to waste with his "'obsession' with genocide."[29]

Indeed, Lemkin's colleagues continued to lash out at his work for legal, political, or personal reasons. Some lamented that he had not analyzed the real content of the laws described, as if compiling them was enough for an understanding of how Nazism worked in Europe or to judge those responsible. In a review of *Axis Rule*, Melchior Palyi, an economics professor at the University of Chicago, was venomous:

> This case is typical of the conflict between the impassionate pursuit of a political goal and the purposeful political approach. It is the case of the ethically indignant prosecutor who unconsciously assumes the role of the judge—so common among students of law doubling as "social scientists." The field of international law, in its vague incompleteness and its lack of positive authority, is especially fit for the confusion of ultimate standards. Dr. Lemkin's case is a tragic one, too. His highly refined legal apparatus which is to serve against the Nazis could be turned on the Allies as well. Almost every one of the . . . international crimes he charges to the Nazis has been duplicated . . . by Allied occupational authorities.[30]

Palyi seized on the lack of precision in the definition of genocide, which made it an easily manipulated concept: "Allied practices include, in effect, even the worst of Nazi excesses—'genocide,' the mass extinction of civilians, as the fate of millions of Germans driven, under inhuman conditions, from their homes in east-central Europe. Of course, there is this substantial difference: that the Nazis shamelessly displayed their intentionally planned misdeeds, while the western Allies stumble into illegal practices and cover them with humanitarian or other formulas."[31] He was alluding—rightly—to the Soviets' lies at Nuremberg, starting with their transfer of responsibility for the murders in Katyn to the Nazis.

The French jurist Eugène Aroneanu, who had performed the enormous task of compiling Nazi crimes for Nuremberg and done pioneering work on witnesses (even though he mixed up "ordinary" concentration camps and extermination sites), would deliver the mortal blow against the term "genocide":

> Too narrow to embrace all crimes against humanity . . . but motivated by true legal imperialism, this vaunted "genocide" adapts to every reality to accomplish its conquests. For instance, it is proposed that we allow "biological genocide," "cultural genocide," etc., which, in my opinion, is a real monstrosity. . . . Only the introduction of crimes against humanity will impede a policy of the crime in the future, as it has already triumphed, in the past, over Nazi officials. To rechristen the "crime against humanity" . . . is to try to destroy a living reality through a quarrel over words. I am pointing out the double danger that there would be in replacing the law itself by a convention and the institution of the crime against humanity by an ersatz.[32]

Genocide of the Jews: A Singular Event?

"Ersatz," "monstrosity": the concept of genocide seemed to be destined for stillbirth and Lemkin for a return to oblivion. He did find allies, however. At Nuremberg, due to differences of interpretation among the four Allies, including on the notion of the "Jewish people"—some felt that Jews had nothing in common but religion—and on crimes against humanity, the coherence and centrality of the crimes against Jews could not be recognized as "as a unit in fact and in law."[33]

Lemkin then crossed paths with the lawyer Jacob Robinson, a Lithuanian Jew who had created the Institute of Jewish Affairs in New York, where he had arrived as a refugee in 1940. Robinson, like Lemkin, thought that during the early discriminatory measures and violence the Jews had served as "lab rats" for Hitler's war in a "cold pogrom," starting in 1933.[34] The failure of the future Allies to agree on the refugees, for instance at the Évian conference in 1938, had armed Hitler with a detestable argument, which was reiterated in following years. The entire world claimed not to understand the specificity of the Jews' fate, even after 1941 and 1942, when it involved physical, biological, and cultural extermination—what Lemkin was now calling "genocide."

Robinson and Lemkin agreed on the factual aspects of the extermination and on the comparisons with the massacres of Armenians in the preceding war, as well as on the impossibility of a legal sanction for the Turks' crimes. Where they diverged was in Robinson's single-minded interest in the Jews. Lemkin, due to his obsession with bringing the word "genocide" to global awareness and into the international legal vocabulary, "de-Judaized" it in order to universalize it. It became necessary to relativize the burden of the Jewish catastrophe, even though it weighed so heavily upon him. Breaking away from the time span of the war and proving that acts of genocide had been committed starting in 1933, he wanted to apply the crime during peacetime. Robinson wanted above all to establish a "conspiracy against the Jewish people": the Nazis had intentionally thought out a grand plan of destruction of the Jews "directed not only against the Jews under their control but also against those beyond their reach."[35]

Jewish survivors closely followed the Nuremberg trials. Although some found them balanced, others felt that the main victims of the Nazis were not made central to the deliberations, as there was more talk of the executioners than of them. And yet, the accumulation of testimony on the Einsatzgruppen, Treblinka, Birkenau, the Warsaw ghetto, and other locations had given a real Jewish flavor to the tribunals. Moyshe Feigenbaum, who participated in the historic commissions on the displaced persons camps, felt that it was also up to Jews to make up for the deficiencies in the verdicts with their personal, private experiences. There would have to be a transition from the "final solution"—the expression of the executioners—to *Hrbn* ("destruction" in Yiddish) or "catastrophe," the victims' expression:

[The documents in the trial] show only how the murderers behaved toward us, how they treated us and what they did with us. Do our lives in those nightmarish days consist only of such fragments? On what basis will the historian be able to create an image of what happened in the ghettos? . . . Therefore each testimony of a saved Jew, every song from the Nazi era, every proverb, every anecdote and joke, every photograph is for us of tremendous value.[36]

Toward the Convention on the Prevention and Punishment of the Crime of Genocide, Paris, 1948

It is always an arduous task to have a new concept admitted into international law. It was even more difficult at the beginning of the Cold War: how could pro-Americans and pro-Soviets be brought together to reflect, at a time when negotiations on the creation of the state of Israel were concluding, by a Polish Jewish refugee in the United States? No nation wanted to be looked into in peacetime—the Soviets no more than the Americans. And yet, Lemkin succeeded. The editor of the *Washington Post* wrote a portrait of him that became a portrait of the concept itself: "'The crime of genocide.' The word invented by a refugee will become a treaty. There is not a bomb, bullet, or torpedo in Raphael Lemkin's story. Yet this is one of the more fantastic stories of World War II. It is the story of an idea and a word."[37]

Lemkin was particularly satisfied by the UN declaration on December 11, 1946, on the "crime of genocide": it both laid the groundwork for a convention and finally distinguished genocide from crimes against humanity, to which it had been confined in Nuremberg the previous year. The Convention on the Prevention and Punishment of the Crime of Genocide was adopted on December 9, 1948, by the UN General Assembly in Paris.

For Lemkin, what was now essential was the prevention of genocide. He emphasized this in an interview in the French newspaper *Le Monde*: "never again" could not serve simply as a mantra; it was necessary to take action for peace through international law. His determination was never as strong as during these years. He was convinced that Hitler had intended to exterminate the Jews; in fact, "he had begun to exterminate German Jews" in 1933. Although criminals were punished in Nuremberg—not fully, because the crime of genocide had not been recognized—now, no criminal in power could become a Hitler. Under the convention, "a new Hitler could be arrested as an international criminal long before he had crossed any border with his armies." And in the *Washington Post* Lemkin ironically recalled the words of his detractors in Madrid in 1933: "But there is no such thing as exterminating whole groups of people."[38]

Lemkin doggedly returned to his compilation work. For example, he annotated a report on Czechoslovakia: "Horrible crimes done by Germans about looting and kidnapping of children from all nationalities in the occupied countries have been uncovered. Special orders have been issued concerning the germanisation of Polish and Czech children and families." He made a list of the names of children from the Czech villages of Lidice and Lezaky kidnapped after their parents were killed and placed with German families and of fifty-seven Germans, from nursery-school employees to directors of *Lebensborn*, from the director of the Lodz ghetto prison to members of the Gestapo to simple truck drivers.[39] The fate of the children would be central to the definition of genocide in the UN convention, which the Economic and Social Council was charged with writing.

During the preparatory sessions, Lemkin stood toe to toe with his opponents, both lawyers and politicians. In the more than two thousand pages of reports and debates, the Cold War and the year 1948 figured more prominently than the first half of the twentieth century: there was no allusion to the Armenians and few to World War II and the extermination of the Jews, even though the Soviet delegate remarked that his own country knew the most about genocide: "We know all about Maidanek and Babiy Yar. We waged this struggle in actual fact. . . . We shall carry on with the struggle."[40]

Lemkin, meanwhile, was using the word "civilization" to add universal scope: "I realized that the real issue at stake in the war was civilization not as a propaganda slogan but as a palpable reality."[41] Civilization stripped of propaganda: here again, World War I, when barbarity was the essence of the German Other, surfaced, and in World War II the reality of the Nazi crimes enabled the Soviets to camouflage their own crimes. Lemkin wanted to give real meaning to the overly manipulated terms "humanity," "civilization," and "culture"; in his drafts he constantly scribbled "cultural genocide."

In his essays on cultural genocide, he took Jewish culture as a first example, with the Bible as the founding document:

In 1939 the Germans burned the great library of the Jewish Theological Seminary at Lublin, Poland. This was reported by the Germans as follows: "For us it was a matter of special pride to destroy the Talmudic Academy. . . . We threw out of the building the great Talmudic library. . . . We set fire to the books. . . . The Jews of Lublin were assembled around and cried bitterly. . . . We summoned the military band and the joyful shouts of the soldiers silenced the sound of the Jewish cries."[42]

Then, he exalted European culture:

How impoverished our culture would have been if the people condemned by Germany, like the Jews, had not been capable of creating the Bible or bringing into the world an Einstein, a Spinoza; if the Poles had been unable to offer the world a Copernicus, a Chopin, a Curie; the Czechs . . . Huss, Dvorak; the Greeks . . . Plato, Socrates; the Russians . . . Tolstoy, Rimsky-Korsakov; the French . . . Voltaire, Montesquieu, Pasteur; the Dutch, Erasmus, Grotius, Rembrandt; the Belgians, Rubens, Maeterlinck; the Norwegians, Grieg; the Yugoslavs, Negosti; the Danes, Kierkegaard.[43]

No example was given from outside Europe; although the peoples of Africa and Asia were still largely under colonization, Latin America had been of great assistance to the UN. The first signatory state of the convention, in December 1948, was the Dominican Republic.

"Camouflaged genocide"?

Lemkin made a living teaching at various universities, but he was only a guest lecturer for limited terms, looked down on by his colleagues. He tried to find a position via the Emergency Committee in Aid of Displaced Foreign Scholars, which had assisted him so generously in 1941. He put forth his main specialty, financial law and international payments, convinced of its importance in settling the war.[44] He lashed out at legal scholars who disdained him and clung to the Nuremberg categories—not including genocide—in order to "reap jobs, honors, and Mandarin ceremonies." As for his political and diplomatic opponents—particularly the British and the Soviets—they joined forces to bury the convention project "in perfumed coffin committees."[45]

The reporter for *The New Yorker* in Paris for the 1948 UN session sketched Lemkin aptly: "Lemkin is a sad, witty, man born in eastern Poland. . . . He became a lawyer, which he now regrets, because he feels that lawyers are against progress. In the course of studying genocide, he has, he says, discovered that when authorities burn books, they are likely to start burning people next, and he wants a law against both."[46] Burning books, burning human beings: Lemkin, shameless, did not credit the German poet Heinrich Heine, but he plainly showed his disappointment. At first, he had divided evil, crime, into seven "fields of genocide techniques"—political, social, economic, biological, physical, religious, and moral—which he subsequently reduced to three: physical, biological, and cultural genocide, "a violation of the integrity of the group and selected members of this group. . . . If one kills a man without regard to the fact that he is Polish, Armenian, Huguenot, or Muslim, this is a simple murder, but if one kills a man because he is Polish, Armenian, Huguenot, or Muslim, it is a case of genocide."[47]

To emphasize intentionality, the delegate from the Netherlands invented the incisive formula of "camouflaged genocide": "It will have to be established beyond doubt, however, that so-called camouflaged genocide will equally be punishable; this covers cases in which the defendant might plead that the incriminated action, although it did in fact lead to the destruction or frustration of a group, was not aimed against that group."[48]

But, by the time it was being adopted, the convention no longer really corresponded to what Lemkin was arguing for. When he began his work, he took the example of other peoples to prove the universality of genocide and had his articles translated into many languages. In an interview during the UN session in December 1948, he talked about the consequences of the "crime of crimes" in relation to the forced departure of victims (a subject as current in 2018 as in 1948): "The victims of genocide do not simply wait patiently for death to arrive. They flee to other countries that are not always prepared to accept them. The problem of displaced persons and children in distress is only one direct result of genocide. Certain countries are called upon to pay the costs of crimes committed elsewhere. This crime is thus international because of its ramifications for international life."[49]

ſ

Lemkin was plagued by bad luck: on the eve of the vote on the convention, the Universal Declaration of Human Rights was itself voted on. After
suffering the blows of Lauterpacht and Jackson, he had to face competition
from René Cassin and Eleanor Roosevelt.[50] Indeed, many thought that the
first fight of the twentieth century, the protection of minorities under the law,
should now give way to protection of individual rights—a feeling shared
also among Lemkin's supporters, although he was convinced of the contrary:

> The Declaration of Human Rights is only an enunciation of general princi-
> ples. It has no binding force as international law. . . . The Genocide Con-
> vention is an international treaty. It can be enforced both as an international
> law and as a domestic law. Dealing with international crime, it carries with
> itself penalties and the highest degree of legal and moral condemnation. The
> Genocide Convention is a definite and precise commitment before the world
> not to murder peoples and races. . . . The Declaration of Human Rights is only
> an engagement; the Genocide Convention is a marriage.[51]

This was quite ironic, coming from a man who had never married. Perhaps he had never even had a love affair, except with his concept.

"There are some jurists who are still hesitating . . . but there are fewer of them
than of those who are horrified by genocide and want to stop it. The convention
must become a living force in the global community."[52]

After the vote in December 1948, the fight for ratification began, as the sig-
natures of twenty nations were necessary for the convention to become law.
Given the combination of the word "genocide" and its new legal definition,
the reticence of legal scholars, and the reality of planned extermination, the
"founder of the movement to outlaw genocide" looked in every direction.
He dared to lie outright to Eleanor Roosevelt, telling her that in 1943 his
memorandum had convinced her husband of the relevance of the concept;
as we recall, he was furious when he learned that Roosevelt likely hadn't
read it! One of his colleagues, Betty Hight, reported to him, though, that "the
President expressed his great interest . . . and that he believed in this cause;
that such a treaty would not apply to past genocides cases but would be very
beneficial for the future."[53]

Persuaded that his argument was legitimate, and sometimes not without bad faith, he wrote relentlessly. For instance, to Léon Blum: "You know about this tragic problem, alas, better than any statesman in the world. Your entire life you have fought for the principles that are the essence of this convention.... If France ratifies it, quickly, I am convinced that all other members will follow its example."[54] France was indeed an example, but of what all nations were thinking: the crime of genocide was always for others. As a French member of the human rights mission to the UN wrote at the time of ratification in 1950, "Genocide, which is the systematic destruction of a human group, is a crime that France will never commit and that it will never approve nor excuse. There is no reason for France to defer its ratification."[55]

Even though twenty nations ratified the convention in 1951, it was quickly weakened by the lack of an international tribunal, notably, and by the prolonged refusal of major states, including the United States, to ratify it. Up to the present, United Nations bodies have made scant use of the concept, in inverse proportion to its common and often inappropriate use by the public.

Lemkin remained the target of attacks. Some felt that the notion of genocide contributed nothing tangible. Others, conversely, felt that he was minimizing their own persecution by not characterizing it as genocide. These debates have continued for seventy years. For instance, at a time when segregation had just been abolished in the US army but remained legal throughout the country, certain African Americans wanted to appropriate the concept: "Yet this powerful weapon [racist hysteria] is responsible for the extermination of three million European Jews, what a prominent jurist, Dr. Raphael Lemkin, calls 'genocide.' Warsaw and Brooklyn may not be the same, but it can happen here and with the most appalling consequences for the Negro people."[56] In 1951, William Patterson, secretary of a civil rights association, went even further, presenting the UN with a petition accusing the United States of genocide on behalf of "fifteen million black Americans, the vast majority of whose lives are deliberately warped and distorted by the willful creation of conditions making for premature death, poverty, and disease."[57]

Again in 1953, after Lemkin had once again maladroitly evoked discrimination against blacks in the South in an article on the "nature of genocide," Oakley Johnson asked him to reexamine his definition of the term in a country involved in "terrorizing colored people, that is terrorizing a whole race of people who are colored. . . . They terrorize all Negroes, regularly, systematically, all the time. . . . We have here discrimination as a factor in genocide, just as the yellow badge of racial inferiority was forced on Jews by the Nazis." And Johnson added, "In view of the importance of this subject in the United States and its international importance too (South Africa; the whole colonial set-up) . . . you and other authorities should clear up the meaning and application of the term 'genocide.'"[58] This gave rise to a current of thought that has come to prominence in the early twenty-first century, a current that aims to define the slave trade and racialized enslavement not only as crimes against humanity but also as genocides.[59] Even though Lemkin rarely addressed racism, colonialization, and colonialism, his term has been seized upon—proof of recognition of its effectiveness. The concept has become more political than legal, which explains why some social sciences researchers hesitate to use it, even today.

Tirelessly, until the end of his life, Lemkin justified his body of work. For he had only one goal: to have the convention ratified.

Like any new concept, genocide was amalgamated with others. Some confuse genocide and discrimination. That is false:

a) Genocide implies destruction, death, annihilation, whereas discrimination is a *regrettable*[60] denial of certain life possibilities. Being treated unequally is not the same thing as being dead.

b) Genocide is an international crime whereas discrimination is comparatively minor; it is not a criminal phenomenon.[61]

Lemkin was not without political cunning. His correspondence gives multiple examples of his about-faces. For instance, he wrote to Andrey Vyshinsky, the Soviet representative at the UN and a prosecutor at the trials in Moscow. Not hesitating to use medical metaphors, as was the style of the day, he tried to cajole the mass criminal by explaining that not all progress meant a plot against the USSR: would Vyshinsky vote against penicillin?[62]

Yet, he supported peoples—such as the Greeks and the Baltic peoples—who were accusing the Soviets or their satellites of crimes of genocide. In a text sent to the International Labour Conference in London, he protested against communist "genocidal ideology": "Although human rights violations

exist in democracies in different forms of discrimination, genocide is practiced only in Russia."[63] And when African Americans returned to the fray,
he explained to them that they were directing blame against the United
States, when the real tragedy was happening to peoples dominated by the
Soviets.[64] "From the present communist campaign it becomes clear that
action is directed against the Jews in the entire area under communist control. Although Genocide affects now parts of the Jewish people, there is a
danger that under the influence of Soviet propaganda, which assumed the
dimensions and techniques applied by Streicher and Goebbels, the action
will spread rapidly so as to cause the destruction of the entire Jewry."[65] Lemkin did not deny the local anti-Semitism in different Soviet and Sovietized
territories; on the contrary, he rightly emphasized in his writings of the
time that both ancestral and recent lands were susceptible to this new campaign: "The communist campaign is facilitated by the pogrom traditions
in the areas involved which have developed and matured through centuries.
The Russian soil is saturated with the blood of hundreds of thousands of
Jews, and the local population can be easily aroused to participate now in a
large scale genocide action."[66]

Therefore, when the USSR ratified the convention, in 1954 (one year after
Stalin's death), Lemkin could not rejoice fully, as he realized that this signature invalidated his work. But the attacks against Jews by the Soviets
and their satellites (Lemkin cited the Czechs, the Poles, the Hungarians, the
Romanians, and the Bulgarians) were not the only reason for his uneasiness, and his argument was far from being only about the Cold War. In 1951,
he pointed out the major error by the United States, which stubbornly refused to sign the 1948 Convention. He concurred with Adolph Berle, former
assistant secretary of state and now chair of the International Law Committee of the New York City Bar Association: "Failure to ratify the convention
deprives us of a powerful weapon against communism. . . . The Communists unquestionably would use our reluctance to accept the convention in
an attempt to undermine our moral leadership. . . . There is evidence that
the Soviet Union was engaged in genocidal acts against the population of the
Baltic Republics—Lithuania, Estonia and Latvia. Thousands upon thousands
of their male citizens were being deported to Siberia, and their women to
Turkestan. . . . Lemkin warned against the delusion that the crime of mass
extermination had died with the Hitler Regime."[67] Berle, an eminent figure,

was briefed by Lemkin, who was still obsessed with "his" genocide, and he pointed out two fundamental aspects: the convention had a moral, ethical aspect, and American democracy had to recognize it to prove its superiority over Soviet communism. In addition, the Soviet Union was continuing to practice genocide against its own peoples, in particular in reprisal for their "collaboration" with the Nazis during World War II. Lemkin spoke out publicly about the Baltic states, but he also mentioned the Crimea-Tartars, the Caucasian people, and the Volga Germans.

This was when Lemkin turned to examine the Soviet past, and it led to his decision to campaign to have the Great Famine in Ukraine in 1933 declared a genocide. He gave a well-documented speech for the anniversary of the Great Famine in Ukraine on September 20, 1953, six months after Stalin's death: "It is the classic example of Soviet Genocide, its longest and broadest experiment in Russification—the destruction of the Ukrainian Nation." He described the genocide of the Ukrainians in three parts, starting with the destruction of its

> religious, intellectual, political [elites]. . . . The first blow is aimed at the intelligentsia, the national brain, so as to paralyze the rest of the body. In 1920, 1926, and again in 1933, teachers, writers, artists, thinkers, political leaders were liquidated, imprisoned or deported. . . . Second an offensive against the churches, priests, and hierarchy, the "soul" of Ukraine. . . . The third prong of the Soviet plan was aimed at the farmers, the large mass of independent peasants who are the repository of the tradition, folklore and music, the national language and literature, the national spirit of Ukraine. The weapon used is perhaps the most terrible of all—starvation. Between 1932 and 1933, 5,000,000 Ukrainians starved to death.[68]

Lemkin's vision was true: the famine sponsored by Stalin—the Holodomor, as the Ukrainians called it—was a "classic" genocide, with no doubt as to its intention. Prominent historians are unanimous on this fact today, even as the debate over the legal qualification of the crime of genocide continues.[69] For although Lemkin did indeed include political and cultural motivations in his personal definition of genocide, it must be said that the historically recognized definition was not that used by the legal scholars in 1948—whence the debates continuing to the present day, and not just on Ukraine.

The Ukrainian Parliament voted to recognize the Holodomor "as a deliberate act of genocide" in 2006, and many monuments memorializing the famine, the most imposing of which is the Museum-Memorial of Kiev, bear lines from Lemkin's "Soviet Genocide in Ukraine." Nevertheless, some Ukrainians see the events in Babi Yar, in Kiev—site of the largest open-air massacre of Jews—and of the extermination of Jews by Nazis in general—in which many Ukrainians participated—as unfair competition for victimization: had the Ukrainians not suffered enough? These Ukrainians don't like to remember that Lemkin, whom they are happy to canonize as inventor of the term "genocide," was Jewish and Polish and that he had studied in Lvov, now Lviv.

The Armenians Appropriate the Word "Genocide"

How happy Lemkin would have been had he known that Chavarche Missakian, who had been tortured and had survived the first deportations from Constantinople on April 24, 1915, and who had become editor of the Armenian daily in Paris, *Haratch*, had titled his editorial of December 9, 1945, "Genocide":

> A new word . . . coined by an American professor, Lemkin, who explains its meaning in a recently published book. . . . We follow the Nuremberg trials and our mind draws us to a distant world, where "war crimes" were similarly committed according to a plan designed and premeditated yesterday—actually, thirty years ago—to annihilate a people abandoned and left defenseless during the Great War. . . . At that time, where were the lawyers and judges of today? Had they not discovered the word, or was the bloodthirsty monster so powerful and beyond apprehension that they could not grasp it? . . . Has the world improved, from Istanbul and Malta to Nuremberg, Berlin, or Auschwitz? . . . These hyenas of genocide should be summarily judged and sentenced! But where was the first "exemplary" lesson of the present-day genocide inaugurated?[70]

Missakian wrote "war crimes" in scare quotes and adopted the word "genocide"—the neologism *Tséghasbanoutyoun* in Armenian—the word that he would have so wished for in 1915.

Disaster? Massacre? That was yesterday! A genius would have to be born to conceive of this form of extermination and transmit it to barbarians. Another genius was now necessary to find the word describing the fait accompli. No modern language had this word. . . . Today's words seem risible to characterize this catastrophe. "Massacre," "slaughter," and "war" are all innocent words.[71]

To make his case for the urgent need for the Convention on Genocide, Lemkin, the "genius," now oriented his campaign to Christian institutions. In a letter to the Council of Methodist Women, he linked the catastrophes affecting Christians in the two world wars:

This convention is a matter of our conscience and is a test of our relationship to evil. I know it is very hot in July for work. . . . Let us not forget that the heat of this month is less unbearable to us than the heat in the ovens of Auschwitz and Dachau and more lenient than the murderous heat in the desert of Aleppo that burned to death the bodies of hundreds of thousands of Christian Armenians victims of genocide in 1915.[72]

Lemkin was well known at the time, as he had given an interview broadcast on the CBS television network. After summarizing the principles of the convention, he gave a long description of the Armenian genocide. In the background were images of Ottoman soldiers hunting down Armenian children and adults, over which the moderator, Quincy Howe, commented, "These folks . . . are running for their lives. . . . Men on horseback . . . let's say they are modern cavalry out on orders of their commanders. They are huntsmen out on the chase. Only the prey doesn't happen to be a fox. The prey is people. These [Armenians] were the victims. . . . Why? Well, the reason given was that they were friendly to the enemy of their rulers; that they were a fifth column; that they were spies. Every one of the 2 million of them—women, men, and children." Then, Lemkin explained that the annihilation of the Armenians and the impossibility of indicting the criminals had led to his interest in genocide. He recalled Soghmon Tehlirian, the murderer of Talaat Pasha in 1921, with whom he identified directly; both had lost their mother and their native tongue and culture. "[His] mother was killed in the genocide. . . . And he told the court that he did it because his mother came in his sleep . . . many times. . . . The murder of your mother, you would do something about it! So he committed a crime. So, you see, as a lawyer, I thought that a crime should not be punished by the victims, but should be punished by a court."[73]

Lemkin sought in history the intellectual arguments needed for ratification of the convention, even though he knew that it was a political act—whence his complementary readings, in particular on the Armenians. By allying with the Christians, he was pursuing the universalization of his concept, and in looking back at 1915 he was defining his mission to span the entire century. It was in these years that the Armenian genocide returned to being the matrix of his intellectual scaffolding, as it had been in the 1920s and 1930s. Thus, he wrote, in reference to cultural genocide, "The Armenians tried to assemble the names from all their communities who were victims of the genocide. Libraries around the world are collecting all these facts. It would be morally wrong to think that they are being collected for purely scientific and historical reasons. Each Armenian finds himself in each of the documents of the time."[74]

In Lemkin's papers is a book by James J. Mandolian, *What Do the Armenians Want?* (1946), in which Lemkin would have read, "The Armenian case is an old case and a forgotten case which is being revived."[75] He was still emphasizing his affinity with the Armenians in his last published work, a book review that can be read as a testament:

> Father Naslian expresses a judgment that is particularly close to the author's heart. It is that the victims of genocide through the ages have filled history with their pain to the point that humanity can no longer evade either identification of the consequences or its moral responsibility. . . . The sufferings of Armenian men, women, and children thrown into the Euphrates or massacred on the road from Deir Ez-Zor prepared the way for adoption of the Convention on Genocide by the United Nations and morally forced Turkey to ratify it. . . . A million Armenians died, but a law against the murder of peoples has been written with the ink of their blood and in the spirit of their ordeal.[76]

Satisfied that fifty countries had ratified the convention by 1959, Lemkin forgot that it might be absolutely counterproductive. Indeed, the Turks had signed in July 1950, but with the certainty that the Armenians had not suffered a genocide, as Lemkin had made sure not to speak to them about it.[77] Up to the present day, the Turkish state has maintained its position of genocide denial.

"Mr. Lemkin of the Genocide" (Mgr. Roncalli)

Lemkin twice met with Monsignor Roncalli, the future Pope John XXIII, who offered him a beautiful title of nobility, "Mr. Lemkin of the Genocide."[78] Convinced more than ever that the "genocide catastrophe"—the constantly recurring killing of "other" people—formed the nucleus of world history, Lemkin launched himself into writing, publishing numerous articles and planning two books, an autobiography and a history of the concept of genocide, designed as a kind of encyclopedia, in which he intended to describe every destruction of peoples from antiquity to contemporary times.[79] For the latter book, he created or adopted a number of concepts in order to clarify his thought on genocide, revealing himself to be an original cultural researcher. His transdisciplinary vision brought together history, demography, international relations, anthropology, art history, geography, law, sociology, and political science, and his subjects ranged from the Assyrians to the Tasmanians, in alphabetical order. Unfortunately, only a few fragments and a detailed table of contents remain from the original work.

As he was particularly interested in psychology, Lemkin sought to define the interrelationships among three groups: "victims," "genocidists," and the "outside world." There is little chance that Raul Hilberg had read his manuscript when he created his three categories for destruction of the European Jews: "victims," "perpetrators," and "bystanders." Hilberg's "bystanders," analogous to Lemkin's "outside world," reflected more accurately the ambivalent reality than did the concept of the French word *témoin* (witness), as it encompassed seeing, not seeing, participating in the crime, resisting.[80] At the same time as he was theorizing genocides for the final time, Lemkin was also writing his autobiography: in the Belarusian, then Polish, village of his youth, he had been able to observe his disreputable neighbors (or bystanders).[81]

Like the psychiatrist William Niederland, Lemkin described "survivor syndrome," from which he was trying to recover.[82] He knew from experience that the extreme situations with which combatants were confronted had little in common with those facing victims of genocide. After a war, the number of survivors—male, uniformed veterans—is always higher than the number of dead. Coming home from the military front, they return to domestic life and their families. As Lucien Febvre wrote in 1946, "I, a survivor, confronted with cemeteries where the dead of two generations, mown down in their prime, rest uneasily."[83] Conversely, there are very few survivors of a genocide, and they are without family, without support, often forced to go into exile, without a home, without photographs, without personal effects.[84] This explains why so many of them have problems that Lemkin called the "psychological responses of fear; defeatism; loss of self-respect; resistance; and revenge."[85] True to his method, he took specific examples from his readings, encounters, the Nuremberg trial records. It was a prodigious work, in which everything led to genocide. He also alluded to the sense of guilt for having survived, explored in depth in the 1960s by authors from Niederland to Primo Levi. The catastrophe—*Shoah* in Hebrew—was irreparable, it was still spreading, and again, one did not live (*vit*), one survived (*sur-vit*), a semantic nuance that Soazig Aaron reinvented as "subviving" (*sous-vivant*).[86] *Introduction to the History of Genocides* was to be the masterpiece that Lemkin, who had crossed the Atlantic in time, would offer to victims of the crime of crimes: "The very fact of having survived thanks to geography leads to the perpetuation of painful memories." At the time of the Eichmann trial, in 1961, there were some who missed him: "Lemkin, the man who could have abolished future Eichmanns; the man who fought, the fight of a single man, for a single science. A modern Don Quixote who charged the windmills of the world and offered a major contribution to save humanity."[87]

But Lemkin died in 1959. Although the last people to visit him claimed that descriptions of his misery and solitude were being exaggerated—he had even been nominated for the Nobel Peace Prize—his strong feeling of exclusion was like a metaphor for the general indifference to the word "genocide" for many years, inversely proportional to its excessive use today.

> "I was alone, with no money, in a foreign country.
> I had to start my life over." (Jan Karski)

While Lemkin was fighting to save his conception of genocide, Karski was losing his Poland. In May 1944, as he was feverishly writing his memoir, he sent a telegram to London suggesting that "his impressions of England and the United States be publicized in Poland, including the political problems with postwar aid to Poland in world opinion."[88] His book *Story of a Secret State*, a call for mobilization in his country, an implicit order, was intended to be used to prove the rights of the democratic Poland arising from the government in exile. "Poland grew no Quislings, but under the Nazi terror there has grown a secret democratic state. This book is the story of a people who for four years have lived and worked under an invisible government."[89]

But the Soviets who let the Nazis crush the resistance would soon occupy Poland, bringing it under their domination. After Yalta, Karski, the militant patriot, was quoted as saying, "Another Munich for Poland."[90]

For American communists guided by remote control from Moscow, the Warsaw insurrection was a trap, and the resisters who had worked for the government in exile in London were traitors to the true nation and true Poles. Karski was a perfect example. His book was the subject of a critical review in *Soviet Russia Today*, "Not the Whole Story," the author of which paid scant tribute to the courier's courage, presenting him as a naive puppet in the hands of the government in exile. The offspring of a "rather well-to-do family," he was incapable of understanding anything about the struggle of the Polish people and the grandeur of the Soviet sacrifice in 1940.

"In spite of excellent treatment when he was sent to a [prisoners'] camp by the Russians, Karski decides to go back to German-occupied Poland. . . . There he encounters Nazi terror and brutality." While recognizing the importance of his testimony, notably in the two chapters concerning the Warsaw ghetto and Belzec, the critic evoked Karski's treachery: he left Poland in 1943 (in reality in 1942, which would have further reinforced the magazine's point of view) and thus knew nothing further about his country; he was able to survive "easily" thanks to his networks, whereas true Poles were "collectively held responsible for acts of resistance" and massacred. Finally, Karski was working under the auspices of the National Democratic Party: "Every Pole knows that the foundations of this party were laid on anti-Semitism and political and economic struggle against the Jews." Why so much hate, even though the anti-Semitism of certain Polish political parties, before and after the war, cannot be denied? Because Karski was advocating for an Inter-Allied Committee that would administer Polish affairs until free elections were held, which, he hoped, would give birth to a democratic Poland.

For the proponents of a Sovietized Poland, therefore, he lost all the value that he had acquired as a resister. He was no longer anything but "an instrument for the propaganda apparatus of the London Government-in-Exile."[91]

Serving the CIA

So, it is not surprising that Karski agreed to work for former president Herbert Hoover. Hoover, whose political career had been ended by his inability to grapple with the 1929 crisis, in 1945 regained all the energy of his remarkable organization that had supplied occupied Belgium and northern France during the Great War. The neutral powers had sent humanitarian aid to populations threatened with famine and had sold their agricultural production, while accomplishing the feat of having most of the receipts go to the French and Belgian governments. Hoover had also largely saved the Russians from famine in 1921, following the civil war.[92]

Now, in 1945, the important thing was to rescue archives. The documents of former governments in exile, starting with those that the couriers, the agents, often risking their lives, had transported, were in danger of disappearing. Karski accepted this repatriation mission and was to leave for Europe in early summer 1945. On July 5, however, the United States recognized the new Sovietized Poland; the country for which he had fought no longer existed. His mentor, Jan Ciechanowski, handed in the keys to the embassy in Washington. Karski, like most of the staff, did not want to pledge allegiance to the new regime. From refugee, he became stateless.

It was in the service of the United States, of which he became a citizen in 1954—and where his pseudonym "Karski" definitively replaced the name Kozielewski, because that was how he had entered the country—that he went to Europe with the hope, an insane hope for many years (until 1989), of finding a Poland that he knew.

In this context, the search for archives that he conducted from July to December 1945 resembled Dubnow's or Ringelblum's. When all was lost, the traces of the glorious past struggle against the Nazis—and the communists—remained proof of life, of struggle, of hope.[93]

In London, Paris, and Rome, Karski collected hundreds of leaflets during this final trip as a courier. The main thrust of these documents, of course, was anti-Soviet more than anti-Nazi. In *Poland Accuses: An Indictment of the Major German War Criminals*, Poles, who had been absent from Nuremberg in accordance with the wishes of the Soviets, insisted on looking back at 1939 and the German-Soviet agreement on the dismantling of Poland.[94] The time of the Nazis seemed to have been only a short parenthesis in the larger struggle of Polish patriots against the Russians and then the Soviets.

However, Karski continued to carry within himself the great massacre of the Jews. With them he shared an early memory, from immediately after the catastrophe, a private memory recorded in accounts hastily written in 1945–46 and marked by numerous commemorations, especially in Yiddish, in the different countries—France, Belgium, the United States, Australia, Argentina, the Yishuv and then Israel—in which several tens of thousands of survivors found themselves.[95]

Professor Karski

Karski had dreamed of becoming a Polish diplomat, but this was now impossible. So, he returned to studying political science under the aegis of the regent of Georgetown University in Washington, the Jesuit priest Edmund Walsh, whom he had met in 1943. He used his personal documents for his dissertation, "The Great Powers and Poland, 1919–1945," a typewritten copy of which was presented in 1953 at Georgetown University and numerous editions of which formed the basis of his teaching throughout his academic career.

His work as a student and then as a professor was in line with his citizen engagement since 1939: to show the calamities faced by independent Poland, from its resurrection in 1919 to its obliteration by the Soviets in 1945. In chapter 28 of his dissertation, "British and American Attitudes toward Poland, 1941–1943," he explained how Roosevelt's and Churchill's "pragmatism" in winning the war led them to prefer an alliance with the Soviets, who were indispensable to defeating the Nazis, over their commitments to Poland: "Polish interests, whenever in conflict with Russia's demands, rarely seemed important enough to risk antagonizing the Soviet dictator. Stalin realized his worth, and whenever it came to Polish matters, he took full advantage of his position."[96] Military strategy dominated, and, if Poland had to be sacrificed, Poland would be sacrificed. Karski quoted himself:

In August 1943, a courier from the Polish Underground, Jan Karski, was dispatched to Washington with a mission to report on the situation in Poland

and on the Nazi extermination of the Jews. Roosevelt received him with both
interest and sympathy. True, he pointed out, Poland would have to concede
some territory to Russia, but he was sure that Stalin would demand no more
than what was necessary "to save face." . . . "Tell the leaders of the resistance,"
the president concluded, "that their indomitable attitude has been duly appreciated. Tell them that they will never have cause to regret their brave decision
to reject any collaboration with the enemy and that Poland will live to reap the
reward of its heroism and sacrifice.[97]

It was 1953, the year of Stalin's death, but the Cold War continued. The
fate of the Polish Jews was now secondary. And yet, when, twice in his imposing volume, Karski spoke of the Holocaust, it was as an eyewitness: "In
enslaved Poland people lived in abjection, humiliation, lawlessness, and terror. Concentration camps grew larger and more numerous every month. Nazi
atrocities were unspeakable. Forsaken by all and totally helpless, Poland's
Jews—three and a half million of them—were about to begin their last exodus from the ghettoes to gas chambers." This passage was footnoted: "For an
eyewitness testimony as to conditions in the Warsaw and Belzec ghettoes,
see Karski, *Story of a Secret State.*"[98]

Karski the academic used classic archives; when he quoted himself, it
was with regard to the fate of Poland—his dissertation subject—and that of
the Polish Jews. In the ensuing years, however, the extermination of the
Jews disappeared completely from his academic and public discourse. For
it was the prisoner who had escaped the Soviets and the Polish exile who
interested Radio Free Europe and other activist audiences: "Jan Karski will
present the methods of Soviet indoctrination in satellite countries."[99] Karski
used his oratorical talents for the CIA on a lecture tour across Asia and
Europe. In 1956, he testified in front of the House Un-American Activities
Committee, where he presented himself as an academic expert with direct
experience of the war. The former resister and author of *Story of a Secret
State* went to testify about "Communism and the Soviet methods of conquest in the Eastern European area" during the year of uprising and revolts
in Poland and Hungary. He found the committee too discreet, acknowledged its "very, very good work," and promised to speak out even more.[100]

Karski continued to tell the story of his meeting with Roosevelt in 1943,
from which he excerpted only the passages on the Poles, the war, and the

resistance. In 1957, he wrote to the newspapers, as he would do often, about the "false election in Poland" after the disturbances of 1956. He pointed out that this nonelection hid the true aspirations of the "Polish nation, which has not experienced such misery in half a century and has no hope for the future." He saw a clear paradox: "There is certain confusion, strangely enough, caused by a combination of communist propaganda and American traditional sympathy for the Polish People."[101] This concerned a different Poland, one that no longer existed.

In 1961, Karski, an anticommunist so virulent that his students nicknamed him "McCarthski," was invited to the Maxwell Air Force Academy. A photograph shows him equipped for flight at the side of an instructor, a colonel. Then he gave a lecture on communism. He introduced himself this way: "In 1943, I personally reported to President Roosevelt and other British and American officials."[102] In 1943, during World War II, what had he "reported"?

Karski, the new American, with his strong accent and particular habits, left no doubt about where his heart belonged. Thus he described himself, in French and not without humor, at the time he was undertaking a tour for the CIA:

> I am a Catholic by religion, believing and practicing. I completed my university studies in Poland, in the faculty of law. . . .
>
> During the war, I fought as a soldier against the Germans and became a prisoner of war. . . . in Russia. In 1939, Stalin's Russia collaborated with Hitler's Germany. The two countries attacked Poland from two sides.
>
> I escaped, and once back in Poland I joined the resistance against the Nazis. . . . I traveled around Europe a number of times, naturally in secret. In 1940, I was arrested by the Gestapo. I escaped, without my teeth and with several ribs broken during torture. In 1943, I was sent to the United States to inform President Roosevelt and the American government about the situation in Poland. When the English and American governments recognized the communist regime in Poland, in 1945 . . . I left the embassy and suddenly I became an immigrant. I was alone, with no money, in a foreign country. I had to start my life over.[103]

6

Becoming Karski,
Becoming Lemkin

1978–2018

The losses of war may be repaired, but the losses of genocide are irreparable.[1]

—Lemkin

The messengers had borne witness. By his invention of the term "genocide" and his fight for the UN convention, Lemkin built a memorial for the annihilated through his writings. Karski, the Catholic resister, never failed to remember the Jewish origins of his wife, Pola Nirenska, and her people wiped out in the catastrophe: "But I reported what I saw."[2] In the late 1970s, he began to take part in public commemorations of the destruction of the Jews in Europe.

"There is no testimony without some involvement of oath . . . and without sworn faith. . . . The witness *promises* to say or to manifest something to another, his addressee: a truth, a sense which has been or is in some way present to him as a unique and irreplaceable witness."[3] Is it necessary to recall that the French word for "witness," *témoin*, is etymologically related to the word "martyr"?

"All murdered Jews have become my family"

Although Jan Karski's two days in front of the filmmaker Claude Lanzmann's camera took place in 1978, Lanzmann was still editing his film in the early 1980s. The filming of the interview probably catalyzed in Karski, who had remained more or less silent on the subject since the war, the desire to speak out once again. The psychiatrist Dori Laub acknowledged such desires in an essay titled "Not Knowing Is an Active Process of Destruction. Why the Testimonial Procedure Is of So Much Importance";[4] elsewhere, he wrote, "Memory leads to memory, perhaps even to an explosion of memories."[5] Karski was feeling a sense of urgency: fewer and fewer survivors were still alive, and what they had lived through was further and further in the past. The struggle against time was accompanied by a sense of guilt for not having testified earlier. In a *Washington Post* article titled "Holocaust: So Horrible No One Believed It Was True," Abe Karp, professor of Jewish studies at the University of Rochester, described a colloquium in which Karski participated in 1980: "'How would one know an event so horrible that a special term had to be fashioned to describe it?'" This referral to a "special term," "Holocaust," followed by two years the broadcast of the television series of the same name. Lemkin would not have been happy that the producers of the series had refused to use his neologism. Whether holocaust or genocide, Karp added that, even long after 1945, it remained impossible to believe that the event had occurred. It was a denial that Karski, now a professor at Georgetown University and "a Polish citizen during the war," confirmed, as he recounted yet again his mission to Washington and his meetings with Roosevelt and Frankfurter.[6]

Karski did not speak in a major public arena devoted to the extermination of the Jews until 1981, when he sat on a panel at "Discovering the 'Final Solution,'" also called the International Liberators' Conference, the first symposium organized by the forerunner of the United States Holocaust Memorial Museum.[7] On the first day, the organizer, Miles Lerman, recounted how he had survived, which meant that he was one of those alive in Poland in 1945, and described how he had come to be involved with this conference, which, even in 1981, was groundbreaking.

> On the day of my liberation, I returned to my hometown on the top of a tank of the advancing Soviet and Polish armies. I should have been jubilant, for Hitler's defeat was imminent, but I was not. How could I be? For of the 16,000 Jews who lived in my hometown before the Nazi onslaught, I found on my return home 11 surviving Jews, wandering around aimlessly, hoping to find some of their families alive. Unfortunately, most of them perished in the gas

chambers of the death camp of Belzec. Among them were my mother, my sister and her husband, three of her young boys—ages six, eight, and 13—plus 29 other members of my immediate family.[8]

Lerman then made two promises to the dead: to remember their fate on the site of their ordeal—whence his commitment to commemorating Belzec—and, above all, to speak history aloud: "We [are] to bear witness and tell the story of their agony and their torture and their painful deaths . . . to ensure that this shameful chapter in the history of mankind remains unaltered and undistorted forever and ever."[9]

"Shameful," "mankind": Lerman positioned himself as a moral witness, as did most of the delegates from the fourteen Allied nations who spoke: survivors, resisters, officers, war correspondents, doctors, and military chaplains, including many from the Eastern Bloc—a first in Washington. The conference was possible because Elie Wiesel had met General Vasily Petrenko, liberator of Auschwitz, in Moscow in 1979. It was Wiesel's wish that liberated and liberators would fight together against Holocaust denial, and he felt that testimony from Jewish survivors was necessary, even though he was not taken in by certain political agendas. In his own speech, Wiesel remembered the arrival of the first Americans in Buchenwald, where he had himself arrived, the only survivor of his family, after the death march from Auschwitz. Barely a teenager, he had seen these soldiers, grown men, crack; the experience of extermination overturned the generational pyramid, inverted values and meaning, as all life had been crushed: "You broke down, you wept. You wept and wept uncontrollably, unashamedly. You were our children then. . . . You wept. We could not. We had no more tears left. We had nothing left. In a way we were dead, and we knew it."[10]

Karski's speech made a big impression in the assembly hall of the State Department. So, this man was living in Washington? How was it that he wasn't known? He took his time, giving details on dates, places, people encountered, articles published, lectures given. He retraced every step of an eyewitness account that no one had listened to; he went so far as to replay scenes. Wiesel reported on his speech: "There was laughter when he imitated Roosevelt, and there were tears when he described the Warsaw ghetto and its misery."[11] Asked what he thought about the lack of action by those to whom he had spoken in London and Washington, Karski said that he no longer felt anything: "At that time, I was a recording machine. I was a tape recorder. If I had any human feelings—surprise, shock—I would have gone crazy a long time ago. I had no feelings at all. So, don't ask me was I surprised or not. I was not surprised about anything."[12]

Karski didn't ask "Who knew what?" He knew better than anyone what the answer was. On the other hand, his question was "When?" The precise instant when things became known transformed him the more he spoke. He began to reconstruct his identity, in a form of self-Judaization that he pursued until his death, twenty years later:

> Many of you at this conference gave testimony on the Jewish Gehenna. Respect is due to you.
>
> The Lord assigned me a role to speak and write during the war, when—as it seemed to me—it might help. It did not. . . .
>
> Furthermore, when the war came to its end, I learned that the governments, the leaders, the scholars, the writers did not know what had been happening to the Jews. They were taken by surprise. The murder of six million innocents was a secret. . . .
>
> Then, I became a Jew like the family of my wife, who is sitting in this audience—all of them perished in the ghettos, in the concentration camps, in the gas chambers—so all murdered Jews became my family.
>
> But I am a Christian Jew. I am a practicing Catholic. And, although not a heretic, still my faith tells me: the second Original Sin had been committed by humanity: through commission, or omission, or self-imposed ignorance, or insensitivity, or self-interest, or hypocrisy, or heartless rationalization.
>
> This sin will haunt humanity to the end of time.
>
> It does haunt me. And I want it to be so.[13]

Haunted by the sin of the abandonment of the Jews, the Catholic who had nevertheless testified for their survival since 1942 now proclaimed himself a Jew—an emotional, cultural, political Jew, not a religious one. It was not the term "Holocaust" that came to his mind to designate the catastrophe, however, but "Jewish Gehenna," an assumed pleonasm, a vision of hellfire both Christianized and harking back to the retributions of the Old Testament.

"Righteous Among the Nations"

Karski's prominence did not escape two Israelis present at the International Liberators' Conference: Gideon Hausner, the prosecutor at the Eichmann trial, and Yitzhak Arad, director of Yad Vashem. They invited him to Israel, where he received the title of Righteous Among the Nations the following year, in 1982.

In 1942, when Karski was in the Warsaw ghetto and Izbica and Lemkin was writing the first draft of *Axis Rule*, a Jew from the Yishuv, Mordecai Shenhabi, was already conceptualizing the commemoration of the killings and the rescuers by formulating the notion of "Righteous Among the Nations" coupled with a memorial to the extermination of the Jews, "Yad Vashem": "I will give them, in my house and within my walls, a memorial [*Yad*] and a name [*Shem*] . . . that will not be cut off" (Isaiah 56:5). Shenhabi proposed, in addition to a list of Jewish victims, a "list of the Righteous Among the Nations who saved souls or belongings" of destroyed Jewish communities.[14]

It would take almost ten years for the notion of the "Righteous" to become rooted in Israeli culture: "Rescuers came from all social strata. . . . All those who came to our aid are dear to us, and when the history of the Holocaust is written, an eternal monument will also be erected in honor of these Righteous among the Nations."[15] In the Martyrs' and Heroes Remembrance (Yad Vashem) Law passed in August 1953, the definition was founded on the idea of personal heroism: "The Righteous among the Nations who risked themselves to save Jews."

The extermination of the Jews, mentioned in the Constitution of Israel in 1948 (*Shoah* in Hebrew, *Holocaust* in English), did not become part of the nation's civic religion until the late 1970s. The Eichmann trial was one of the main steps in this evolution.[16] Ben Gurion wanted the victims of the genocide to be identified with the state of Israel, which was presented as rampart and recourse for all oppressed and persecuted Jews. The trial had barely gotten under way when it was suspended for the commemoration of Yom HaShoah[17]—the day of the Shoah—when, for the first time, the Righteous Among the Nations were named.

In his closing argument at the trial, Hausner "paid a tribute to these Gentiles who helped us" and listed the "non-Jews" who had rescued them:[18] "In the dark, horrible night which descended on Europe with Hitler's rise to power, there were also some rays of light. And the Jewish people will not forget its benefactors.[19] . . . And those kindly Poles who were hiding Jews right in the middle of the valley of death, under fearful danger, braving the wave of hellish hate which had enveloped all Poland; there were others also, there was the Polish underground, and there were ordinary people who helped, who concealed, who saved, who kept others alive [in Lithuania, Germany, Yugoslavia, Greece, Bulgaria, Romania]."[20] Hausner quoted Karski, who was not yet, in the strict sense of the term, a patented Righteous Among the Nations. Although he had suffered for and with Jews, although he had testified for their survival, he had not literally saved any. The eyewitness became the moral witness, the "courageous emissary of the Jewish resistance," thanks to whom "everyone had an account from a non-Jewish eyewitness."[21]

The state of Israel gradually transformed this individual recognition into a diplomatic tool. In 1962, David Alcalay, director of the bureau of testimony on Jewish victims, took over the Department of the Righteous. He alone was responsible for the two faces of Yad Vashem: the names of the victims, written, intoned, howled, and the names of the saviors, become the "Righteous," still very few in number at the time. The presiding judge at the Eichmann trial, Moshe Landau, was appointed to head the Commission for Designation of the Righteous. Later came the planting of trees—the roots of sacrifice—in the Garden of the Righteous and increasingly sophisticated ceremonies in Jerusalem as the perimeter of Yad Vashem expanded. Hausner was to be one of Jan Karski's sponsors—one of those who put together the dossier proposing him for the status of Righteous Among the Nations.

Jan Karski: The Righteous Among the Righteous

Like the processes involved in canonization, the dossiers of the Righteous Among the Nations contained testimonials. For instance, Irving Sorkin lauded Karski's exemplary life: "I am certain that you will consider Mr. Karski perfectly worthy of such an honor, as he is a rightful Gentile."[22] The biblical term "Gentile" was not chosen at random.

In 1982, Karski began to speak publicly about American affairs, particularly everything connected with World War II and the genocide of the Jews. Right after the war, he had been practically silent. Now, he talked and he wrote. In April 1985, during President Reagan's visit to Bitburg, Germany, Karski shared the opinion of a number of his compatriots: the necessary reconciliation with the Germans could not be concluded in a cemetery that contained the graves of SS soldiers, especially if Reagan did not go to visit an extermination site.[23] In the *Washington Post*, he recalled his war missions in London and Washington, concluding with a judgment that was unusually bitter for him:

> I brought information on the fate of Jews in Nazi-dominated Poland as well as desperate requests for help from Jews, addressed to the Allied governments, to save those who could still be saved. . . . The Jewish requests for help came to naught—the inactivity of the powerful Allied governments having been determined by war priorities, self-controlled ignorance, self-imposed disbelief or soulless rationality. Thus, 6 million Jews, helpless and abandoned by humanity, perished in agony. Today, some 40 years later, as an old man coming to the end of his earthly journey, I cannot but raise my voice. We must pursue peace, cooperation, justice and freedom. But our pursuit can never be based on *self-imposed forgetfulness* of what happened to the Jews during World War II.[24]

A few months later, *Shoah*, finally completed, was released worldwide, and Karski gave his point of view about being a character in the film in a letter to the editor in the *Washington Post* titled "Holocaust: The leaders knew." The letter was framed and placed in the middle of the page. Karski listed all those with whom he had met and concluded, "The widely spread opinion that the Western leaders were unaware of what happened to the Jews is no more than a myth. They knew."[25]

Claude Lanzmann's Karskis: 1978, 1985, 2010

Claude Lanzmann filmed Karski extensively in 1978. In his 1985 edit, he abandoned the heroic resister in the midst of his mission on behalf of Poland (Karski's choice in his memoir) and as the bearer of messages to the Allies trying to convince the president of the United States of the reality of the extermination. The second day of the interview, during which Karski described his missions outside Poland, was completely set aside, as was the account of his hallucinatory visit to Belzec-Izbica. Lanzmann assigned him only the task of reporting what he had seen with his own eyes in the ghetto, echoing what the Jews in Warsaw had asked of him in 1942: "You are going to deal with the English. Now you will give them your oral reports. I'm sure it will strengthen your report if you will be able to say 'I saw it myself.'"[26]

Lanzmann intended *Shoah* not only to show the uniqueness of the Shoah but also to stand as the only work on the uniqueness of the Shoah, through the "exemplarity of the singular."[27] In the spare narrative of the film, the former courier had only one role: to talk about his mission in the ghetto. It was up to him not to report everything he had gone through but to play his part in the symphony composed and orchestrated by Lanzmann, who had designed *Shoah* to start with the first death centers—Chelmno, Treblinka, Sobibor, and the gas chambers at Birkenau. This was why he left Karski's testimony about the ghetto to the end and retained only forty minutes of the rushes in the edit.[28]

> It was important to position the ghetto after the radical nature of the death was known, to show that extermination was included in the logic of the ghettos, in which people were dying of hunger. There was another reason: for there to be tragedy, and for there also to be suspense, the end had to be known from the beginning. Viewers had to know what would happen while at the same time having the feeling that it could not happen.[29]

However, Karski was resistant to Lanzmann's demands, just as he had refused to meet with him until after more than a year of Lanzmann's insistent correspondence.

Karski weeps. "Now, I go back thirty-five years. No, I don't go back no, no"—three nos. He leaves the couch, the library, the screen. Lanzmann is alone; a traveling shot down the empty hallway. Then Karski reappears, sitting: "I am ready." But he doesn't look at Lanzmann, and he still objects: "Even now I don't want . . . I understand your role. I am here. I don't go back in my memory. I couldn't tell any more."[30]

Karski mixes present and past: 1978: "I don't go back"; the war, "I couldn't tell any more."[31] He has a linguistic tic. Most of his sentences begin with "now," as if he were encouraging himself to speak—to make the past present. He sets out next to himself his cigarettes, notes, evidence of what he is advancing. Close by is the reassuring presence of his wife. Lanzmann edited all of this out. He did, however, exploit Karski's initial refusal to let himself be submerged in his memories, cutting from the dramatic "No!" to the serenity of the new citizen of the United States, land of liberty. In a telling illustration, a cutaway shot overflies the Statue of Liberty, the port of New York, and the south end of Manhattan, and then we discover, via the Stars and Stripes on the White House flagpole, the capital of the most powerful country in the world: the Lincoln and Jefferson memorials, the Washington Monument, and Capitol Hill.[32] Lanzmann's camera becomes Frank Capra's, and Karski's voice becomes James Stewart's; we fluctuate between *Mr. Smith Goes to Washington* and *Why We Fight*, in the democratic and valorous America that Karski had served. He was the only Polish Catholic whom Lanzmann interviewed at length, and he was presented as Righteous even before Yad Vashem recognized him as such.

Karski describes the ghetto on the soundtrack as images of Warsaw in the 1980s appear on screen: the buildings, both modern and decrepit, of a popular democracy, brick houses, empty lots. Close-up on a street sign, a backyard. At the back, in the basement, was there once a passage to the ghetto like the one on Muranowska Street through which Karski had gone? "Indeed, at that time, the building had become like a modern version of the River Styx which connected the world of the living with the world of the dead."[33]

Karski never went to Auschwitz. Yet, images from Birkenau and Auschwitz—piles of forks, spoons, pots, suitcases, shoes, glasses, shaving brushes, archives of objects, traces that reeked of evil, that cried out—formed a long montage that accompanied his words.[34] These heaps were substitutes for the archives that Lanzmann did not allow himself to use in his film. The items crammed into the showcases of the museum that Auschwitz I had become were now metonyms for the uniqueness of the Jewish catastrophe that, far from reifying it, offered a glimpse of the daily life of those who had been murdered.

Dialogue between Lanzmann and Karski:

JK: It is one thing to know statistics. There were hundreds of thousands of Poles also killed—of Russians, Serbians, Greeks. We knew about it. But it was a question of statistics.

CL: Did they insist on the complete uniqueness?

JK: This was their problem: to impress upon me—and that was my mission—to impress upon all the people whom I am going to see that the Jewish situation is unprecedented in history.[35]

JK: The question could be asked—and at various stages of this film this question emerged—is there any comparison between what happened to the European Jews during the second world war, and any happening in past history? Whatever I know about history, it is totally unique. It was a problem in itself unprecedented historically.[36]

Lanzmann hoped that by having not only listened but also recorded and filmed, he would spur memories. By cutting together multiple testimonies that were so different and so similar, he hoped to encounter history between personal truth and heuristic value. And so he returned again and again to the same questions, trying to break down his interviewees to the point that a movie critic, though moved by the "terrible urgency of 'Shoah,'" lambasted him: "Lanzmann seems needlessly cruel. . . . While the length of the film is certainly justified by the subject matter, Lanzmann seems almost arrogant in protracting some sequences . . . reflect[ing] his sometimes unreasoning fanaticism. . . . The fourth night, when the subject turns mainly to the Warsaw Ghetto, is the weakest, except that it does include the riveting, eloquent testimony of Jan Karski."[37]

But why did Lanzmann not use all of Karski's words—in particular those on the Warsaw ghetto and Izbica—even though he was excited at the idea of meeting him? "I remember the strong feelings that washed over me when I realized . . . that Jan Karski was alive. . . . So, Karski was living, the emotion intensified when I saw him and began to shoot with him, forgetting how long it had taken to convince him to accept."[38] Lanzmann knew that Izbica, which Karski had visited, was not an extermination site with a gas chamber but a place of transit where people were murdered "incidentally." So why claim to have asked him about Belzec?

In later years, Karski became a Righteous Among the Nations. When he was interviewed for the Spielberg Archive, and then more and more often until his death in 2000, he affirmed the uniqueness of the extermination of the Jews: "The Holocaust is unique . . . the Holocaust is Jewish."[39] Although, as a professor of political science, Karski was aware of other genocides (Bosnia, Armenia, Poland), he always dwelled on the exceptional nature of the genocide of the Jews, extending the thought of Elie Wiesel: "Destruction of the Jews was a unique phenomenon of World War II. As Elie Wiesel said:

'All nations under Nazi domination were victims, but all Jews were victims.'"[40] Thirty years after Lemkin's death, Karski fell short of his reflections on genocides by elevating the genocide of the Jews.

It is not surprising that in the new Yad Vashem museum—an imposing concrete triangle that leads from night to day, from death to life, from dark times in Europe to the bright light of Jerusalem—Karski appears in a filmed sequence.[41] The scene, chosen from the rushes of *Shoah* donated by Lanzmann, is that in which he described his meeting with Roosevelt. He creates a forceful presence on screen through his choice of tone of voice and gesture. He draws himself up in his seat to embody the "'Grand Seigneur' . . . the majesty of power and grandeur." Then he shrinks before the deluge of weighty words on the certain military defeat of Nazi Germany. But he is not satisfied. As he is about to leave, he knows that he has to talk about the Jews, as "it is not a secondary question." "I stood up and told him, Mr. President, I will return to Poland, I will say that I have met with President Roosevelt, I need a strong message, everyone will ask me, 'What did he say?'" Karski once again imitates Roosevelt: he draws himself up a bit more, takes a puff of an imaginary cigar, makes a hand gesture so that the smoke of his cigarette rises toward an infinite grandeur: "You tell them that we will win this war, the guilty will be punished for their acts, and justice will win out." This scene, which Lanzmann did not include in *Shoah*—deeming that Karski was overacting—became central to Yad Vashem.

In one section of the museum, Raphael Lemkin, his concept of genocide, and a 1944 aerial photograph of the Auschwitz-Birkenau complex before its deadly purpose was known are presented, along with this question: "Why wasn't Auschwitz bombed?"

Karski and Lemkin figure together in this staging of the "when" and "why." Why had the world not heard the cries of the murdered Jews? Why had it not listened to the messengers, and why had it let the Jews die? An essay by Avraham Levite is placed above the TV monitor on which Karski appears: "All of us [are] dying here in polar, ice-cold indifference of nations, forgotten by the world and its hustle and bustle."[42] Karski had understood; in 1978, evoking Lord Selborne, the master of propaganda who saw in his 1942 mission only the successful poisoning of minds, he said, with both humor and bitterness, "You would probably actually have to take Lord Selborne and place him in Belzec! Of course this is impossible—Lord Selbornes do not end their lives in Belzec, they end their lives in bed, regardless of whether war was won or lost."[43]

Late in life, Karski gave more and more interviews and attended many conferences; in Washington, DC, in 1999, he said, "Being a resister was very dangerous then. But I want to respond about the Jews. The Jews were abandoned by governments, by churches, by societies. But they were not abandoned by all of humanity. There were thousands of individuals in Poland, Denmark, Holland, France, Greece, and Hungary who tried to help. Most of them perished. I survived, with some luck." In his speech he repeated once again that his principal mission had been not for Poland but for the Jews: "abandonment of the Jews," "the example of the *St. Louis*," "the bombing of Auschwitz," "the resisters for humanity."[44]

Karski's popularity in the United States, and then in Europe, is easily explained. He embodied the questions that were being asked in the 1990s and 2000s. And people turned to him because he confirmed, rather than contradicted, their existing vision of the history of the Shoah. Karski also understood that people's ideas change over time. For instance, he expressed his admiration for Roosevelt, despite his immense disappointment in 1943: "The greatest president of the United States. He was an American president, not a Jewish or Polish or Estonian president. He acted for what he considered to be the interests of the American people."[45]

Wiesel and Karski were close friends at the time: "In truth, you have long ago become an honorary citizen of Jewish history, which will forever remember your courageous and noble activities on behalf of persecuted and doomed Jews during the German occupation of Europe," Wiesel said. "To me, you represent the tragic condition of the messenger whose message has been transmitted but not accepted."[46] He made the transition to witness, in the literal and figurative senses, a moral duty that was similarly incumbent upon those listening. At the inauguration of the Yad Vashem museum, in March 2005, five years after Karski's death, Wiesel said, "There is something more frightening than the messenger who tried to deliver the message and is unable to do so. . . . It is when the messenger has delivered the message and nothing has changed. . . . What is our role? We must become the messengers."[47]

Karski never embodied the tragedy better than when he became an honorary citizen of Israel in 1994, fifty-two years after he had arrived in England with his "message." The foreign minister, Shimon Peres, welcomed him with these words:

> You, sir, proved by your very actions that you rank High in the all too brief list of such great and unique personalities who stood out in the darkest age of Jewish history. Had the Jewish People been blessed with more courageous individuals such as yourself, with more "Righteous among the Nations," its decimation would certainly have been tempered yet further.[48]

Peres's use of a religious vocabulary did not escape Karski, who responded,

> This is the proudest and most meaningful day in my life. Through the honorary citizenship of the State of Israel, I have reached the spiritual source of my Christian faith. In a way, I have also become a part of the Jewish community. . . . And now I, Jan Karski—by birth Kozielewski—a Pole, and American, a Catholic, have also become an Israelite.[49]

Being Righteous had made him universal, he had saved "men and thus all humanity"; being an Israeli citizen returned him to his Christian—that is, Jewish—origins.

All those who visit his grave at the Mount Olivet cemetery in Washington share his convictions. At the grave, decorated with a cross, can be found fresh flowers—a Christian ritual—but also stones and candles—a Jewish ritual.

After Karski died, Karol Badyna, a Polish artist who specialized in likenesses of John Paul II, produced a sculpture of him sitting on a bench in Washington in 1943, as he had portrayed the scene in the final pages of his memoir. The bronze likeness is playing chess, the passion of Karski's life; the pieces on the board are configured in such a way that he wins no matter what play an adversary who sits down opposite him might make, in a synthesis of the metamorphosis of Jan Kozielewski into Jan Karski. Indeed, even in the face of strong opposition, he had always won: a pawn at the beginning of the war, a knight serving the resistance, then a court jester in his missions, he finally became Righteous Among the Nations and then Righteous of the Righteous, in an absolute moral coronation. The first Karski was that of World War II; the second Karski was the one discovered by Elie Wiesel and Claude Lanzmann; the third Karski, after his death in 2000, was at once American, Polish, Israeli, Catholic, and Jewish. When alive, he wanted to be everything at once; in death, he was instrumentalized by each identity in different ways.

Karski and Lemkin Enter the Realm of Literature

Bruno Tessarech and Yannick Haenel brought the character of Karski to French literature in 2009. The form of the novel allowed each author to deal with the polyphony of situations by offering multiple points of view. Tessarech's *Les Sentinelles* did not leave much open to debate, perhaps because the character of Karski was quite artificial—a highly romanticized version of the Catholic resister. Haenel was bolder in *Jan Karski*,[50] fashioning Karski as a new type of eyewitness who saw what others did not, without blind spots. Horrified, he watched the death of the Jews, the theophoric people, and touched God.

As an epigraph for his book, Haenel slightly shifted the meaning of Paul Celan's pessimistic "No one bears witness for the witness" to "Who witnesses for the witness?"[51] The question emphasized the fact that Karski narrated his own truth, that the images of him in the 1985 film were edited by Lanzmann, that chronology counts, and that 1943 was a long way from 1978—and an even longer way from 2009. In another of Haenel's novels, *Cercles*, a character actually refers to Shoah:

> I looked for traces of the ghetto. It was difficult because, in fact, there were no traces left. . . . There was nothing there, and yet he said that this was exactly where it had taken place. Was it possible that someone, in Warsaw, could designate a place, point to an empty lot, indicate a street, a part of a street, a hole in the street, and say, "There it is—that's where it took place"? Because even if you don't see anything—even if there's nothing to see—it was that nothing that I wanted to see.[52]

When *Shoah* was released, Lanzmann himself declared, in an American newspaper, "'That's the subject of the film, the fact that there's nothing left.'" As the article's author noted, "There are no pictures of gas chambers, of Auschwitz or Treblinka at their work of extermination. Many of the sites have been cleared, returned to pasture and silent woods. What Lanzmann did was seek out those who saw the death machine: especially the few survivors of the Jewish *Sonderkommando.*" Remembering this "nothing" was Karski's mission in the Warsaw ghetto: "Remember, Remember."[53]

Why had the world abandoned the Jews? Haenel's approach was quite similar to that of the Yad Vashem museum. In returning to the meeting with Roosevelt, he chose satire and parable. A disillusioned and wounded Karski says again and again, in a long monologue, that the Jews of Europe were not saved. In Arthur Nauzyciel's fascinating direction of the adaptation for the stage, Karski finds himself alone sitting, once again, in the lobby of a large theater; soon, his Jewish wife will be dancing.[54] Dancing when Jews are dead? The actor Laurent Poitrenaux, playing Karski, almost chants his lines: the fate of six million Jews was sealed in 1942, despite Karski, Lemkin, Riegner, and the president of the United States. In this sense, Haenel concurs with the greatest historian of extermination as a global phenomenon, Saul Friedländer, who observed that, although Hitler lost the war against the Allies (a statement made by Roosevelt to Karski), he won the war against the Jews by destroying not only six million human beings but also a civilization and a language: cultural genocide, Lemkin's term.[55] Lemkin also had his turn in the spotlight in New York, in 2010, in a play by Catherine Filloux. Haunted by the genocides of the Armenians and the Jews, Lemkin, who had said sixty years earlier that "we will never be free of genocide," returns to the world to discover, horrified, the killings of Bosnians and Tutsis.[56]

In France, the success of *Jan Karski*—which was translated into dozens of languages—provoked bitter debate. Lanzmann, who considered the witnesses in *Shoah* to be his property, could not bear the idea that someone else would use their words to subvert, as he saw it, the message of his film.[57] Particularly insulted by the dialogue between Roosevelt and Karski as reinvented by Haenel, he decided to edit together an hour-long film from the second day of the 1978 interview, which he titled *The Karski Report.* As he had in *Un vivant qui passe*; *Sobibor 14 octobre 1943, 16 heures*; and *Le Dernier des injustes*,[58] Lanzmann brought his "truth" to bear against the falsifiers. Haenel, who had reconstructed much of both Karski and the content of his message in his novel, was attacked severely for having made himself the ventriloquist of history—and for having taken liberties with Lanzmann's work.[59]

Lanzmann introduced his new edit on screen:

I decided as such, because it seemed absolutely essential to bring back the truth. By relating the reactions to his reports from both his American and British listeners, Karski makes us face a fundamental and deeply grave question: What does it mean to know? What does knowledge of an unfathomable horror do to the person that's hearing about it for the first time—one who's necessarily not ready to face a series of crimes that were unprecedented in the history of mankind? Whatever has been said, the majority of Jews could not be rescued once Hitler started to launch his war against them. Such is the tragedy of History, which leaves no room for retrospective illusion hiding the complexity, the heaviness, the opaqueness of an époque, veritable configuration of the impossible.[60]

If Haenel had engaged in a betrayal, Lanzmann, by invoking the absolute truth of what the witness had said in front of his camera, was doing no different. In the 1985 version of *Shoah*, Karski's words had been edited with other images, truncated, cut; now they were to become the historical truth, without superimposed images of Warsaw or New York, with the intent of raw testimony, so far from the sophisticated visual work of *Shoah*. And yet, when one studies the rushes, one sees that editing choices—that is, cuts—were made again in 2000. So, for Lanzmann, which were Karski's "true" words? And which was the "true" Karski—that is, to which era did this Karski belong?

Indeed, Lanzmann recently revisited the meaning of his film: "The question of time is central to *Shoah*. The film is a struggle with time, against time, and for time, too, from the beginning to the end, and even today." The film was shot in the present: "The action takes place today"—that is, in 1985, when it was released—and it continues to be seen in the present. The images came out of "a *treasure*, in the Greek sense of the word." Lanzmann, the archeologist as filmmaker, spent days, even weeks, with some of his characters, his "inventions" in the archeological sense—the sense of unearthing. Karski, Murmelstein, and Lerner were part of it: "Their presence could not be fit within the time of *Shoah*. Or else I would have needed hours and hours more."[61] And so there were new edits of these figures beyond the

Shoah timeline. The time of the encounter between them and Lanzmann to retell the past time of their journey through the Shoah becomes the present time of the spectator. Was the filmmaker Lanzmann coming to resemble the novelist who wrote about his own deportation, Jorge Semprun? "We made this voyage in fiction, and I thus erased my solitude in reality. What good is writing books if one does not invent the truth? Or else, plausibility."[62] The witnesses did not claim to offer anything but the plausibility born of their memories. Philippe Mesnard has masterfully shown how Levi the survivor became Primo the witness by understanding how authenticity had to be reconciled with his readers' horizon of expectation.[63] And what is the writing of history if not another way of reconstructing such plausibility in another time, ours, the here and now? As Walter Benjamin put it,

> To articulate the past historically does not mean to recognize it "the way it really was." It means to seize hold of a memory as it flashes up at a moment of danger. . . . In every era the attempt must be made anew to wrest tradition away from a conformism that is about to overpower it. Only that historian will have the gift of fanning the spark of hope in the past who is firmly convinced that *even the dead* will not be safe from the enemy if he wins [this was written in 1940]. And this enemy has not ceased to be victorious.[64]

The "victory of the enemy" is that "nothing" remains in Warsaw, Poland. How can the traces be reconstructed? Far from "nothing"—from omission— Nathan Rapoport, creator of the first memorial to the Warsaw ghetto in 1948, chose an elegy on the pain of Jews faced with the destruction of the temple: "Could I have made a stone with a hole in it and said, 'Voilà! The heroism of the Jews.' . . . My task was to re-create the shadows of mother and fathers, young and old. Their tragic and epic end should stay in the memory of generations to come."[65] Today, the ghetto monument is no longer situated in front of "nothing," an immense empty lot. Constructed there, not without difficulty, was a contemporary building that houses the POLIN Museum of the History of the Polish Jews, covering centuries and not just the time of their extermination.[66] Between the monument and the museum, Karol Badyna created an elderly Karski, the book *Story of a Secret State* sitting on the arm of his armchair. This "talking" bronze Karski speaks of his mission in Polish, not in English as he did in his interviews. He who said he was a "machine" in the service of his message has been transformed into an automaton for posterity.

Karski: Polish Once Again

After 1945, Karski faced almost certain death, as did many resisters in the secret army, if he returned to Poland.[67] And so, he became an American. Until 1989, he was invisible in the country of his birth; then, when democracy returned, he was turned into a model citizen. Some leaders easily twisted the historical truth a bit to make his exceptional story the symbol of the true Poland; this was expressed, for instance, in a letter to him from the foreign minister, Andrzej Olechowski, congratulating him on becoming an honorary citizen of Israel: "Thanks to your extraordinary contribution, we have taken a new step toward eliminating false interpretations of the history of Polish–Jewish relations."[68]

Yet, some Polish associations, less scrupulous historians, and recent governments have tried to minimize or erase the aspect of Karski's mission in which he reported specifically on the fate of the Jews; instead, he is held up mainly as a hero of the resistance—which is true of the first Karski, but not the second one. It was in this spirit that he was recently awarded, posthumously, the title of colonel in the Polish army.

But these tributes can take another path: the hero is instrumentalized in a political combat that denies Polish collaboration in the genocide of the Jews—a collaboration minimized in the name of the suffering of all Poles. This new campaign began in 2012, when President Barack Obama posthumously awarded Karski the highest American civilian honor, the Presidential Medal of Freedom. In his announcement, made on April 23 while visiting the Holocaust Memorial in Washington with Elie Wiesel, Obama emphasized the need to tell young generations about a "crime unique in the history of humanity": "We must tell our children about how this evil was allowed to happen—because so many people succumbed to their darkest instincts; because so many others stood silent. But let us also tell our children about the Righteous Among the Nations. Among them was Jan Karski—a young Polish Catholic—who witnessed Jews being put on cattle cars, who saw the killings, and who told the truth, all the way to President Roosevelt himself."[69] At the medal ceremony on May 29, Obama used the term "Polish death camp," drawing fire from Polish authorities, who then went on to attack all those who did not specify that the death camps had belonged to the Nazis, who were occupying Poland, and that Auschwitz-Birkenau had been part of the Nazi Reich at that time. In early 2017, a German television network was sued for Holocaust denial for using the same term: "Do not mistake the victim for the killer. The death camps were Nazi, never Polish." The goal, obviously, was to insist upon the sole responsibility of the Nazis for the extermination of Jews—and for the unprecedented suffering of Poles during the war. There was no mention of the various types of complicity by Poles in the extermination of their Jewish neighbors; nor is the subject broached by the Institute of National Remembrance in Poland.[70]

Paradoxically, it was because he was not Jewish that Karski made such an impression on public opinion. In the era of the Righteous, he was the Righteous Among the Righteous. His likeness in sculpture can be seen in New York, in Lodz, at the University of Tel Aviv, and in the Krakow ghetto reconstructed for the shooting of Steven Spielberg's film on another Righteous of a very different type, Oskar Schindler. In the main square of the ghetto, Karski watches over Jewish and/or Israeli restaurants reinvented for tourists. And on book covers, in graphic novels, in movies, and on numerous websites, he has become *Karski: How One Man Tried to Stop the Holocaust*.[71]

Karski, Righteous Among the Righteous, paragon of moral integrity. In a vehement article, his American biographer and friend Tom Wood did not hesitate to use his voice to urge Americans to resist President Trump's anti-immigration measures: "Too many . . . of us . . . are silent in the presence of a malignant force. They shirk their duty. In the language of Holocaust scholarship, they are bystanders. Some, even, may turn out to be perpetrators." And Wood gave the final word to Karski, quoting him from their last meeting before Karski's death in 2000, seventeen years earlier: "People, all of us probably, we have infinite power to do good. And we have infinite power to follow evil. We are all schizophrenic, as I see our nature. We have a choice. We can choose to be robbers. We can choose to be good people. And our Lord left us the choice. Many people chose evil."[72]

Conclusion

Armenians, Jews, Tutsis

The perpetuation of the psychological scar: I realized that the function of
memory is not only to record past events but to stimulate human conscience.
                                                              —Lemkin, 1950

Who knows about Raphael Lemkin today, outside of a few intellectual and
legal circles? Despite his invention of the word "genocide," or because of
its problematic definition, the Polish Jewish lawyer, who died in the United
States, has not yet found his place in the global consciousness. Studied and
quoted mainly by those who advocated to have the catastrophe that befell
them called genocide, he often serves as a moral and intellectual cautionary
figure, for better or, sometimes, for worse.

In 2015, Armenian national and religious communities scattered around
the world commemorated the hundredth anniversary of the genocide. They
accorded a place of honor to Lemkin, who had begun his intellectual and
activist career with the Armenians and who returned to them always, including for cultural genocide:

> The cultural losses caused by the genocide of the Armenians in Turkey were
> stupefying. As the intellectual nucleus of Turkey, the Armenians owned in-
> valuable personal libraries, archives, and historical manuscripts, which have
> been dispersed and lost. Churches, convents, and monuments of great artistic
> and historical value were destroyed.[1]

The Armenian Genocide Museum-Institute in Yerevan offers Lemkin
Scholarship grants to students and researchers who specialize in genocide

studies. If Armenians are leaders in studying the legacy of the inventor of the word "genocide," it is because their own genocide is still being denied. It is not recurrently thrown into doubt, as is the genocide of the Jews, by those nostalgic for the Nazi order and by Islamist sycophants of the destruction of Israel, assassins, and "murderers of memory." In the case of the extermination of the Armenians, it is Turkey, which inherited and perpetuated the state that conducted the genocide, that stubbornly clings to denial.

"I transformed my personal disaster into a moral striking force. Was I not under a moral duty to repay my mother for having stimulated in me the interest in Genocide? Was it not the best form of gratitude to make a 'Genocide pact' as an epitaph on her symbolic grave and as a common recognition that she and many millions did not die in vain? I redoubled my efforts and found temporary relief from my grief in this work."[2] By inventing the word "genocide," Lemkin was able to make his personal sorrow universal. Beyond the inclusion of genocide in the legal field, its cultural and psychological ravages—no doubt its most lasting legacy—establish that it is impossible to compensate for: "After a lost war," Lemkin wrote, "a nation may reconstruct its technical and financial resources, restart a new life. But those who were destroyed in a genocide are lost forever. The losses of war may be repaired; the losses of a genocide are irreparable."[3] He also dwelled upon the "shame" and "sense of guilt" felt by those who survived, "often the only one from one's family or group of friends."[4]

How can it be proved that trauma, which is individual in nature, affects all victims as a community? Lemkin found himself in an intellectual situation somewhat similar to that of the sociologist Maurice Halbwachs, who tried in the 1920s to connect individual memory to group memory, later called collective or historical memory.[5] Anticipating what researchers such as François Fourquet have called "worldwide subjectivity," Lemkin wrote that all members of a group, at a particular time, share the same "emotional essence," which is transmitted through heredity.

> The psychological impact of genocide on the victimized group is enormous. . . . Its psychological effect on the group is even bigger than on each individual, because every individual influenced by genocide conveys his feelings to members of his group. Every collectivization of emotions is more

than the mathematical sum of those emotions. It creates a new and stronger emotional essence. To that must be added the refinement of pain, sorrow, the perception of injustice, and, above all, the impossibility of bringing those who have died back to life. This collective grief is hereditary; it is being transmitted to future generations not only by word of mouth between parents and children but also by songs, literature, and music.[6]

Once again, Lemkin took the example of the Armenians, who were divided between passing down the historical narrative to preserve their national identity and perpetuating the trauma as infinite torment: "[They] have tried to assemble names and historic facts relating to every community where genocide took place. . . . It would be morally unjust to think that these data are being collected for purely scientifically historical reasons. Each Armenian finds himself in every new document." And Lemkin added, "Members of the group who found themselves far from the scene of the genocide experienced it as victims."[7] With his encyclopedic mind, this original and attentive social sciences researcher had perceived very early the impact of genocide on members of the group, even those who were distant or absent from the time of the catastrophe. We have only to think, eighty years later, of the Americanization and Australianization of the Holocaust—which involves not only national political aspects but, even more, real identification with the group targeted: Jews.

Today, scholars of what is called postmemory concur with Lemkin; they show that genocides move through all generations because they break apart the basic unit, the family. Parents are "orphaned" of children, orphans are dispossessed of their parents, and extended family—uncles, aunts, cousins—are deprived of their close circle and thus of the possibility of belonging to a community of grief. A vanishing identity? As the Tutsis of Rwanda recover their voices after the prolonged abandonment, animalization, and reification that they have suffered, they are expressing themselves:

A genocide destroys everything, family ties included. . . . A void divides the families who have suffered. The memory of the dead drives them apart. Each member feels lonelier than the next. At school, when I hear classmates describe vacations with their grandparents, it tears at my heart. . . . But still, for me, the chance to become someone has passed. . . . I've pretty much lost my love of myself. I've known the filth of animals, I've seen the ferocity of the hyena and worse still—because animals are never as vile as that. I was forced by a brutal man. I was taken away, out there, to a place about which nothing can be said. But the worst is still there walking in front of me. My heart will always hold suspicions. It knows all too well that destiny can break its promises.[8]

Yet, the survivors struggle; one of them, Émilienne Mukansoro, speaks to all of her exterminated relatives: "I've spent more time with you than with my living family. I've tried to be my father and my mother."[9] Indeed, the survivors, and those who were born after, assume new family roles, replacing grandparents and even parents, brothers and sisters, uncles and aunts who have been killed. Sometimes they are much younger than those whom they are trying to protect in this way, as if inverting the generations could bring something back to life: hope. But it also brings back to life something from the time of the genocide: defeat.

Lemkin took the examples of both Armenian and Jewish survivors to illustrate his devastating idea: there is no future for victims of a genocide. He spoke once more for himself, for all Jewish victims, for all victims throughout the ages, and even for those in the future—as he did not believe in "never again" despite the "preventive" aspect of the 1948 convention. Even though the Tutsis in Rwanda had not read his words, they offer evidence of what he called "the perpetuation of the psychological scar." As Élise Rida Musomandera expressed it, "There are survivors, as the genocide was stopped, but do the survivors really exist?"[10] Or, in the words of the sociologist Esther Mujawayo, "The power of a genocide is exactly that: horror during, but still horror afterward. Within us there is no end to a genocide. There is just the stopping of murders, massacres, pursuits, but there is no end to the destruction."[11] Claudine, in Nyamata, said, "Thanks to the wedding, time wears a kind face at present, but only at present. Because I see clearly that the future has already been eaten up by what I lived through."[12]

As "eaten up" as the survivors who tried to return to live in their region that had been the site of genocide—the Jews in Poland and Ukraine after 1945—the Tutsis in Rwanda after 1994 had to confront, in addition to the denials, the perpetuation of the genocide in the constant presence of their murderous neighbors, with their sense of impunity: "Up to this day I am still living in this genocide that originated with you. . . . But it doesn't intimidate me, it doesn't keep me from talking about all my dead people, for I feel them all around me, even if they no longer speak."[13]

"No one, they can know what we've been through. No one."[14]

Genocide: the victims and the law finally on the same level: endless suffering, imprescriptible crime.

ACKNOWLEDGMENTS

This transnational project was possible thanks to the United States Holocaust Memorial Museum, the British National Archives, and the archives at the following institutions: Yad Vashem, United Nations in New York and Geneva, Stanford University, Columbia University, Georgetown University, and the Centre de documentation Juive contemporaine in Paris. I am particularly grateful to the Center for Advanced Holocaust Studies, directed by Paul Shapiro and Suzanne Brown-Fleming, which awarded me the Miles Lerman Fellowship so that I could work with its permanent and temporary researchers. My thanks to Jan Lambertz, who became the linchpin of the project—no article or archive escaped her—and Elizabeth Anthony, Omer Bartov, Rémy Besson, Mark Celinziak, Jo-Ellyn Decker, Rebecca Carter-Chand, Rebecca Erbelding, Martin Dean, Willa Johnson, Istvan Pal Adam, Emil Kerenji, Jürgen Matthäus, and Sybille Steinbacher, as well as the three wonderful librarians at the center, now the Jack, Joseph and Morton Mandel Center for Advanced Holocaust Studies: Ron Coleman, Megan Lewis, and Vincent Slatt.

In France, Poland, Israel, the United States, Great Britain, Switzerland, and Italy, colleagues and friends were unstintingly generous with their support: Philippe Mesnard (who suggested Jan Karski to me when I was already working on Raphael Lemkin), as well as Vincent Baudriller, Nicolas Beaupré, Georges Bensoussan, Luca Bernardini, Christian Biet, Aimée Brown-Price, Bernard Bruneteau, Bruno Cabanes, Sébastien Carney, the late David Cesarani, Evelyne Cohen, Dorota Dakowska, J. P. Daughton, Octave Debary,

Christian Delage, Bernard Delpal, Juliette Denis, Vincent Duclert, Jacques Ehrenfreund, Isabelle Ernot, Raphael Esrail, Yves Faure, Caroline Fontaine, Étienne Fouilloux, Jacky Fredj, Anne-Marie Gassier, Richard Goodkin, Jan Gross, Atina Grossman, Frédéric Gugelot, Gilles Heuré, the late Sarah Hirschmann and the late Albert Hirschmann, John Horne, Luba Jurgenson, Raymond Kevorkian, Audrey Kichelewski, Anaïs Kien, Alain Kleinberger, Anouche Kunth, Emmanuel Laurentin, Jean Lebrun, Annaig Lefeuvre, Jean-Claude Léon, Gaïdz Minassian, Claire Mouradian, Émilienne Mukansoro, Martine Morris and the late Terry Morris, Sophie Nagiscarde, Arthur Nauzyciel, Philip Nord, Nicolas Patin, Monroe Price, Andy Rabinbach, Nicole Rambourg, Louis Rimrodt, Habie Schwarz, Lior Smadja, Karen Taieb, Mark Tannenbaum, Yves Ternon, Dominique Varma, Paul Weindling, Nicolas Werth, Jay Winter, Alexandre Sumpf, and Slawomir Zurek.

Stéphane Audoin-Rouzeau, Hélène Dumas, Philippe Gumplowicz, the late Paulette Meyer-Moureaux, Renée Poznanski, Valérie Rosoux, Henry Rousso, Julien Serrousi, and Fabien Théofilakis read all or part of the manuscript; Sophie Hogg and Pauline Labey enthusiastically brought the project to Fayard, where it landed on the desk of Anthony Rowley a few days before his death.

I express my immense gratitude to all of you. This book is also yours; the choices remain mine.

This book was translated with extraordinary professionalism by Käthe Roth. My deepest thanks go to her, as well as the entire team in the George L. Mosse Program in History at the University of Wisconsin, starting with its energetic director, Skye Doney, who decided to publish this book and asked Käthe to translate it.

In fond memory of George Mosse, intellectual trailblazer and much more.

NOTES

Introduction

The reader may note that some texts that are cited as being originally in English have been retranslated from the French edition. This is because, despite our best efforts, these original texts remain buried deep in archives, not digitized, or unavailable for other reasons.

1. Charles Péguy, "Notre jeunesse," *Les Cahiers de la Quinzaine*, Cahier 12–11 (1910).

2. Jan Karski, *Story of a Secret State* (Boston: Houghton Mifflin, 1944).

3. Raphael Lemkin, "Destruction of Peoples as an International Crime, Genocide," *Polish Review* 18 (January 1945); *Axis Rule in Occupied Europe: Laws of Occupation, Analysis of Government, Proposal for Redress* (Washington, DC: Carnegie Endowment for International Peace, Department of International Law, 1944).

4. Rushes from *Shoah* conserved at the United States Holocaust Memorial Museum (USHMM) in Washington, DC, p. 61 of the typescript and audio tape, https://collections.ushmm.org/film_findingaids/RG-60.5006_01_trs_en.pdf.

5. Raymond Aron, *Mémoires* (Paris: Julliard, 1983), 176 (our translation). Claude Lanzmann quotes Aron from memory—thus in different words—in his introduction to the film *The Karski Report* (2010) and similarly in *Les Temps modernes* (January–March 2010). See chapter 6.

6. See Renée Poznanski, *Propagandes et persécutions: La Résistance et le "problème juif" 1940–1944* (Paris: Fayard, 2008).

7. Avishai Margalit, *The Ethics of Memory* (Cambridge, MA: Harvard University Press, 2002).

8. Robert Gerwarth, *The Vanquished: Why the First World War Failed to End, 1917–1923* (London: Allen Lane, 2016).

9. Saul Friedländer, *Réflexions sur le nazisme: Entretiens avec Stéphane Bou* (Paris: Seuil, 2016).

10. It was the transit center for Belzec that Karski saw, not the killing center in Belzec. Robert Kuwalek, *Belzec, le premier centre de mise à mort*, trans. Alexendre Dayet (Paris: Calmann-Lévy, 2013).

11. Raphael Lemkin, *Totally Unofficial: The Autobiography of Raphael Lemkin*, ed. Donna-Lee Frieze (New Haven: Yale University Press, 2013).

12. Samuel Beckett, *Worstward Ho* (1983); *The Unnamable*, 1959 (originally published as *L'innommable* [Paris: Minuit, 1953]).

Chapter 1. Karski the Soldier, Lemkin the Lawyer

1. Victor Zaslavsky, *Le Massacre de Katyn* (Paris: Perrin, "Tempus" imprint, 2007). See chapter 5 of this book.

2. Raphael Lemkin, *Totally Unofficial: The Autobiography of Raphael Lemkin*, ed. Donna-Lee Frieze (New Haven: Yale University Press, 2013), 59. This autobiography, edited together from fragments, was written in the 1950s.

3. Ibid., 79–80, 67.

4. Ibid., 70. The filmmaker Axel Corti portrayed this situation accurately in the first part of his trilogy *Welcome in Vienna*, "God Doesn't Believe in Us Anymore" (1982), on Jews trapped by Nazism as they tried to flee Europe.

5. Ibid., 80.

6. Raphael Lemkin, *La Règlementation des paiements internationaux* (Paris: Pedone, 1939).

7. Lemkin, *Totally Unofficial*, 51.

8. An Orthodox Jewish baker in Dubno in conversation with Lemkin, quoted in Lemkin, *Totally Unofficial*, 52.

9. Ibid., 52–54.

10. Ibid., 52.

11. Emanuel Ringelblum quoted in Samuel D. Kassow, *Who Will Write Our History? Emanuel Ringelblum, the Warsaw Ghetto, and the Oyneg Shabes Archive* (Bloomington: Indiana University Press, 2007), 11.

12. Nathan Weistock, "Simon Doubnov (1860–1941): Que faire quand sonne l'heure d'Haman? (1939)," *Revue d'histoire de la Shoah* 174 (2002): 11 (our translation).

13. Esther, III, 13, http://biblescripture.net/Esther.html.

14. The expression used was *Yiddishkeit*.

15. Weistock, "Simon Doubnov," 14–15 (our translation).

16. Varian Fry, "The Massacre of the Jews," *The New Republic* (December 21, 1942): 817.

17. Lepsius's first book, *Bericht über e Lage des armenischen Volkes in der Türkei* (Report on the Situation of the Armenian People in Turkey), was censored in August 1916, but twenty thousand copies had already been distributed. Werfel used the second edition, which included a 1915 interview with Enver Pasha, *Der Todesgang des Armenischen Volkes* (The Death March of the Armenian People).

18. Peter Stephan Jungk, *Franz Werfel: A Life in Prague, Vienna, and Hollywood*, trans. Anselm Hollo (New York: Grove Weidenfeld, 1990), 139.

19. Franz Werfel, *The Forty Days of Musa Dagh*, trans. Geoffrey Dunlop and James Reidel (Jaffrey, NH: Verba Mundi, 2012), 140. In his preface to the French edition, titled "Le crime de l'oubli" (The Crime of Forgetting), Elie Wiesel mentions "striking correspondences" between the fate of the Armenians and that of the Jews: "Is the author evoking a past experienced or a future prophesized? Is not the 'musa dagh' a sort of ghetto in which survivors, in a burst of pride and desperate courage, prepare to die in combat rather than perish in the bloodied dust of distant roads?" In Franz Werfel, *Les 40 jours du Musa Dagh*, trans. Paule Hofer-Bury (Paris: Albin Michel, 2015), 6 (our translation).

20. Werfel, *Forty Days*.

21. Quoted in Peter Stephan Jungk, *Franz Werfel: A Life in Prague, Vienna, and Hollywood*, trans. Anselm Hollo (New York: Fromm International, 1991), 165.

22. *Varian Fry: Mission américaine de sauvetage des intellectuels anti-nazis, Marseille 1940–1942*, exhibition catalogue (Arles: Actes sud, 1999). For another view of Fry, written by one of his assistants in Marseille, see Daniel Bénédite, *Un Chemin vers la liberté sous l'Occupation: Du Comité Varian Fry au débarquement en Méditerranée, 1940–1944* (Paris: Éditions du Félin-résistance, 2017 [1983]).

23. Quoted in the introduction by Otto Friedrich in Franz Werfel, *Cella, or, The Survivors* [1939, unfinished novel] (New York: Henry Holt, 1989).

24. Franz Werfel, "Our Path Continues" (December 27, 1940), in *Jewish Responses to Persecution*, vol. 2, *1938–1940*, ed. A. Garbarini, E. Kerenji, J. Lambertz, and Avinoam Patt (New York: Rowman & Littlefield, 2011), 485–88.

25. Peter Longerich, *Holocaust: The Nazi Persecution and Murder of the Jews* (Oxford: Oxford University Press, 2010); Omer Bartov, *Mirrors of Destruction: War, Genocide, and Modern Identity* (Oxford: Oxford University Press, 2002).

26. Lemkin, *Totally Unofficial*, 71.

27. Ibid., 72.

28. Kassow, *Who Will Write Our History? Oyneg Shabes*, "the joy of the Sabbath," was the code name chosen by Ringelblum for his archival collection in the ghetto. See Emanuel Ringelblum, *Oneg Shubbat, journal du Ghetto de Varsovie* (Paris: Calmann-Lévy/Mémorial de la Shoah, 2017).

29. Edward Raczynski to Lord Winterton, January 13, 1939, quoted in Bernard Wasserstein, "Polish Influences on British Policy Regarding Jewish Rescue Efforts in Poland 1939–1945," in *Polin: Studies in Polish Jewry*, vol. 11, *Focusing on Aspects and Experiences of Religion*, ed. Antony Polonsky (Liverpool: Liverpool University Press, 1998), 185.

30. Roberts quoted in Wasserstein, "Polish Influences," 187.

31. British National Archives (BNA), Kew, HO 213/347, Home Office, Aliens Department. Treatment of Jewish race, general question, January 6, 1942.

32. David Engel, "An Early Account of Polish Jewry under Nazi and Soviet Occupation Presented to the Polish Government-in-Exile, February 1940," *Jewish Social Studies* 45, no. 1 (1983): 1–16. See Joshua Zimmerman, *The Polish Underground and the Jews, 1939–1945* (Cambridge: Cambridge University Press, 2015).

33. Engel, "An Early Account," 6.

34. Ibid., 6–7.

35. Ibid., 8.

36. Jan Tomasz Gross, *Polish Society Under German Occupation: The General-gouvernement, 1939–1944* (Princeton: Princeton University Press, 1979).

37. Engel, "An Early Account," 9.

38. Ibid., 10 (emphasis in original).

39. On the ordeals suffered by Polish Jews at the hands of the Nazis and Soviets, see Julius Margolin, *Voyage au pays des Ze-ka* (Paris: Le Bruit du temps, 2010); Alain Blum, Marta Craveri, and Valérie Nivelon, eds., *Déportés en URSS: Récits d'Européens au Goulag* (Paris: Éditions autrement, 2012).

40. Engel, "An Early Account," 10.

41. Lemkin, *Totally Unofficial*, 57.

42. "The Outbreak of the German-Polish War," in *The Volkovysk Memorial Book* or *Wolkovisker Yizkor Book* or *Hurban Volkovysk*, ed. Moses Einhorn (New York and Tel Aviv: Committee of Volkovysk Émigrés, Katriel Lashowitz, USHMM Collection, 1946, 1947, 1988), chap. 5, p. 330 (our translation from the French; original is in Yiddish). This is a trilogy of three separate works: 1. *Sefer Zikaron Volkovysk*, ed. Moses Einhorn (New York, 1949); 2. *Volkovysk* (Tel Aviv: Committee of Volkovysk Emigres, 1946); 3. *Volkovysk* (Tel Aviv: Katriel Lashowitz, 1988). See http://www.tay tsh.org/bibliography/volkovysk-memorial-book.

43. Letter from Moshe Kleinbaum (who arrived in Geneva after an odyssey lasting several months) to Nahum Goldmann, president of the Administration Committee of the World Jewish Congress, March 12, 140, reproduced in Jürgen Matthäus with Emil Kerenji, *Jewish Responses to Persecution, 1933–1946* (Lanham, MD: Rowman and Littlefield, 2017), 47–48.

44. Calel Perechodnik, *Am I a Murderer? Testament of a Jewish Ghetto Policeman*, trans. and ed. Frank Fox (Boulder, CO: Westview Press, 1996), 2. Perechodnik was writing in 1943, after his family was murdered by the Nazis.

45. *Volkovysk Memorial Book*, 330 (our translation).

46. Engel, "An Early Account," 9.

47. Ibid., 9–10.

48. Ibid., 14.

49. Ibid., 12.

50. Ibid., 14.

51. Jan Lanicek, "Governments-in-Exile and the Jews during and after the Second World War," *Holocaust Studies* 35, no. 2–3 (2012): 73–94.

52. George Orwell, "Antisemitism in Britain," *Contemporary Jewish Record*, London, April 1945.

53. Engel, "An Early Account," 11.

54. Jan Tomasz Gross, *Neighbors: The Destruction of the Polish Community in Jedwabne, Poland* (Princeton: Princeton University Press, 2001).

55. Jan Karski, *Story of a Secret State* (Boston: Houghton Mifflin, 1944), 82.

56. Reports quoted by Saul Friedländer in *Les Années d'extermination: L'Allemagne nazie et les Juifs, 1939–1945* (Paris: Seuil, 2008), 86–87 (our translation).

57. Raphael Lemkin, manuscripts, New York Public Library (NYPL), Collection 922, displaced scholars. I would like to thank Jan Lambertz for telling me about this invaluable archival collection.

58. Dr. Henry Rozenthal, letter on the letterhead of the Adult School of Jewish Studies, Young Men's Hebrew Association (our translation). Raphael Lemkin, manuscripts, NYPL, Collection 922, displaced scholars.

59. Letter from Ms. Drury to President Few of Duke University, July 3, 1940. Raphael Lemkin, manuscripts, NYPL, Collection 922, displaced scholars.

60. Lemkin, *Totally Unofficial*, 97.

61. Michael Ignatieff, "The Danger of a World without Enemies: Lemkin's Word," *New Republic* 226, no. 9 (February 2001): 26–28.

62. Lemkin, *Totally Unofficial*, 80.

Chapter 2. Karski Discovers the Annihilation of Lemkin's World

1. Marian Kozielewski, International Tracing Service file, Bad Arolsen. KZ Oswiecim, 14/8/40–4/4/41.

2. Jan Lanicek, "Governments-in-Exile and the Jews during and after the Second World War," *Holocaust Studies* 35, no. 2–3 (2012): 73–94.

3. Polish Underground Labor Movement, *The Camp of Disappearing Men: A Story of the Oswiecim Concentration Camp, Based on Reports from the Polish Underground Labor Movement* (Office of War Information, Poland Fights, 1944).

4. Ibid., 33–34.

5. Ibid., 43.

6. Prime Minister Winston Churchill's Broadcast to the World about the Meeting with President Roosevelt, August 24, 1941, https://www.ibiblio.org/pha/timeline/410824awp.html.

7. See Catherine Collomp, *Résister au nazisme: Le Jewish Labor Committee, New York, 1934–1945* (Paris: CNRS éditions, 2016).

8. Holocaust Memorial, Washington, DC, Archives, Prm-70, "Memorandum Submitted to the President of the United States . . . by a Delegation of Representative of Jewish Organisations," December 8, 1942.

9. The *New York Times* reported on December 17, 1942, "A joint declaration by members of the United Nations was issued today condemning Germany's 'bestial policy of cold-blooded extermination' of Jews and declaring that 'such events can only strengthen the resolve of all freedom-loving peoples to overthrow the barbarous Hitlerite tyranny.'"

10. British National Archives (BNA), C1240/61/18, December 15, 1942 (our translation).

11. BNA, Kew, letter sent on June 30, 1942, different service stamps, up to July 17, 1942 (our translation).

12. BNA, Kew, report of June 29, 1942.

13. BNA, Kew, Fo. 371, 31097.

14. The same photographs are found in the collections of the United States Holocaust Memorial Museum in Washington, DC, at Yad Vashem in Jerusalem, in the archives of the Polish government in exile at the Hoover Institution, and in Warsaw; archivists have acquired copies of microfilms carried by people smugglers that were prepared and preserved in Poland at the risk of many resisters' lives. Dr. Emil Apfelbaum, in particular, worked at the hospital in Czyste and conducted research on the famine in the Warsaw ghetto in 1942. His working photographs formed the basis for this series.

15. Published following the demonstration on July 22, 1942, in a leaflet by Alfred J. Dobbs et al., *German Atrocities in Poland and Czechoslovakia: Labour's Protest* (London: Liberty Publications, 1942), http://pbc.gda.pl/Content/72811/Labours_pro test.pdf.

16. BNA, Kew, six-page speech (our translation).

17. BNA, Kew, note by D. Allen, September 11, 1942 (emphasis added).

18. Richard Bolchover, *British Jewry and the Holocaust* (Cambridge: Cambridge University Press, 1993); Pamela Shatzkes, *Holocaust and Rescue: Impotent or Indifferent? Anglo-Jewry 1938–1945* (Basingstoke: Palgrave, 2002).

19. Daniel Blatman, "On a Mission against All Odds: Samuel Zygielbojm in London (April 1942–May 1943)," *Yad Vashem Studies* 2 (1990): 237–72.

20. Printed in boldface on the back cover of *Stop Them Now: German Mass Murder of Jews in Poland* (London: Liberty Publications, September 1942), https://www .marxists.org/subject/jewish/stop-murder.pdf.

21. Ibid., 11, 12, 13.

22. Ibid., 5.

23. Ibid.

24. Ibid. (emphasis in original).

25. Ibid., 7.

26. Ibid., 15.

27. Ibid., 9. The cemetery on Okopowa Street was identified through another series of photographs, taken by Heinrich Jöst, a sergeant in the German army, on September 19, 1941. These photographs remained in his possession until 1982 and then were donated to Yad Vashem. In some cases, victims and executioners took similar pictures, for radically different purposes. See the exhibition *Regards sur les ghettos* and its eponymous catalogue (Paris: Mémorial de la Shoah, 2014). Imre Kertesz, for example, describes these carts in *Être sans destin* (Arles: Actes sud, 1998).

28. Jan Karski, *Story of a Secret State* (Boston: Houghton Mifflin, 1944), 332.

29. Samuel Golfard's diary describing an *Aktion* in Galicia. Written January 30, 1943, relating the events of 1942, in *The Diary of Samuel Golfard and the Holocaust in Galicia*, ed. Wendy Lower, USHMM series Jewish Responses to Persecutions, gen. ed. Jürgen Matthäus (Lanham, MD: AltaMira Press, 2011), 64.

30. Marcel Cohen, interview in *Europe* (January 2016): 214.

31. Jacob Sloan, ed., *Notes from the Warsaw Ghetto: The Journal of Emanuel Ringelblum* (New York: McGraw Hill, 1958), 295, 297–98.

32. Jan Karski, *Mon témoignage devant le monde: Histoire d'un État clandestin* (Paris: Robert Laffont, 2010), 275 (our translation).

33. Republic of Poland, Ministry of Foreign Affairs, *The Mass Extermination of Jews in German Occupied Poland: Note Addressed to the Governments of the United Nations on December 10th, 1942, and Other Documents* (London, New York, and Melbourne: Hutchinson and Co., 1942). The Mémorial de la Shoah in Paris recently acquired a copy of this brochure, one of the three copies in the Library of Congress in 1943. It is possible to imagine that Lemkin and Karski consulted this very copy in Washington, DC.

34. George Orwell, *Chroniques du temps de la guerre (1941–1943)* (Paris: Éditions Lebovici, 1988), 245, broadcast of December 12, 1942 (our translation).

35. At least in some form. Ibid., December 17, 1942, 248–49 (our translation).

36. "Défi, l'ordre nouveau en Pologne," *Les Cahiers du Témoignage chrétien*, no. 13–14 (January–February 1943): 12 (emphasis in original; our translation).

37. Our translation. Feiner's second report was probably dated August 31. Daniel Blatman, *Notre liberté et la vôtre: Le mouvement ouvrier juif BUND en Pologne, 1939–1949* (Paris: Cerf, 2002), 185.

38. Karski, in London, sent a message from the Jewish resistance to Sikorski on this subject. Joshua D. Zimmerman, *The Polish Underground and the Jews, 1939–1945* (Cambridge: Cambridge University Press, 2015), 301.

39. Feiner, quoted in Karski, *Story of a Secret State*, 324.

40. Ibid.

41. BNA, Kew, text of telegram of December 12, 1942, copy of the British Censor. The original telegram is available at https://codoh.com/library/document/3336/?lang=en.

42. BNA, Kew, Shmuel Zygielbojm, telegram to Churchill, December 15, 1942.

43. BNA, Kew, telegram of December 4, 1942, to Tartakower and Miller, World Jewish Congress, New York, copy of the British Censor; copy of telegram viewable at http://www.deathcamps.org/reinhard/pic/stupp.jpg.

44. Rushes for *Shoah*, USHMM, reels 310 and 311, typescript, 44–45, https://collections.ushmm.org/film_findingaids/RG-60.5006_01_trs_en.pdf. These reels were devoted entirely to Zygielbojm.

45. Ibid., 48.

46. Nowak wrote his memoir much later, in 1978, but before Karski returned to the spotlight. Logically, he cites Karski in his account of being in London in 1942–43. Jan Nowak, *Courier from Warsaw* (Detroit: Wayne State University Press, 1982).

47. I consulted the proofs of *Story of a Secret State* in the Karski archives in Georgetown. Karski carefully edited every word that he felt inappropriate.

48. Transcription of the radio program in which Karski participated anonymously in London: "The Jewish Mass Executions: Account by an Eye-Witness," in Alexei Tolstoy, *Terror in Europe: The Fate of the Polish Jews* (London: National

Committee for Rescue from Nazi Terror, n.d. [1943]), reprinted in *PL.IT/rassegna italiana di argomenti polacchi* (May 2014): 136–41. I am grateful to one of the foremost experts on Karski, Luca Bernardini, for having found this text for me in the excellent online journal *PL.IT/rassegna italiana di argomenti polacchi*.

49. Ibid., 139.

50. Karski, *Story of a Secret State*, 321 (introduction to the chapter "The Ghetto").

51. *Polish Fortnightly Review*, no. 82 (December 15, 1943): 9.

52. "Le Massacre des Juifs en Pologne: Récit d'un témoin oculaire," *Fraternité*, special issue (September 1943) (our translation). (Translator's note: this text has now undergone one further translation into English.) "Nouvelles arrestations massives et déportations des Juifs de France vers les camps de la torture et de la mort," article on page 1, lower right, and page 2. At the same time, the emissary from the Polish government in exile in unoccupied France, S. Zabiello, was sending accurate reports on deportations of Polish Jews from France to London. *Le Gouvernement polonais en exil et la persécution des Juifs en France en 1942 d'après les documents inédits*, compiled and edited by Pawel Korzec and Jacques Burko (Paris: Cerf, 1997); *Pardès*, no. 16 (1992): 121–33.

53. Alexei Tolstoy, *Terror in Europe: The Fate of the Polish Jews* (London: National Committee for Rescue from Nazi Terror, n.d. [1943]), 139.

54. In Berlin, at the site, destroyed after the war, a memorial—very judiciously transparent for those who do not want to see it—was erected only in 2014.

55. Lemkin Archives, NYPL, loose sheet, 1949 (our translation).

56. *Volkovysk Memorial Book*, 3 vols., ed. Moses Einhorn (New York, 1949); the Yiddish version was published by the Committee of Volkovysk Emigres in Tel Aviv in 1949. The work was reprinted and expanded in English in 2002 (Mahwah, NJ: Jacob Solomon Berger, 2002) with a list of donors, including a number of descendants of Lemkin's brother, Elias. At the time, he stated that he was the only survivor of the family. The Yiddish version has this dedication, in English: "In memoriam dedicated in Love and reverence to the sacred memory of my Family and the Jewish Community of Wolkowysk."

57. Bradfisch quoted in Peter Longerich, *Holocaust: The Nazi Persecution and the Murder of the Jews* (Oxford: Oxford University Press, 2010), 198.

58. Nebe quoted in Peter Longerich, *Heinrich Himmler*, trans. Jeremy Noakes and Lesley Sharpe (Oxford: Oxford University Press, 2012), 525.

59. Quoted in Longerich, *Holocaust*, 152.

60. Ibid., 222.

61. *Volkovysk Memorial Book*, 933 (our translation)

62. Quoted in Raphael Lemkin, *Totally Unofficial: The Autobiography of Raphael Lemkin* (New Haven: Yale University Press, 2013), 55.

63. Izaak Goldberg, *The Miracles versus Tyranny* (New York: Philosophical Library, 1978), 128.

64. Vassili Grossman, "The Hell of Treblinka," translated from Russian by Molly Godwin-Jones and Maxim D. Shrayer, in *Voices of Jewish-Russian Literature: An Anthology*, ed. Maxim D. Shrayer (Boston: Academic Studies Press, 2018), 433.

65. Goldberg, *The Miracles versus Tyranny*, 130. This Czech doctor's wandering through labor camps and ghettos was very typical of the few unlikely survivors—whence the title of his memoir.

66. Grossman, "Hell of Treblinka," 444–45.

67. *Volkovysk Memorial Book*, 918 (our translation).

68. Zalmen Gradowski, "In the Heart of Hell," in *The Literature of Destruction: Jewish Responses to Catastrophe*, ed. David G. Roskies (Philadelphia: Jewish Publication Society, 1988), 563–64.

69. *Volkovysk Memorial Book*, 945 (our translation).

70. Ibid., 929 (our translation).

71. Handwritten letter from Szlamek on the Belzec camp sent to Hersz Wasser, April 1942 (original in Polish and Yiddish), http://www.memorialdelashoah.org/upload/minisites/ringelblum/shoah/documents/document11-en.htm. See Samuel Kassow, *Who Will Write Our History? Rediscovering a Hidden Archive from the Warsaw Ghetto* (New York: Vintage Books, 2009); Kassow, *Who Will Write Our History? Emanuel Ringelblum, the Warsaw Ghetto, and the Oyneg Shabes Archive* (Bloomington: Indiana University Press, 2007).

72. The Yiddish publication *Oyneg Shabes Mitteilungen* reported, in its April 1942 issue, deportations from Lublin to Belzec and the "rumor" of "asphyxia by gas as in Chelmno." Quoted at length in Daniel Blatman, *En direct du ghetto: La presse clandestine juive dans le ghetto de Varsovie, 1940–1943* (Paris: Cerf, 2005), 454–57.

73. Kassow, quoting a report, written in Polish, in the Oyneg Shabes in *Who Will Write Our History?*, 296.

74. Rushes for *Shoah*, reel 305, typescript, p. 32.

75. Karski, *Story of a Secret State*, 324–25.

76. Ibid., 322.

77. Ibid., 330.

78. *The American Mercury* (November 1944): 567–75.

79. Karski, *Story of a Secret State*, 330.

80. George Creel, a veteran newsman—he ran the Committee on Public Information, an American propaganda organ, during World War I—sent the text to Karski to check his reconstruction of Karski's words. That is why the Karski archive at Stanford University contains a document called "Poland's Underground," by "Mr. X," as told to George Creel. The episode was also described more succinctly in another article in *Collier's Weekly*, Martha Gellhorn's "Three Poles," radioed from London in 1943 and published on March 18, 1944. Specific dates did not seem terribly important; articles on the situation in Poland were being published with information that was already quite out of date.

81. Mr. B., as told to George Creel, "Revenge in Poland," *Collier's Weekly*, November 6, 1943, 34.

82. Ibid., 32–33. See also Mr. X, "Poland's Underground." Karski's decision to discuss homosexuality—it seems that he was unaware that it was punishable by death or imprisonment in a concentration camp in the Reich—is striking. Karski is

talking freely to an American journalist and presenting himself as a paragon of Catholic morality in the Polish underground that he is representing. I would like to thank Jean Lebrun for making me aware of the encounter between the playwright Pierre Barillet and Karski in Paris in 1946, when Karski returned to that city to collect Polish underground documents to take to the United States. Barillet recounted their liaison and kept to the end of his life the book that Karski dedicated to him. Pierre Barillet, *À la ville comme à la scène* (Paris: Fallois, 2004), 33–34.

83. "Défi, l'ordre nouveau en Pologne," *Cahiers du Témoignage chrétien*, no. 13–14 (January–February 1943): 11 (our translation).

84. Mr. B., "Revenge in Poland," November 6, 1943, 34.

85. Ibid., 32.

86. Ibid., 20, 32.

87. Mr. B., "Revenge in Poland," October 30, 1943, 11, 69.

88. Robert Kuwalek, *Belzec, le premier centre de mise à mort*, trans. Alexendre Dayet (Paris: Calmann-Lévy, 2013).

89. Samuel Golfard, in *Diary of Samuel Golfard*, went even further, accusing those whom he called the "Jewish Gestapo," the ghetto police officers, of participating in the same system of corruption.

90. Karski, *Story of a Secret State*, 342.

91. Mr. B., "Revenge in Poland," November 6, 1943, 20.

92. Krüger was not killed but replaced; he committed suicide in 1945. I am grateful to Nicolas Patin for these details. See his *Krüger, un bourreau ordinaire* (Paris: Fayard, 2017).

93. David Engel, "An Early Account of Polish Jewry under Nazi and Soviet Occupation Presented to the Polish Government-in-Exile, February 1940," *Jewish Social Studies* 45, no. 1 (1983): 8.

94. USHMM Collection, no. 32057 (our translation).

95. Karski, *Mon témoignage*, 296–97 (our translation).

96. I extend my warmest thanks to Slawomir Zurek, director of the Polish-Jewish Literature Studies Centre at the John Paul II Catholic University of Lublin, who took me to Izbica and Belzec. In both cases, the train tracks were still in the same place. In 1942, these two small towns had an 80 percent Jewish population.

97. Golfard, *Diary of Samuel Golfard*, 56 (Eastern Galicia, August 1942). Electrocution was also mentioned in the report "The Mass Extermination of Jews in German-Occupied Poland," report sent by the Polish Ministry of Foreign Affairs to the United Nations, December 10, 1942.

98. In fact, small gas chambers had been used in the late nineteenth century to suffocate stray dogs in Paris, and then in Mexico. Arnaud Exbalin, *La grande tuerie des chiens. Enquête sur les canicides dans le Mexique colonial* (Ceyzérieux: Champ Vallon, 2021), chapter 3, "Décanisations."

99. *The Ghetto Speaks*, no. 20, February 1, 1944 (our translation).

100. "Le Massacre des Juifs en Pologne," 2 (our translation). The French underground newspaper *Fraternité* was relaying the BBC's interview with Karski. We see that the resistance in France was well informed via London—even if it was, in this

case, a year late—and supported actions against mass deportations from France. See Renée Poznanski, *Propagandes et persécutions: La Résistance et le "problème juif,"* *1940–1944* (Paris: Fayard, 2008).

101. Karski, *Story of a Secret State*, 348–49.

102. "Le Massacre des Juifs en Pologne" (our translation).

103. Karski, *Story of a Secret State*, 349–50.

104. I am grateful to Martin Dean, who opened so many avenues to me and answered my questions with all of his formidable knowledge of the extermination of the Jews.

105. Yitzhak Arad, *The Operation Reinhard Death Camps* (Bloomington: Indiana University Press, 1987), 350–51.

106. "Memorandum Submitted to the President of the United States," December 8, 1942, n.p., https://www.jewishvirtuallibrary.org/memo-from-jewish-leader -press-president-roosevelt-to-act.

107. Republic of Poland, Ministry of Foreign Affairs, *Mass Extermination*, 9.

108. Karski quoted in Frank Baron, "The 'Myth' and Reality of Rescue from the Holocaust: The Karski-Koestler and Vrba-Wetzler Reports," in *German-Speaking Exiles in Great Britain*, vol. 2, ed. Anthony Grenville (Amsterdam and Atlanta: Editions Rodopi B.V., 2000), 173.

109. Testimony of Myeczyslaw Sekiewicz, forced Sonderkommando laborer, after the war, in Patrick Montague, *Chelmno and the Holocaust: The History of Hitler's First Death Camp* (London and New York: I. B. Tauris, 2012), 44 (translation adapted).

110. Captain Withold Pilecki, *Witold's Report from Auschwitz*, trans. Karolina Linda Potocka and Witold Wybranski (Zabki, Poland: Apostolicum Publishing House, 2017), 5. The report was written in 1945. http://rtmpilecki.eu/wp-content/ uploads/2018/05/RAPORT_WITOLDA_GB_WWW.pdf.

111. The organ of the American Representation of the General Jewish Workers' Union of Poland. I consulted this issue at the Princeton University library, where it was received on July 21, 1943. It is likely that intellectuals at Princeton, such as Albert Einstein and Jacques Maritain, read issues of *The Ghetto Speaks*. In the British National Archives, it can be seen that by August 1942 there were questions about the use of gas and about the accounts that had come from Poland. Diplomatic prudence, apparently, was called for: "I think we shall surely have to return a very guarded reply on the lines that our attention has been drawn to the report in question, but that H.M.G. has no means of confirming it" (BNA, Kew, September 7, 1942). This is around the date when Karski arrived in Izbica.

112. *The Ghetto Speaks*, no. 2 (August 5, 1942), 2.

113. This scene was cut from the final edit of *Shoah*. It can be found in the film rushes at USHMM, Washington, DC.

114. Rushes for *Shoah*, USHMM, 43.

115. Karski, *Story of a Secret State*, 349.

116. Ibid., 354.

117. Ibid., 321–22.

118. Arthur Koestler, *Arrival and Departure* (New York: Macmillan, 1943), 69. The French-language version of the book was titled *Croisade sans croix* [Crusade without a Cross] (Paris: Calmann-Lévy, 1946)—a rather inaccurate translation, although it referred to the almost Christ-like figure of the hero of the book. Koestler referred to what he also called "the great anti-Fascist crusade which, with drums and fanfares, advanced from defeat to defeat."

119. Koestler quoted in Baron, "The 'Myth' and Reality," 174. See also David Cesarani, *Arthur Koestler: The Homeless Mind* (Cambridge: Free Press, 1999), 202–3.

120. Koestler, *Arrival*, 69.

121. Ibid., 71.

122. Ibid., 71–72.

123. Ibid., 75–78.

124. George Orwell, "Arthur Koestler," *New York Times*, 1944. Reprinted in George Orwell, *Critical Essays* (London: Secker and Warburg, 1946). This was not only the opinion of British critics; in his review of the book for the *New York Times* on November 21, 1943, the Jewish American author Saul Bellow spoke of it only in terms of political morals and made no mention of the specific fate of the Jews in the train episode.

125. *Manchester Evening News*, December 9, 1943, reproduced in George Orwell, "Arthur Koestler," in *George Orwell: The Collected Essays, Journalism & Letters*, vol. 3, *As I Please, 1943–1946*, ed. Sonia Orwell and Ian Angus (Boston: Nonpareil Books, 2000), 234 (emphasis in original).

126. George Orwell, "Arthur Koestler," http://orwell.ru/library/reviews/koestler/english/e_ak.

127. Bottome quoted in Cesarani, *Arthur Koestler*, 208.

128. "Arthur Koestler" [late 1943], reprinted in *Hiéroglyphes* [1944] (Paris: Les Belles Lettres, 2012) (our translation). Koestler is in fact citing three million Jews killed. Sitwell was gay, whence Koestler's snide allusion to Proust.

129. Osbert Sitwell, quoted in Cesarani, *Arthur Koestler*, 208.

Chapter 3. Flashback

1. George Orwell [1943], "Looking Back on the Spanish War," in *Orwell: My Country Right or Left, 1940–1943*, vol. 2, *Essays, Journalism & Letters*, ed. Sonia Orwell and Ian Angus (Jaffrey, NH: Nonpareil, 2000), 253.

2. NYPL, Manuscripts, Col. 922, Displaced Scholars, Marc Bloch (our translation). Bloch, an illustrious historian to whom an American visa was immediately granted in 1940, refused it because his mother and oldest son were excluded; instead, he entered the French resistance.

3. The legacy of the Great War has been rediscovered from the executioners' point of view. This recent past has also been explored from the point of view of the victims and "witnesses," or "accomplices," on site or very far away. See Gerd Krumeich, ed., *Nationalsozialismus and Erster Weltkrieg* (Essen: Klartext-Verlag,

2010); Christian Ingrao, *Croire et détruire: Les intellectuels dans la machine de guerre nazie* (Paris: Fayard, 2009).

4. Charles de Gaulle, London Radio, September 18, 1941, in *De Gaulle: Discours et messages*, vol. 1, *Pendant la guerre* (Paris: Plon, 1970), 102–3 (our translation).

5. British National Archives (BNA), Kew, Sikorski, June 9, 1942, speech, 6 (our translation).

6. *The Times* (London), December 4, 1942, 3.

7. "Nazi War on Jews. The New Barbarism. Response of Civilized World," *The Times* (London), December 5, 1942.

8. Professors of Germany, "To the Civilized World," *North American Review* 201, no. 765 (August 1919): 285, https://www.jstor.org/stable/25122278.

9. Among them Roger Casement, who wrote the "Casement Report" (1903), in *Correspondence and Report from His Majesty's Consul at Boma Respecting the Administration of the Independent State of the Congo* (London: His Majesty's Stationery Office), 21–81, https://archive.org/details/CasementReport/page/n1. A testimonial in *The Times* (London) read as follows: "[The rubber] is collected by force. The soldiers drive the people into the bush. If they will not go they are shot down, and their left hands cut off and taken as trophies to the commissaire. The soldiers do not care who they shoot down, and they more often shoot poor helpless women and harmless children. These hands, the hands of men, women, and children, are placed in rows before the commissaire, who counts them to see that the soldiers have not wasted the cartridges. The commissaire is paid a commission of about 1d. a pound upon all the rubber he gets. It is therefore to his interest to get as much as he can" (November 18, 1895).

10. The African American journalist and legal expert Washington Williams, in a letter written in 1890 to the Secretary of State of the United States, was the first to use the term "crimes against humanity" in relation to the atrocities committed in the Congo under King Leopold II of Belgium.

11. Roundell Palmer, 3rd Earl of Selborne, an officer during World War I, was a personal friend of Winston Churchill's. In 1942, he was supposed to be minister of economic warfare but instead became the chief of the Special Operations Executive, which was tasked with countering anticommunist propaganda in Eastern Europe, and thus in Poland, in parallel with the fight against the Nazis.

12. Rushes for *Shoah*, USHMM, reel 316, typescript, 62–63, https://collections.ushmm.org/film_findingaids/RG-60.5006_01_trs_en.pdf.

13. See the pioneering book by John Horne and Alan Kramer, *German Atrocities, 1914: A History of Denial* (New Haven: Yale University Press, 2001). See also Annette Becker, *Les Cicatrices rouges, 14–18: France et Belgique occupées* (Paris: Fayard, 2010). Even as experienced a historian as Deborah Lipstadt thought, at the time she wrote *Beyond Belief: The American Press and the Coming of the Holocaust (1933–1945)* (New York: Free Press, 1986), that the atrocities of World War I were pure propaganda, that they had not taken place. Contemporary historiography contradicts her.

14. Marc Bloch, "Réflexions d'un historien sur les fausses nouvelles de la guerre," *Revue de synthèse historique*, 33 (1921): 32 (our translation).

15. *Evening Standard*, October 15, 1942.

16. Bloch, "Réflexions," note 24 (our translation).

17. Annette Becker, *Voir la Grande Guerre, un autre récit* (Paris: Armand Colin, 2014).

18. This was a common practice, as shown in a 1917 film by the Section ciné-matographique des armées in which French soldiers made candles, with this de-scription: "Making candles with fat from military abattoirs to light up the foxholes." A German promotional film shows a woman rubbing her hands with glycerin extracted from animal bones. Beside her is the Eiffel Tower: the pride of producing substitutes to win the war.

19. *The Times* (London), April 17, 1917, 5, cited in Joachim Neander and Randal Marlin, "Media and Propaganda: The Northcliffe Press and the Corpse Factory Story of World War I," *Global Media Journal—Canadian Edition* 3, no. 2 (2010): 73–74, https://core.ac.uk/download/pdf/26945870.pdf.

20. Adrian Gregory, *The Last Great War: British Society and the First World War* (Cambridge: Cambridge University Press, 2008), 57.

21. Bertrand Russell, "Government Propaganda," in *These Eventful Years*, vol. 1, *The Twentieth Century in the Making, as Told by Many of Its Makers* (Encyclopaedia Britannica, 1924). See Neander and Marlin, "Media and Propaganda."

22. Adolf Hitler, *Mein Kampf* (New York: Reynal & Hitchcock, 1940), 237–38.

23. Victor Klemperer, *The Language of the Third Reich, LTI—Lingua Tertii Impe-rii: A Philologist's Notebook*, trans. Martin Brady (London: Athlone Press, 2000), 26–27.

24. Report cited in chapter 2. BNA, Kew, Poland, C 8789, September 11, 1942.

25. *New York Times*, November 26, 1942, 16; Rafael Medoff, *The Anguish of a Jew-ish Leader: Stephen S. Wise and the Holocaust* (Washington, DC: David S. Wyman Institute for Holocaust Studies, 2015).

26. Our translation. Three *Christian Century* editorials from 1942 to 1944 returned to this theme: "Horror Stories from Poland" (December 9, 1942); "Polish Atrocities Are Entered in the Books" (December 30, 1942); "Biggest Atrocity Story Breaks in Poland" (September 13, 1944).

27. Raymond Arthur Davies, "The Human Soap Factory," in *The Truth about Poland* (1946), chapter 5 (our translation). "Raymond Arthur Davies" was a pseud-onym used by Rudolph Shohan, convicted of fraud in Canada and likely a Soviet agent. I would like to thank the Canadian Holocaust scholar Mark Celinscak for this information.

28. J. Neander, "The Danzig Soap Case: Facts and Legends around 'Professor Spanner' and the Danzig Anatomic Institute 1944–1945," *German Studies Review* 29, no. 1 (February 2006): 63–86.

29. Victor Gollancz, *"Let My People Go": Some Practical Proposals for Dealing with Hitler's Massacre of the Jews and an Appeal to the British Public* (London: Victor

Gollancz Ltd., 1943), 10, 1 (emphasis in original). The text was dated "Christmas Day, 1942"—a date deliberately chosen.

30. Jacques Maritain, "Anti-Semitism as a Problem for the Jew," *The Commonweal*, September 25, 1942, in Jacques Maritain and Raissa Maritain, *Œuvres complètes*, vol. 8, *1944–1946* (Fribourg: Éditions Universitaires, 1989) (our translation). See also Jacques Maritain, "Le Droit raciste à l'assaut de la civilization," in *Le Droit raciste à l'assaut de la civilisation*, ed. E. Hamburger, M. Gottschalk, P. Jacob, J. Maritain, and B. Mirkine-Guétzevitch (New York: Éditions de la Maison française, 1943), 111.

31. William Shirer, "The Propaganda Front," *Washington Post*, February 14, 1943, https://www.justice.gov/sites/default/files/criminal/legacy/2010/04/11/ezra-pound -p4.pdf.

32. Gollancz, *"Let My People Go,"* 29.

33. William L. Shirer, "The Propaganda Front," *Washington Post*, January 3, 1943, B7.

34. William L. Shirer, "The Propaganda Front: No Atrocity Stories, Facts," *Washington Post*, March 21, 1943, B7.

35. Gerhart M. Riegner, *Never Despair: Sixty Years in the Service of the Jewish People and the Cause of Human Rights*, trans. William Sayers (Chicago: Ivan R. Dee, 2006), 56–57.

36. Raymond Aron, *Memoirs: Fifty Years of Political Reflection*, trans. George Holoch (New York: Holmes & Meier, 1990), 122.

37. Varian Fry, "The Massacre of the Jews," *New Republic* (December 21, 1942): 816. See also Thomas Weber, *La Première Guerre d'Hitler* (Paris: Perrin, 2012).

38. Fry, "Massacre of the Jews," 818. See Becker, *Les Cicatrices rouges, 14–18*.

39. Eleanor Roosevelt asked Welles on September 12, 1942, cited by Andy Marino in *A Quiet American: The Secret War of Varian Fry* (New York: St. Martin's Press, 1999). In her daily column, "My Day," Roosevelt in fact did not mention Fry. On December 5, 1942, she mentioned the extermination of two-thirds of the Jews in Poland, the exact information that had come to her. She added that protesting was useless and that Hitler would have to be punished by death. Eleanor Roosevelt, *My Day: The Best of Eleanor Roosevelt's Acclaimed Newspaper Columns, 1936–1962*, ed. David Emblidge (Cambridge, MA: Da Capo Press, 2009).

40. Raphael Lemkin, *Totally Unofficial: The Autobiography of Raphael Lemkin*, ed. Donna-Lee Frieze (New Haven: Yale University Press, 2013), 113. Lemkin's use of the word "genocide" here is an anachronism, as he had not yet invented the term at this time.

41. Raphael Lemkin, *Axis Rule in Occupied Europe: Laws of Occupation, Analysis of Government, Proposals for Redress* (Washington, DC: Carnegie Endowment for International Peace, 1944). The preface was written in 1943, and the book was published in the fall of 1944.

42. Hayim Nahman Bialik, "City of the Killings," in *Songs from Bialik: Selected Poems of Hayim Nahman Bialik*, ed. and trans. Atar Hadari (Syracuse: Syracuse University Press, 2000), 1.

43. The term was first used in the United States to describe what was happening in the wars in the former Yugoslavia in the 1990s.

44. Abel Pann, *Autobiographie: Le roman d'un Juif* (Paris: Cerf, 1996), 119–20 (our translation). See also Abel Pann, *In the Name of the Czar: 24 Original Pictures* (American Jewish Chronicle, 1918); Becker, *Voir la Grande Guerre*, 89–91.

45. Simon Dubnow, *Le Livre de ma vie: Souvenirs et réflexions, matériaux pour l'histoire de mon temps* (Paris: Cerf, 2000), 720–22 (our translation); the passage was written May 16–17, 1915. The word "Judeophobia" appears in the Russian original; Dubnow also used the expression "hate of the Jew." I thank Alexandre Sumpf for these linguistic details.

46. Alexandre Sumpf, *La Grande Guerre oubliée: Russie, 1914–1918* (Paris: Perrin, 2014); Nicolas Werth, "Dans l'ombre de la Shoah, les pogroms des guerres civiles russes," introduction to *Livre des pogroms: Antichambre d'un génocide, Ukraine, Russie, Biélorussie,1917–1922* (Paris: Calmann-Lévy, 2010), 36–37, and "Les Déportations des 'populations suspectes' dans les espaces russes et soviétiques, 1914–1953," *Communisme*, no. 78–79 (2004): 11–43. This was the third wave of pogroms in Russia, after those in 1884 and 1908. My warm thanks to Nicolas Werth, who, more than cited here, is followed to the letter.

47. *Volkovysk Memorial Book*, 107–9.

48. Mark von Hagen, "The Moral Economy of Ethnic Violence: The Pogrom in Lwow, November 1918," *Geschichte und Gesellschaft* 31 (2005): 203–26.

49. *La Baïonnette*, September 7, 1916 (our translation).

50. Turkish document sent to Pope Benedict XV, Vatican Archives (VA), asV, guerra 14–18, 244, fasc. 110. Author unknown, *Vérité sur le mouvement révolutionnaire arménien et les mesures gouvernementales* (Constantinople, 1916).

51. *Hilal*, March 14, 1918 (our translation). Copy conserved in the VA, secretariat of state, guerra 14–18, 244, fasc. 112.

52. Philippe Burrin, *Ressentiment et apocalypse: Essai sur l'antisémitisme nazi* (Paris: Seuil, 2004), 71–75.

53. Jean Jaurès, speech to the Assemblée, December 3, 1886 (our translation). Vincent Duclert, *La France face au génocide des Arméniens* (Paris: Fayard, 2015), 140–49.

54. Paul Painlevé quoting René Pinon (our translation).

55. Quoted in Richard Breitman and Allan J. Lichtman, *FDR and the Jews* (Cambridge, MA: Belknap Press of Harvard University Press, 2013), 214.

56. Annette Becker and Jay Winter, "Le Génocide arménien et les réactions de l'opinion internationale," in *Vers la guerre totale: Le tournant de 1914–1915*, ed. John Horne and the Centre international de recherche de l'Historial de la Grande Guerre (Paris: Éditions Tallandier, 2010).

57. Breitman and Lichtman, *FDR and the Jews*, 214. As president, Roosevelt discussed the Armenians with his secretary of the treasury, Henry Morgenthau Jr.—none other than the son of Henry Morgenthau Sr., the American ambassador to the Ottoman Empire and real-time witness to the massacres. I shall return to this. See

Keith Pomakoy, *Helping Humanity: American Policy and Genocide Rescue* (Lanham, MD: Lexington Books, 2011).

58. Elisabeth Kontogiorgi, *Population Exchange in Greek Macedonia: The Rural Settlement of Refugees 1922–1930* (Oxford: Oxford University Press, 2006), 54. Kontogiorgi attributes the quotation in a footnote to Martin Gilbert, *Winston S. Churchill*, vol. 4, *World in Torment, 1916–1922* (Hillsdale, MI: Hillsdale College Press, 1975), 854.

59. Charles Graves, *Mr. Punch's History of the Great War* (New York: Frederick A. Stokes, 1919), 270.

60. Heinrich Vierbücher, *Arménie 1915: Ce que le gouvernement impérial a caché aux sujets allemands: le massacre d'un peuple civilisé par les Turcs*, 1930 (our translation).

61. UK Parliament, House of Lords Hansard, December 17, 1942, https://hansard.parliament.uk/Lords/1942-12-17/debates/af4d15ee-1598-4a11-a46e-ae0af284604/PersecutionOfTheJewsAlliesDeclaration.

62. See the different works by Dzovinar Kevonian and Sevane Garibian, in particular "Ailleurs, hier, autrement, connaissance et reconnaissance du génocide des Arméniens," *Revue d'histoire de la Shoah*, no. 277–78 (2003); Taner Akçam, *A Shameful Act: The Armenian Genocide and the Question of Turkish Responsibility*, trans. Paul Bessemer (New York: Metropolitan Books, 2006). Akçam recently wrote another remarkable book, in which he proves the intention and the responsibility of the Young Turks, and especially Talaat Pasha, in the extermination of the Armenians: *Killing Orders: Talaat Pasha's Telegrams and the Armenian Genocide* (London: Palgrave Macmillan, Palgrave Studies in the History of Genocides imprint, 2018). This book has been translated into French, with an original preface by Annette Becker (Paris: CNRS Editions, 2020).

63. Lemkin, *Totally Unofficial*, 19.

64. Vahakn N. Dadrian and Taner Akçam, *Judgment at Istanbul: The Armenian Genocide Trials* (New York and Oxford: Berghahn Books, 2011). At the time, Armenian activists were on a mission to eliminate former perpetrators.

65. Lemkin, *Totally Unofficial*, 20.

66. Joseph Kessel, "Témoignage de M. Joseph Kessel au procès Schwartzbard," in *Reportages, Romans*, ed. Gilles Heuré (Paris: Gallimard, Quarto imprint, 2010), 635 (our translation).

67. Lepsius's testimony was drawn from his *Report on the Situation of the Armenian People in Turkey*, published in 1916.

68. Half-hour interview with Lemkin by Quincy Howe, broadcast 1949, CBS archives. Quotation from http://www.armeniapedia.org/wiki/Lemkin_Discusses_Armenian_Genocide_In_Newly-Found_1949_CBS_Interview.

69. Lemkin, *Totally Unofficial*, 20.

70. Wolf Gruner, "'Peregrinations into the Void?' German Jews and Their Knowledge about the Armenian Genocide during the Third Reich," *Central European*

History 45 (2012): 1–26. See also Stefan Ihrig, *Atatürk in the Nazi Imagination* (Cambridge, MA: Harvard University Press, 2014).

71. Klemperer quoted in Gruner, "'Peregrinations into the Void?,'" 2 (Gruner's translation).

72. *Convention (II) with Respect to the Laws and Customs of War on Land*, The Hague, 1899, Preamble, https://ihl-databases.icrc.org/applic/ihl/ihl.nsf/ART/150-11 0001?OpenDocument.

73. The clause was included, with slight changes, in the 1907 preamble to the convention, which was to become, once ratified in 1909, the basis for international law on warfare in 1914. Rupert Ticehurst, "The Martens Clause and the Laws of Armed Conflict," *International Review of the Red Cross* 37, no. 317 (1997): 125–34; Vladimir Pustogarov, "Fyodor Fyodorovich Martens (1845–1909)—A Humanist of Modern Times," *International Review of the Red Cross* 36, no. 312 (1996): 300–314.

74. Raphael Lemkin, "Acts Constituting a General (Transnational) Danger Considered as Offences against the Law of Nations," trans. Jim Fussell, http://www.pre ventgenocide.org/lemkin/madrid1933-english.htm; "A Report on Terrorism," trans. Vincent Chanethom, http://watchersofthesky.com/wp-content/uploads/2014/10/ lemkins-madrid-report-in-1933.pdf.

75. Lemkin, "Acts Constituting."

76. Lemkin, "Report on Terrorism," "Acts Constituting."

77. Lemkin, "Report on Terrorism" (emphasis added).

78. Provisions for minimal protection of cultural assets had existed since the Hague Convention (IX) of 1907. Following the suggestion by the Russian painter and lawyer Nicholas Roerich, the Roerich Museum in New York asked Georges Chklaver, of the Institut des hautes études internationales at the Université de Paris, to draft a convention for discussion by international bodies. The Roerich Pact (also known as the Treaty on the Protection of Artistic and Scientific Institutions and Historic Monuments) was signed on April 15, 1935.

79. Lemkin cited Pella's book *The Repression of the Crimes against the Personality of the State* (1930), which became a legal classic. Ironically, Pella would be accused— rightly or wrongly—of anti-Semitism after World War II, and he and Lemkin had a falling-out.

80. Lemkin, "Report on Terrorism" (emphasis added).

81. A term used by Hugo Grotius but also a reference to the Torah and the Talmud that Lemkin, former student in the *heder* (Jewish school), knew well. Intention of the evil act: Exodus 21, 12–14.

82. Lemkin, "Acts Constituting" (emphasis in original).

83. Ibid.

84. Jan Karski, *The Great Powers and Poland, 1919–1945: From Versailles to Yalta* (Lanham, MD: University Press of America, 1985). I consulted the typewritten manuscript at Georgetown University.

85. Lemkin, "Acts Constituting" (emphasis in original).

86. NYPL, microfilm 2, notes from the 1950s (our translation).

87. *Washington Post*, December 3, 1944 (our translation).

88. Jan Karski, *Story of a Secret State* (Boston: Houghton Mifflin, 1944), 384. This was one of the numerous passages that Karski added or modified when the first edition was published. See the proofs in the Georgetown University archives. Chapter 33, "My Report to the World," is one of the most heavily marked up in the entire book, proving its importance to the publication in the United States in wartime.

89. Stephen Wise, *The Personal Letters of Stephen Wise* (Boston: Beacon Press, 1956), 166.

90. Ibid., 260.

91. Calel Perechodnik, *Am I a Murderer? Testament of a Jewish Ghetto Policeman*, trans. Frank Fox (Boulder, CO: Westview Press, 1996).

92. Emanuel Ringelblum cites Maxence Van der Meersch's *Invasion 14*, published in 1935 (published in English as *Invasion*, trans. Gerard Hopkins [New York: Viking, 1937]) in *Chronique du ghetto de Varsovie* (Paris: Payot, 1958), 312–13 (our translation). Seven hundred thousand Poles emigrated to work in the mines in northern France after World War I, giving rise to their interest in the period of occupation in 1914–18.

93. Library of Congress, Pehle, John, memorandum for the Secretary's Files, 1944 January 16; the Morgenthau Diaries (microfilm Publication Bethesda, MD: University Publications of America, c. 1995–97) (our translation). Microfilm 23, 392–73P, volume 694, document 190–192. I am grateful to Rebecca Erbelding of the USHMM, who tracked down all references to Armenians and to Lemkin in the archives of the War Refugee Board for me. Her doctoral dissertation, "About Time: The History of the War Refugee Board," has been published by UMI Dissertation Publishing (2015). (See chapter 4.)

94. Letter from Randolph Paul to Bruce Bliven, February 4, 1944, Papers of the War Refugee Board (Bethesda, MD: University Publications of America, 2002) (our translation). Microfilm LM0305, reel 25, Folder 7, documents 692–695, USHMM.

95. Frankfurter participated as a Zionist, although an ambivalent one—a view he always held. H. N. Hirsch, *The Enigma of Felix Frankfurter* (New York: Basic Books, 1981).

Chapter 4. Naming a Nameless Crime

1. British National Archives (BNA), Kew, Fo. 371 1942. Germany. *Treatment of War criminals*, telegram no. 7686. For the chronology, see chapter 2.

2. USHMM, copy of the archives of the Polish government in exile deposited at Stanford University, dossier 70, 19–20.

3. Chaim Weizmann, speech given at Madison Square Garden, New York, March 1, 1943 (our translation).

4. Quoted in "35,000 Slain Jews Honored at Rally. Speakers Condemn Warsaw Persecutions as the Most Barbarous in History," *New York Times*, June 20, 1943, 34.

5. BNA, Kew, Shmuel Zygielbojm, telegram to Churchill, December 15, 1942. See chapter 2.

6. Shmuel Zygielbojm's letter published in the *Polish Review*, June 14, 1943, https://www.marxists.org/subject/jewish/zygielbojm-suicide-letter.pdf. The October 4, 1943, issue of the *Polish Review* began with a series of poems "to the Jews, to the memory of Shmuel Zygielbojm."

7. Adolph Held, quoted in "35,000 Slain Jews."

8. Jan Ciechanowski, *Defeat in Victory* (New York: Doubleday, 1947), 179.

9. General Sikorski, 9, I 1943, File 111, government in exile, Polish archives, USHMM.

10. *Memorandum*, Assistant Secretary, Department of State, July 10, 1943, USHMM (our translation).

11. Jan Karski, *Story of a Secret State: My Report to the World* (London: Penguin Books, 2012), 419.

12. Rushes for *Shoah*, USHMM, reel 313. Lanzmann did not use in *Shoah* the material from the second day of his interview with Karski, during which he spoke about his meetings at the White House with Roosevelt and at the Supreme Court with Justice Frankfurter. In 2010, he used some parts of this 1978 interview in a new film, *The Karski Report*. See chapter 6.

13. Ibid.

14. Ibid., reel 314.

15. Library of Congress, Manuscript Division.

16. Rushes for *Shoah*, USHMM, reel 315. Understandably, Lanzmann did not keep these remarks, even in his new edit in 2010.

17. Ibid. On the "nos" of Karski and Frankfurter, see the introduction and chapter 6.

18. *Minutes of Meeting of Representation of Polish Jewry, on Occasion of the Visit of Mr. Jan Karski*, Cincinnati, American Jewish Archives, August 9, 1943, 1 (our translation).

19. Whom he had met in London; see chapters 2 and 6.

20. *Minutes of Meeting of Representation of Polish Jewry*, 5 (our translation).

21. Schwarzbart quoted in E. Thomas Wood and Stanislaw M. Jankowski, *Karski: How One Man Tried to Stop the Holocaust* (New York: Wiley, 1994), 178.

22. *Minutes of Meeting of Representation of Polish Jewry*, 8 (our translation).

23. Ibid., 5, 7.

24. *Oswiecim* (*Camp of Death*) (New York: Poland Fights [Polish labor group], 1944), 41–48, https://archive.org/details/OswiecimCampOfDeath. The original Polish-language version was published by the resistance in 1942. The 1944 translation was conserved by Karski, Georgetown University archives.

25. "Jewish evacuation," internal verbatim record, Treasury Department, in the presence of Henry Morgenthau Jr., Treasury Secretary, December 19, 1943, USHMM archives, 14 and 21. See Rebecca Erbelding, "About Time: The History of the War Refugee Board," PhD dissertation, George Mason University, 2015, published as *Rescue Board: The Untold Story of America's Efforts to Save the Jews of Europe* (New York: Penguin Random House, 2019).

26. "Jewish evacuation," 13.

27. Letter from the World Jewish Congress dated April 13, 1944, signed by its president, Nahum Goldmann, including a memo from December 3, 1943 (our translation). Copy at the USHMM. I will not discuss here the well-known issue of negotiations between the Nazis and the Hungarian Jewish aid organizations. See Z. Vagi, L. Csosz, and G. Kadar, *The Holocaust in Hungary: Evolution of a Genocide*, trans. Zsofia Zvolensky (Lanham, MD: AltaMira Press, 2013).

28. Vagi, Csosz, and Kadar, *The Holocaust in Hungary*, 11.

29. The report was dated January 13, 1944. It is reproduced in Michael Mashberg, "Documents Concerning the American State Department and the Stateless European Jews, 1942–1944," *Jewish Social Studies* 39, no.1–2 (Winter–Spring 1977): 163–82. The quotation is on 164.

30. Ibid., 167 (emphasis in original).

31. Richard Breitman, *Official Secrets: What the Nazis Planned, What the British and Americans Knew* (New York: Farrar, Straus and Giroux, 1999).

32. Mashberg, "Documents Concerning the American State Department," 174.

33. Message from President Roosevelt to the president of the World Jewish Congress, July 31, 1944, Truman Library, Jta no. 176 (emphasis added).

34. It is also what John Pehle would wonder all his life. In 1981, he said, "But by and large, I am afraid that the American effort to save the oppressed people of Europe was too little and too late." In *The Liberation of the Nazi Concentration Camps 1945: Eyewitness Accounts of the Liberators*, ed. Brewster Chamberlin and Marica Feldman (Washington, DC: United States Holocaust Memorial Council, 1987), 175.

35. USHMM archives, Board of Economic Warfare (our translation).

36. Raphael Lemkin, *Totally Unofficial: The Autobiography of Raphael Lemkin* (New Haven: Yale University Press, 2013), 114.

37. Ibid., 115.

38. Ibid., 115, 117.

39. *The Diary of Samuel Golfard and the Holocaust in Galicia*, ed. Wendy Lower, USHMM series Jewish Responses to Persecutions, gen. ed. Jürgen Matthäus (Lanham, MD: AltaMira Press, 2011), 94–95.

40. Isaac Schneersohn, Foreword, in *La Persécution des Juifs dans les pays de l'Est présentée à Nuremberg*, a collection of documents edited by Henri Monneray, preface by General Telford Taylor, introduction by René Cassin (Paris: Éditions du Centre, CdJC, 1949), 8 (our translation).

41. *New York Times*, February 7, 1943, section M, pp. 1, 16.

42. Arthur Koestler, *New York Times*, January 9, 1944, reprinted in his *The Yogi and the Commissar, and Other Essays* (New York: Macmillan, 1945), 90.

43. This is the "rule" of the distance-compassion ratio that contemporary humanitarian experts often denounce: the farther away the evil is, geographically or socially, the less one is interested in it. Only events within one's close circle can arouse compassion.

44. Koestler, *The Yogi and the Commissar*, 91.

45. Ibid., 93.

46. Lemkin, *Totally Unofficial*, 58.

47. Lemkin, note in the Collection of the NYPL.

48. Lemkin, *Totally Unofficial*, 115, 116.

49. NYPL, Lemkin Papers, microfilm no. 2, n.d. Some words are crossed out or illegible, and the text was probably written under huge stress and at a time when Lemkin had not fully mastered English.

50. Raphael Lemkin, "Le crime de génocide," *Notes documentaires et études*, no. 417, La documentation française (1946) (our translation).

51. Title of chapter 7 in the provisional outline of *Totally Unofficial*.

52. Several fragments at the NYPL.

53. Lemkin, *Totally Unofficial*, 1.

54. Raphael Lemkin, *Axis Rule in Occupied Europe: Laws of Occupation, Proposals for Redress* (Washington, DC: Carnegie Endowment for international Peace, Division of International Law, 1944), 77. Articles 46 and 52 (confiscations and forced labor) of The Hague Conventions were cited.

55. Ibid., 78.

56. Ibid., 79 (emphasis added).

57. Raphael Lemkin, *Key Laws, Decrees, and Regulations Issued by the Axis in Occupied Europe* (Board of Economic Warfare, Blockade and Supply Branch, Reoccupation Division, December 1942), typescript, USHMM.

58. Johann Chapoutot, *La Loi du sang: Penser et agir en nazi* (Paris: Gallimard, "Bibliothèque des Histoires," 2014).

59. Lemkin, *Key Laws*, 8800.

60. Lemkin, "Le crime de génocide," *Notes documentaires et études*, no. 417 (September 24, 1946), 3 (emphasis added; our translation).

61. Abram de Swaan, *Diviser pour tuer: Les régimes génocidaires et leurs hommes de main* (Paris: Seuil, 2016); Christian Ingrao, *La Promesse de l'Est: Espérance nazie et génocide, 1939–1943* (Paris: Seuil, 2017).

62. "Bits of This and That," *Washington Post*, September 16, 1943. Lemkin probably wrote this notice himself.

63. Lemkin, *Axis Rule*, 338.

64. Ibid.

65. Ibid., 128.

66. "Report of Minister Whitlock," in *German War Practices*, part 1, *Treatment of Civilians*, ed. D. C. Munro, G. C. Sellery, and A. C. Krey (Committee on Public Information, 1918), 78. See also James Wilford Garner, *International Law and the World Order* (New York: Longmans Green, 1920), 184n1, in which he quotes the "opinion of the American minister to Belgium in a report to the department of state in April 1917."

67. General Ludendorff, *The General Staff and Its Problems*, vol. 1, 156, 157, quoted in Lemkin, *Axis Rule*, 67n2. Lemkin also quoted Roosevelt at the conference of the

International Labor Organization on November 6, 1941, reminding his audience that two million foreign forced laborers were replacing Germans who had left for the front.

68. Lemkin, *Axis Rule*, 67.

69. French-language manuscript, NYPL, 4 (our translation). See Annette Becker, "La 'Grosse Bertha' frappe Saint-Gervais," in Annette Becker et al., *La Très Grande Guerre* (Paris: Le Monde Éditions, 1994).

70. Lemkin to Jackson, May 4, 1945, Lemkin Archives, NYPL.

71. "Secret Field Marshal v. Reichenau Order, Subject: Conduct of Troops in Eastern Territories, October 10, 1941," https://phdn.org/archives/www.ess.uwe.ac .uk/genocide/USSR2.htm. Lemkin cited the order in a letter dated October 12, 1941 (Office of US Chief Committee for War Crimes), in *The Holocaust: Selected Documents*, vol. 10, *The Einsatzgruppen or Murder Commandos* (New York and London: Garland, 1982), 6, document 2. See also Telford Taylor, "Cross-Examination of von Rundstedt at Nuremberg by General Telford Taylor," in *The Anatomy of the Nuremberg Trials: A Personal Memoir* (London: Bloomsbury, 1993), 520–21.

72. Von Rundstedt quoted in Raphael Lemkin, "Genocide—A Modern Crime," *Free World* 4 (April 1945): 39.

73. Ibid. In a *Washington Post* article titled "Retribution," no doubt inspired by Lemkin, von Rundstedt was quoted again about the punishments that awaited the Germans.

74. Letter from Wallace to Lemkin, February 11, 1946, Library of Congress Archives, Wallace fonds. In 1944, Wallace was involved mainly in deliveries of matériel to the Soviet Union in a lend-lease arrangement, whence his visit to the Kolyma gulag, where he saw Potemkin Village–type experiments on detainees (whom he took for actual laborers) subjected to extreme forced labor. Related by Varlam Shalamov in *Kolyma Tales*, trans. John Glad (London: Penguin Books, 1994). Wallace obviously did not understand the meaning of mass violence.

75. Taken from the title of chapter 7 of Lemkin, *Totally Unofficial*.

76. *Washington Post*, December 3, 1944.

77. Norman Bentwich, "The Law of War Crimes," *Palestine Post*, November 23, 1945.

78. Lemkin's response in the *Washington Post* on December 14, 1944, to a letter to the editor in that newspaper written by "army officer, Virginia," dated December 3, 1944, and published on December 10. We see the use that different prosecutors of the post–World War II trials might have made of Lemkin's clear response.

79. Sterling North, *Washington Post*, December 24, 1944.

80. Otto D. Tolischus, "Twentieth-Century Moloch: The Nazi-Inspired Totalitarian State, Devourer of Progress—and of Itself," *New York Times Book Review*, January 21, 1945.

81. P. O. Douglas, "Genocide," *Washington Post*, December 29, 1944 (letter written December 20).

82. Letter to the editor, *Washington Post*, December 29, 1944.

83. Review of Jan Karski's book *Story of a Secret State* (Boston: Houghton Mifflin, 1944), in *Polish Review*, January 18, 1945.

84. Advertisement in the *New York Times*, February 4, 1945.

85. *New York Times*, December 3, 1944.

86. Advertisement in the *Chicago Tribune*, December 3, 1944.

87. "Poland's 'Underground State' Exhibition," *Polish Review*, September 4, 1944.

88. New York exhibition, May 10–June 8, 1944, *Polish Review* (our translation).

89. For example, in the *Polish Review*, March 28, 1944, and in all sorts of underground leaflets exhibited or reproduced. Karski's archives contain a large number, which he collected in Europe in 1946.

90. Sterling North, "The Post's Book of the Week," *Washington Post*, December 31, 1944, section S, p. 5.

91. *Chicago Daily* (in Polish), January 25, 1945.

92. Karski, *Story of a Secret State* (2012), 320.

93. Unsigned book review of *Story of a Secret State* in the Ogden [Utah] *Standard-Examiner*, January 7, 1945, 18, https://www.newspapers.com/clip/31390595/the-ogden-standard-examiner/ (emphasis added).

94. There was just about no one to liberate, whence the choice of the word "opened." In fact, "liberate" would signify a political will, that of making the camps central to the war. This was never the case for the Allies.

95. Daniel Blatman, *The Death Marches: The Final Phase of Nazi Genocide*, trans. Chaya Galai (Cambridge: Belknap Press, 2011).

96. *New York Times*, January 9, 1944, p. sm5.

97. Exhibition catalogue for *Filmer la guerre: Les Soviétiques face à la Shoah 1941–1946* (Paris: Mémorial de la Shoah, 2014).

98. Canadians were also present at Bergen-Belsen. See Mark Celinsack, *Distance from the Belsen Heap: Allied Forces and the Liberation of a Nazi Concentration Camp* (Toronto: University of Toronto Press, 2015).

99. Elie Wiesel, *Night*, trans. Marion Wiesel (New York: Hill and Wang, 2012); originally published in Yiddish in 1955. See chapter 6.

100. John Dower, *War without Mercy: Race and Power in the Pacific War* (New York: Pantheon Books, 1986).

101. Paul Winkler, "Torture Camps," *Washington Post*, February 12, 1944, p. 6.

102. Cartoon by Garner Rea, *Colliers*, February 19, 1944.

103. Cartoons by Helen Hokinson, *The New Yorker*, May 13 and May 20, 1944.

104. Edmund Wilson, *The New Yorker*, November 25, 1944, p. 92.

105. "Gallup Finds Most Believe Atrocity Tales," *Washington Post*, December 3, 1944.

106. Edward T. Folliard, "Skeptic Yanks See Proof of Nazi Atrocities," *Washington Post*, April 16, 1945, p. 1.

107. William L. Shirer, "The Propaganda Front," *Washington Post*, January 3, 1943, p. B7 (our translation).

108. "Atrocities of World War One," *Washington Post*, May 6, 1945, p. B4 (our translation). Wittenberg, Luther's city, was a military prison camp during World War I. On the reality of and propaganda about these camps, see Heather Jones, *Violence against Prisoners of War, in the First World War, Britain, France and Germany, 1914–1920* (Cambridge: Cambridge University Press, 2013).

109. "Gazing into the Pit," *The Christian Century*, May 9, 1945.

110. Marcel Cohen, "Faire avec presque rien ou le métier d'un écrivain stupéfait," *Europe*, January 2016, p. 207 (our translation).

Chapter 5. The War Is Over

1. Lemkin, critical reading of *Les Mémoires de Mgr Jean Naslian*, 2 vols. (Imprimerie mechithariste, 1955) (our translation).

2. United Nations General Assembly, "Resolution 96 (1). The Crime of Genocide," December 11, 1946.

3. Jan Gross, *Fear: Anti-Semitism in Poland after Auschwitz* (New York: Random House, 2007); Gross, *Golden Harvest: Events at the Periphery of the Holocaust* (Oxford: Oxford University Press, 2012); Aude Kichelewski, *Les Survivants: Être juif en Pologne de 1945 à nos jours* (Paris: Vendémiaire, 2016).

4. Translator's note: *Survivant* is, directly, a survivor. *Rescapé* has the additional nuance of "being safe, uninjured."

5. Henry Rousso, ed., *Après la Shoah, rescapés, réfugiés, survivants, 1944–47*, catalogue for an exhibition, curated by Henry Rousso at the Mémorial de la Shoah in Paris, 2016.

6. USHMM archives, report of Earl G. Harrison to President Truman, August 24, 1945, https://www.ushmm.org/exhibition/displaced-persons/resourc1.htm.

7. The amateur film is in the USHMM archives.

8. Letter in the file of Raphael Lemkin at the International Tracing Service, Bad Arolsen, No. 228134 (our translation).

9. "All wiped out. No more family." File of the International Tracing Service, Bad Arolsen. Elias Lemkin, No. 3763; Lea, No. 690424; Samuel, No. 696053; Sholom/Saul, No. 794 636.

10. I am grateful to Juliette Denis, expert in the wartime USSR, for these details. See Catherine Gousseff, *Échanger les peuples: Le déplacement des minorités aux confins polono-soviétiques, 1944–1947* (Paris: Fayard, 2015).

11. Memo of December 19, 1943, USHMM, p. 26 (our translation).

12. See chapter 4.

13. Files of the International Tracing Service, Bad Arolsen, Daniel Lemkin, No. 474146.

14. Anonymous, "Retribution," *Washington Post*, May 6, 1945 (our translation).

15. Raphael Lemkin, "The Legal Case against Hitler, Part I," *The Nation*, February 24, 1945, p. 206.

16. In 1942, Franz Neumann wrote a prescient book on Nazism, *Behemoth: The Structure and Practice of National Socialism* (Oxford: Oxford University Press,

1942). He was later Raul Hilberg's dissertation adviser at Columbia University, New York.

17. Telford Taylor, *The Anatomy of the Nuremberg Trials: A Personal Memoir* (London: Bloomsbury, 1993), 49.

18. Ibid., 50.

19. Ibid., 103.

20. Hersch Lauterpacht, *An International Bill of the Rights of Man* (New York: Columbia University Press, 1944). He criticized *Axis Rule* in the *Cambridge Law Journal*. See Philippe Sands, *East West Street: On the Origins of Genocide and Crimes against Humanity* (London: Weidenfeld and Nicolson, 2016).

21. Interview with Professor Lemkin at United Nations Radio, June 12, 1957, p. 1. World Jewish Congress Collection, box H276, file 10.

22. Our translation.

23. Alexander also wrote the Nuremberg code on ethical medical experiments. "Science under dictatorship," he wrote, "becomes subordinated to the guiding philosophy of the dictatorship." Leo Alexander, "Medical Science under Dictatorship," *New England Journal of Medicine* 241, No. 2 (July 14, 1949): 39.

24. Paul Julian Weindling, *Nazi Medicine and the Nuremberg Trials: From Medical War Crimes to Informed Consent* (Basingstoke: Palgrave Macmillan, 2004), 85. I am grateful to Paul Weindling for confirming my hypothesis of barbarism assumed by Lemkin.

25. Raphael Lemkin, "The Significance of the Concept of Genocide in the Trial of War Criminals," 1946, Lemkin Archives, Columbia University, New York City, box 4, file 4.

26. Letter from Egon Schneller to Raphael Lemkin to thank him with ten copies of his article "International Film for Discovery of War Criminals," Lemkin Archives, Columbia University, New York City, box 5, file 5. See Christian Delage, *La Vérité par l'image, de Nuremberg au procès Milosevic* (Paris: Denoël, 2006).

27. Quoted by Mark Lewis, *The Birth of the New Justice: The Internationalization of Crime and Punishment, 1939–1950* (Oxford: Oxford University Press, 2014) 205.

28. Letter from Lemkin to David Maxwell Fyfe, assistant general prosecutor, August 26, 1946, AJHS, Lemkin Papers, quoted in Anson Rabinbach, "Raphael Lemkin et le concept de genocide," *Revue d'histoire de la Shoah* (July 2008): 541 (our translation).

29. Sands, *East West Street*, 301.

30. Melchior Palyi, book review of *Axis Rule*, *American Journal of Sociology* 51, no. 5 (March 1946): 496–97. See also Melchior Palyi, *Papers*, Special Collections Research Center, University of Chicago Library. We may admire Palyi's scholarly prescience, as it would not be until the 1980s that the Nazism of the occupation would be studied in this way, via the local and regional decisions more or less arbitrated by Berlin.

31. Ibid., 497.

32. Eugène Aroneanu, "Les Nations Unies et le crime contre l'humanité," *Le Monde*, December 10, 1948 (our translation).

33. Jacob Robinson, "The International Military Tribunal and the Holocaust: Some Legal Reflections," *Israel Law Review* 7, no. 1 (January 1972): 7.

34. Jacob Robinson cited by Mark Lewis in *Birth of the New Justice*, 155, 159.

35. Robinson, text written in 1945, quoted in Michael Marrus, "A Jewish Lobby at Nuremberg: Jacob Robinson and the Institute for Jewish Affairs, 1945–1946," *Cardozo Law Review* 27 (April 2006): 1654.

36. Quoted in David Cesarani, *Final Solution: The Fate of the Jews 1933–1949* (New York: St. Martin's Press, 2016), 786. See, for example, Benjamin Fondane [1942], "Préface en prose," in *L'Exode: Super Flumina Babylonis* (Paris: La Fenêtre ardent, 1965).

37. Sigrid Arne, "Nazi Victim Helps Repay Debt," *Portland Press Herald*, March 16, 1947, quoted in Raphael Lemkin, *Totally Unofficial: The Autobiography of Raphael Lemkin* (New Haven: Yale University Press, 2013), xxi.

38. Sigrid Arne, interview with Raphael Lemkin, *Washington Post*, March 16, 1947, section B, p. 3.

39. American report for the United National Relief and Rehabilitation Administration, July 29, 1946, UN Archives, New York.

40. Hirad Abtahi and Philippa Webb, *The Genocide Convention: The Travaux préparatoires*, vol. 1 (Boston: Martinus Nijhoff, 2009), 459. The quotation is by Mr. Durdenevsky (USSR), speaking at the 123rd plenary meeting, November 21, 1946.

41. Lemkin, *Totally Unofficial*, 80.

42. Raphael Lemkin, *Axis Rule* (Washington, DC: Carnegie Endowment for International Peace, 1944), 84–85. Lemkin is quoting *Le Frankfurter Zeitung*, March 28, 1941.

43. Lemkin, "Le Crime de génocide," *Notes documentaires et études*, no. 417 (September 24, 1946) (our translation).

44. Letter from Raphael Lemkin to the Emergency Committee in Aid of Displaced Foreign Scholars, June 21, 1944, NYPL.

45. Quoted in Lewis, *Birth of the New Justice*, 204.

46. Genet [pen name of Janet Flanner], "Letter from Paris," *The New Yorker*, October 16, 1948, p. 111.

47. Raphael Lemkin, "Encyclopédie des génocides," French-language manuscript, in *Caractères juridiques du genocide*, chap. 2, p. 5 (our translation).

48. "Observations Concerning the Articles," in Abtahi and Webb, *Genocide Convention*, 636.

49. Radio-Lille, December 1948, French-language transcript in the Lemkin Archives, Jacob Rader Marcus Center, Cincinnati (our translation).

50. Mark Mazower, *No Enchanted Palace: The End of Empire and the Ideological Origins of the United Nations* (Princeton: Princeton University Press, 2009).

51. Raphael Lemkin, "Totally Unofficial Man," in *Pioneers of Genocide Studies*, ed. Samuel Totten and Steven Leonard Jacobs (New Brunswick, NJ: Transaction Publishers, 2002), 392–93.

52. Our translation.

53. Letter to Eleanor Roosevelt, February 1, 1950, Lemkin Archives, Cincinnati (Lemkin reminds E. Roosevelt of the past).

54. Lemkin to Léon Blum, February 18, 1950, Lemkin Archives, Cincinnati (our translation).

55. Letter to François de Menthon, January 3, 1950. Quoted in Lewis, *Birth of the New Justice*, 182.

56. Eugene Holmes, "Anti-Semitism," review of *Must Men Hate?* by Sigmund Livingston, *Journal of Negro Education* 15, no. 2 (Spring 1946): 207.

57. "US Accused in UN of Negro Genocide," *New York Times*, December 18, 1951, p. 13.

58. Letter from Oakley Johnson, of New York, June 24, 1953, Lemkin Archives, Cincinnati. See Guillaume Mouralis, *Le Moment Nuremberg: Le procès international, les lawyers et la question raciale* (Paris: Les Presses de Sciences Po, 2019). An English translation is to be published in 2021 by Oxford University Press.

59. See the works by Myriam Cottias, in particular "La Traite et l'esclavage racialisé comme genocide," in *Rapport de la Mission d'étude en France sur la recherche et l'enseignement des génocides et des crimes de masse*, ed. Vincent Duclert (Paris: CNRS Éditions, 2018).

60. Lemkin added "regrettable" by hand on the typescript.

61. NYPL, sparse notes from the 1950s, microfilm 4 (our translation).

62. Lemkin, *Totally Unofficial*, 128. In fact, Vyshinsky had written a short book in the 1930s on the interference of international criminal law in the internal politics of the Soviet Union.

63. Text written November 16, 1949, for the International Labour Conference, London, Lemkin Archives, Cincinnati (our translation).

64. "Charge of US Genocide Called Red Smoke Screen," *Washington Post*, December 16, 1951, p. m6.

65. "Communist Genocide Campaign," notes by Lemkin, Reel 4, Lemkin Archives, NYPL, 1951.

66. Ibid.

67. "Berle Chides U.S. on Genocide Issue," *New York Times*, January 13, 1951, p. 2.

68. Raphael Lemkin, NYPL, Manuscripts and Archives Division, Reel 3. Published in L. Y. Luciuk, ed., *Holodomor: Reflections on the Great Famine of 1932–1933 in Soviet Ukraine* (Kingston, ON: Kashtan Press, 2008), 237–38.

69. Cf. Nicolas Werth's conclusion in *Les Grandes Famines soviétiques* (Paris: Que sais-je, 2020). For a more journalistic approach, see Ann Applebaum, *Red Famine: Stalin's War on Ukraine* (London: Penguin, 2018).

70. *Haratch*, no. 208, December 9, 1945, in Chavarche Missakian, *Face à l'innommable, avril 1915* (Marseille: Éditions Parenthèses, 2015) (our translation).

71. Chavarche Missakian, "La Grande Crise," excerpts of letters written in August 1915, translated by Krikor Beledian, *Europe*, special issue *Témoigner en littérature*, ed. Frédérik Detue and Charlotte Lacoste, no. 1041–42 (2016): 57, 58.

72. Letter to Thelma Stevens, member of the Council of Methodist Women, July 26, 1950, NYPL. Numerous priests, in particular, were deported to Dachau.

73. CBS, "U.N. Casebook," documentary series, broadcast February 13, 1949. Interview with Lemkin on the UN convention and the Armenian genocide. A partial transcript is available at http://www.armeniapedia.org/wiki/Lemkin_Discusses_Armenian_Genocide_In_Newly-Found_1949_CBS_Interview. Part of the interview can be viewed at https://vimeo.com/125514772.

74. Raphael Lemkin, "Prolongement de la cicatrice psychologique," manuscript, NYPL, n.p. (our translation).

75. Quoted in Tanya Elder, "Documenting Lemkin's Life by Exploring His Archival Papers," in *The Origins of Genocide: Raphael Lemkin as a Historian of Mass Violence*, ed. Dominik J. Schaller and Jürgen Zimmerer (London and New York: Routledge, 2009), 45.

76. Raphael Lemkin, 1958 review of *Les Mémoires de Mgr Jean Naslian*, 2 vols. (Imprimerie mechithariste, 1955) (our translation), Lemkin Archives, Cincinnati.

77. John Cooper, *Raphael Lemkin and the Struggle for the Genocide Convention* (Basingstoke: Palgrave Macmillan, 2008).

78. The meetings were on October 27 and November 9, 1948: "I spoke for an hour with Professor Raphael Lemkin, who told me about 'genocide,' in which I was very interested. . . . Received Professor Lemkin, of the genocide." Angelo Giuseppe Roncalli, *Journal de France*, vol. 1, *1945–1948* (Paris: Cerf, 2006), introduction and annotation by Étienne Fouilloux (to whom I extend my warm thanks), 563–69 (our translation).

79. Lemkin, *Totally Unofficial*, and *Lemkin on Genocide*, ed. Leonard Jacobs (Lanham, MD: Lexington Books, 2012).

80. *Investigation of the Psychological Reactions of Three Areas: The Victimized Group / The Genocidist / The Outside World.* Manuscript, Lemkin Archives, NYPL.

81. Here, I use the word "neighbor" as defined by Jan Gross in *Neighbors: The Destruction of the Jewish Community in Jedwabne, Poland* (Princeton: Princeton University Press, 2000).

82. The concept was "invented" by Niederland in 1961. See Bruno Cabanes, "Le Syndrome du survivant: Histoire et usages d'une notion," in *Retour à l'intime au sortir de la guerre*, ed. Bruno Cabanes and Guillaume Picketty (Paris: Tallandier, 2009), 199–211.

83. Lucien Febvre, "Face au vent" (1946), in *Combats pour l'histoire* (Paris: Armand Colin, 1953), 41 (our translation).

84. Anouche Kunth, *Exils arméniens, du Caucase à Paris, 1920–1945* (Paris: Belin, 2016).

85. Quoted in Steven L. Jacobs, ed., *Raphael Lemkin's Thoughts on Nazi Genocide: Not Guilty?* (Lewiston, NY: Edwin Mellen Press, 1992), xx.

86. Soazig Aaron, *Le Non de Klara* (Babelio, 2002).

87. Lemkin Archives, Cincinnati (our translation).

88. British National Archives, Kew, 1532 Kar, 19/5/1944 (our translation).

89. Ad in the *New York Times*, November 28, 1944.

90. Quoted in E. Thomas Wood and Stanislaw M. Jankowski, *Karski: How One Man Tried to Stop the Holocaust* (Hoboken: John Wiley & Sons, 1994), 240.

91. Eve Grot, "Not the Whole Story," *Soviet Russia Today*, March 1945, p. 28.

92. Annette Becker, "Avoir faim/ravitailler," in *Les Cicatrices rouges, 14–18: Belgique et France occupées* (Paris: Fayard, 2010), 131–58; Bruno Cabanes, "The Hungry and the Sick: Herbert Hoover, the Russian Famine, and the Professionalization of Humanitarian Aid," in *The Great War and the Origins of Humanitarianism, 1918–1924* (Cambridge: Cambridge University Press, 2014), 189–247.

93. Poor Lemkin suffered a similar disaster with his archives—due in this case to American liberalism: he had stored nine boxes of documents in Washington and was unable to go to retrieve them. They were "put up for auction for scrap." By a stroke of luck there was in the auction hall a "Mr. Blondell who knew Dr. Rafael Lemkin's achievements"; he bought the papers for twenty dollars and found Lemkin, who was "delighted" to recover them. "They are of great sentimental value for me. They are not worth much money now, I guess. Just documents. But perhaps after I'm dead, someday, they may be worth something." "Owner Will Regain Genocide Documents," *Washington Post*, October 14, 1953, p. 15.

94. Council of Polish Political Parties, *Poland Accuses: An Indictment of the Major German War Criminals* (London: The Montgomery Printing & Stationery Co., 1946).

95. Rousso, *Après la Shoah*; Hasia Diner, *We Remember with Reverence and Love: American Jews and the Myth of Silence after the Holocaust, 1945–1962* (New York: New York University Press, 2009), and "Origins and Meanings of the Myth of Silence," in *After the Holocaust: Challenging the Myth of Silence*, ed. David Cesarani and Eric J. Sundquist (London and New York: Routledge, 2012), 192–201; Simon Perego, *Pleurons-les. Les Juifs de Paris et la commémoration de la Shoah (1944–1967)* (Paris: Champvallon, 2020).

96. Jan Karski, "The Great Powers and Poland, 1919–1945," PhD dissertation, Georgetown University, 1953, 415. Also available in Jan Karski, *The Great Powers and Poland: From Versailles to Yalta* (Lanham, MD: Rowman and Littlefield, 2014), 357.

97. Ibid., 461. Quotation taken from Karski, *Great Powers*, 365–66.

98. Ibid., 415.

99. *Washington Post*, March 3, 1952, section B, p. 5 (our translation).

100. Monday, October 29, 1956, US House of Representatives, Committee on Un-American Activities, International Communism (Revolt in the Satellites), testimony of Dr. Jan Karski, Library of Congress, https://babel.hathitrust.org/cgi/pt?id=uc1.$b654273&view=1up&seq=11.

101. Jan Karski, "Poland's Election: Results Rejected as Not Reflecting Desires of the Nation," "Letters to the Times," *New York Times*, January 20, 1957.

102. Jan Karski, personal archives, Georgetown University.

103. Handwritten note in French, n.d. (around 1956), Karski Archives, George-town University (our translation).

Chapter 6. Becoming Karski, Becoming Lemkin

1. Raphael Lemkin, NYPL, microfilm reel no. 2, *Perpetuation of the Psycho-logical Scar*, 1950s typescript.

2. Claude Lanzmann, *Shoah, an Oral History of the Holocaust: The Complete Text of the Film* (New York: Pantheon Books, 1985), 174.

3. Jacques Derrida, "A Self-Unsealing Poetic Text," trans. Rachel Bowlby, in *Revenge of the Aesthetic: The Place of Literature in Theory Today*, ed. Michael P. Clark (Berkeley: University of California Press, 2000), 194.

4. Dori Laub, "Not Knowing Is an Active Process of Destruction. Why the Testimonial Procedure Is of So Much Importance," in *Trauma Research Newsletter* 1, Hamburg Institute for Social Research, July 2000. Laub, an American psychia-trist, was one of the founders of the Fortunoff Video Archive for Holocaust Testi-monies at Yale University, named after Alan A. Fortunoff, who made a generous endowment gift.

5. Dori Laub, "Psychoanalysis and Genocide: Two Essays," Genocide Studies Program, Yale University, 2002, https://gsp.yale.edu/sites/default/files/gs20_21_-_psychoanalysis_and_genocide_two_essays.pdf.

6. Marjorie Hyer, "Holocaust: So Horrible No One Believed It Was True," *Washington Post*, March 28, 1980, https://www.washingtonpost.com/archive/local/1980/03/28/holocaust-so-horrible-no-one-believed-it-was-true/9501ed7c-b463-45e6-8e04-88c0f94100b4/.

7. President Jimmy Carter appointed Elie Wiesel to chair the President's Com-mission on the Holocaust, which gave rise to the United States Holocaust Memorial Museum. Housed in a building designed by the architect James Ingo Freed, it was inaugurated in 1993. Miles Lerman was the project's linchpin.

8. Miles Lerman, foreword to chapter 1, "Opening," in *The Liberation of the Nazi Concentration Camps 1945: Eyewitness Accounts of the Liberators*, ed. Brewster Chamberlin and Marcia Feldman (Washington, DC: United States Holocaust Memorial Council, 1987), 12. Lerman, who arrived in the United States from a dis-placed persons camp in 1947, was the executive director of the United States Holo-caust Memorial Council.

9. Ibid.

10. Elie Wiesel, chapter 1, "Opening," in Chamberlin and Feldman, *Liberation of the Nazi Concentration Camps*, 14.

11. Wiesel quoted in E. Thomas Wood and Stanislaw Jankowski, *Karski: How One Man Tried to Stop the Holocaust* (New York: J. Wiley & Sons, 1994), 255.

12. Jan Karski, participant in panel discussion, "Discovering the 'Final Solu-tion,'" in Chamberlin and Feldman, *Liberation of the Nazi Concentration Camps*, 191.

13. Jan Karski, presentation, in Chamberlin and Feldman, *Liberation of the Nazi Concentration Camps*, 181. The passage is cited by Raul Hilberg in the chapter

titled "Messengers" in his *Perpetrators Victims Bystanders: The Jewish Catastrophe, 1933–1945* (New York: HarperCollins, 1992), 224. Thereafter, Karski repeated these words often. "Righteous" file, Yad Vashem archives. Hilberg was the only historian featured in the film *Shoah*.

14. Yad Vashem website, https://www.yadvashem.org/yv/en/exhibitions/righteous /milestone02.asp.

15. Yona Kesse, elected representative of the Mapai Party, quoted in Sarah Gensburger, *National Policy, Global Memory: The Commemoration of the "Righteous," from Jerusalem to Paris, 1942–2007*, trans. Katharine Throssell (New York: Berghahn, 2016), 9.

16. David Cesarani, *Eichmann: His Life and Crimes* (London: William Heinemann, 2000).

17. The commemoration took place on April 13, 1961. From 1951, when it was created, until 1959, the "Day of Commemoration of the Genocide and the Ghetto Uprising" took place on the date of 27 Nissan in the Jewish calendar. The transition from the notion of celebrating heroism to that of commemorating the catastrophe for Jewish victims is notable.

18. Gideon Hausner, *Justice in Jerusalem* (New York: Harper & Row, 1966), 397. The book was published simultaneously in many languages in 1966, and "the world knew" once more through it. Lanzmann, however, did not mince his words: "The Eichmann trial would be of no use to me. Reading the transcripts, it became clear to me that the trial had been conducted by ignorant people: the historians at the time had done too little research, the president and the judges were poorly informed; Hausner, the chief prosecutor, thought that pompous, moralizing flights of rhetoric compensated for what he lacked in knowledge . . . the tearful witnesses gave a kind of show, making it impossible to recreate what they had truly experienced." Claude Lanzmann, *The Patagonian Hare: A Memoir*, trans. Frank Wynne (New York: Farrar, Straus and Giroux, 2012), 425. I would like to thank Fabien Théofilakis, a foremost Eichmann scholar. See his "Adolf Eichmann à Jérusalem, 1960–1962: La Shoah en France devant la justice," in *Gestapo et polices allemandes: France Europe de l'Ouest, 1939–1945*, ed. P. Arnaud and F. Théofilakis (Paris: CNRS éditions, 2017), and *"Un jour, c'est l'histoire qui jugera"—Eichmann à Jérusalem: La Shoah vue de la cage de verre* (Paris: Odile Jacob, forthcoming).

19. Hausner then listed examples of countries that had been among the Just—Denmark, Belgium, Sweden, France, the Netherlands, Italy—which, Hausner said, "we shall never forget" or "we shall always remember."

20. Hausner quoted in Gensburger, *National Policy, Global Memory*, 16–17. The list of countries at the end of the quotation is included in the original text but was not included in the translation.

21. Hausner, *Justice in Jerusalem*, 236. Translator's note: The translation in this work changes "Jewish resistance" to "Polish underground." We have amended the translation to retain the author's original meaning.

22. Yad Vashem Archives, Karski file.

23. The Bitburg affair was one of the reasons that the United States was pushed to ratify the 1948 convention on genocide. See Ansom Rabinbach, "Raphael Lemkin et le concept de genocide," *Revue d'histoire de la Shoah* (July 2008): 511–54. As most of the extermination sites were situated in Poland or the Soviet Union, Reagan obviously could not visit them during this G7 meeting in West Germany.

24. Jan Karski, *Washington Post*, letters to the editor, April 22, 1985 (emphasis added).

25. Jan Karski (Washington), *Washington Post*, letters to the editor, December 1, 1985.

26. Lanzmann, *Shoah*, 171.

27. Expression by the German philosopher Andris Breitling.

28. See the writings by Rémy Besson: his dissertation, "La Mise en récit de Shoah" (EHESS, adviser: Christian Delage, 2012), "Le Rapport Karski, une voix qui résonne comme une source," *Études photographiques*, no. 27 (May 2011); *Shoah une double référence? Des faits au film, du film aux faits* (Paris: Éditions MkF, 2017).

29. Lanzmann quoted in Aline Alterman, *Visages: Shoah, le film de Claude Lanzmann* (Paris: Cerf, 2006) (our translation). See C. Lanzmann, "Le Lieu et la parole," in Claude Lanzmann, Bernard Cuau, and Michel Deguy, *Au sujet de Shoah, le film de Claude Lanzmann* (Paris: Belin Éditeur, 2011), 304.

30. Lanzmann, *Shoah*, 167, 174.

31. Ibid.

32. The camera literally falls upon the White House by sliding down the flagpole in a camera movement similar to that sliding down a dead tree in the Birkenau camp.

33. Karski, *Story of a Secret State*, 338. In the film, Nowolipki Street, most of which was in the ghetto, is shown. The etymology of the name is no doubt related to the gardens that bordered the street in the seventeenth century (*nowy* means "new" and *lipa* means "linden"). The street's name became known through a 1930s social novel by Pola Gojawiczynska, *Dziewczeta z Nowolipek* (The Girls of Nowolipki), which was adapted for film several times. I would like to thank Dorota Dakowska for her valuable assistance.

34. On the suitcases from the Auschwitz Museum shown elsewhere in the film, see Éric Marty's reflections in *Le Débat* (December 2010), reprinted in *Sur Shoah de Claude Lanzmann (Le marteau sans maître)* (Paris: Éditions Manucius, 2016).

35. Lanzmann, *Shoah*, 168.

36. Rushes for *Shoah*, USHMM, reel 318, p. 70. See "Franklin Delano Roosevelt, un leader du monde," *Les Temps modernes, Le Rapport Karski* (2010): 20.

37. Tom Shales, "Bearing Witness to Horror" (review of the PBS broadcast of *Shoah*), *Washington Post*, April 27, 1987.

38. Claude Lanzmann, "*Jan Karski* de Yannick Haenel, un faux roman," *Les Temps modernes* (January–March 2010): 2 (our translation).

39. The archive created by Steven Spielberg in 1994 is housed at the University of Southern California. It should be noted that although the Tutsi genocide in Rwanda

in 2000 is not on the archive's list of genocides, that of Bosnia, in 1994—the year of the archive's creation—is.

40. Jan Karski, "Foreword," in Ewa Kurek, *Your Life Is Worth Mine: How Polish Nuns Saved Hundreds of Jewish Children in German-Occupied Poland (1939–1945)* (New York: Hippocrene Books, 1997), 9.

41. Inaugurated in March 2005, the museum was designed by Moshe Safdie. See Moshe Safdie, Joan Ockman, and Diana Murphy, *Yad Vashem: Moshe Safdie—The Architecture of Memory* (Zurich: Lars Müller, 2006).

42. Levite's text, written in January 1945, is presented in a new translation by David Suchoff in his "A Yiddish Text from Auschwitz: Critical History and the Anthological Imagination," *Prooftexts* 19, no. 1 (January 1999): 59–69. The quotation is on 63.

43. Rushes for *Shoah*, USHMM, 70. On Lord Selborne, see chapter 3.

44. Speech lasting twenty-three minutes plus questions, USHMM, February 4, 1999 (our translation), Fulbright ceremony, USHMM oral archives.

45. Ibid. (our translation).

46. Elie Wiesel to Jan Karski, May 10, 1994. Yad Vashem archives, Karski file. Also quoted in part in Annette Becker, "Jan Karski from Eye Witness to Moral Witness: What to Do with Your Senses?," in *Modern Conflict and the Senses*, ed. Nicholas J. Saunders and Paul Cornish (Abingdon: Routledge, 2017), 234.

47. Elie Wiesel at the inauguration ceremony for Yad Vashem, March 15, 2005, https://www.yadvashem.org/events/15-march-2005/ceremony.html.

48. Letter from Shimon Peres to Jan Karski, May 12, 1994. Yad Vashem archives.

49. Jan Karski, speech in Washington, May 12, 1994. Yad Vashem archives.

50. Yannick Haenel, *Jan Karski* (Paris: Gallimard, L'Infini imprint, 2009).

51. In the original German, "Niemand zeugt für den Zeugen." Paul Celan, "No One Bears Witness for the Witness," from *Breathturn*, in Paul Célan, *Breathturn into Timestead: The Collected Later Poetry*, trans. Pierre Joris (New York: Farrar, Straus and Giroux, 2014), 65.

52. Yannick Haenel, *Cercles* (Paris: Gallimard, 2007), 485–86 (our translation). See also Yannick Haenel, *The Messenger: A Novel*, trans. Ian Monk (Berkeley, CA: Counterpoint, 2012).

53. Anthony Lewis, "Abroad at Home; 'Remember, Remember,'" *New York Times*, December 2, 1985, section A, p. 15.

54. Karski's second wife, Pola Nirenska, a survivor of the Shoah, was a dancer and then a dance teacher. I extend my warmest thanks to Arthur Nauzyciel (today the director of the Théâtre national de Bretagne), who has involved me since the beginning in this magnificent theatrical adventure. The play, *Jan Karski (mon nom est une fiction)*, has been performed throughout France and in Switzerland and Poland. Nauzyciel has not drawn the critical fire of Lanzmann and revisionist historians; yet, the play is based on Haenel's novel.

55. Saul Friedländer, *The Years of Extermination: Nazi Germany and the Jews, 1939–1945* (New York: HarperCollins, 2007).

56. Catherine Filloux, *Lemkin's House* (2005). The play has nowhere near the strength of Haenel's novel, but its timeliness makes it of great interest.

57. Lanzmann returned to this polemic in 2016, when Elie Wiesel died. Lanzmann rebuked Wiesel for not praising his film enough, which he regarded as a betrayal.

58. Claude Lanzmann, *Un vivant qui passe*, 1997, 1 h 5 m: 1979 interview with Maurice Rossel, delegate from the International Red Cross committee to Theresienstadt in June 1944; *Sobibor 14 octobre 1943, 16 heures*, 2001, 1 h 35 m; *Le Dernier des injustes*, 2013. The transcripts of these films have been published by Gallimard.

59. "These young writers are complaining . . . as distance allows them, they believe, all the indifference and the worst distortions, in the name of a tearful and retrospective moralism," Lanzmann wrote in *"Jan Karski* de Yannick Haenel: Un faux roman," *Les Temps modernes* (January–March 2010), 1 (our translation).

60. Claude Lanzmann, *Le rapport Karski*, 2010, 48 m.

61. Claude Lanzmann, "Autoportrait à quatre-vingt-dix ans," interview with Franck Nouchi and Juliette Simont, in Juliette Simont, ed., *Claude Lanzmann: Un voyant dans le siècle* (Paris: Gallimard, 2017), 278–80 (our translation).

62. Jorge Semprun, *L'Écriture ou la vie* (Paris: Gallimard, 2002), 188 (our translation).

63. Philippe Mesnard, *Primo Levi: Le passage d'un témoin* (Paris: Fayard, 2011).

64. Walter Benjamin, "Theses on the Philosophy of History," in *Illuminations: Essays and Reflections*, trans. Harry Zohn, ed. Hannah Arendt (Boston and New York: Mariner Books, 2019), 198–99 (emphasis in original). In December 2010, Haenel responded to a letter that I had sent him regarding my intentions for this book: "Like you, I think that the name of Jan Karski is one of a becoming—a metamorphosis—that gives us a huge amount to think about in terms of how the twentieth century fits into history. It is an issue essential to understanding, working out, and testing what is the nerve center of our censures. Not only did he bear within himself overlapping temporalities (and you have noted that his interview with Lanzmann in *Shoah* is constantly shaped by shifts between past and present), but he was in himself a palimpsest. Karski was a man of secrets—as such, he was a fiction, his own fiction (starting with the invention of his name)—a fiction that told the truth, that of a formulation (and constant reformulation) of what the world after 1945 was capable of hearing and accepting. . . . Like you, I think that the essential thing is not Jan Karski's message, but the resistance that this message provoked, the discourses that it started, the changes that it revealed in the slow construction of 'what we know' or, rather, 'what we want to know.' Unfolding Karski through time, through transformations of the image that we have of him, and also through the transformations in Karski himself (and his spiritual evolution) is, I believe, your subject: it inverts the rather weighty certainties . . . [of those who] do not want to know how much of what took place under the name of Jan Karski has been kept back and played out through time—that is, up to the present" (our translation). Annette Becker, personal archives.

65. Henry Rousso, ed., *Après la Shoah: Rescapés, réfugiés, survivants (1944–1947)* (Paris: Mémorial de la Shoah, 2016), 134 (our translation). Nathan Rapoport, a refugee in the USSR, had wanted to create a monument to the destruction of the ghetto in 1943; his proposal was deemed too romantic and nationalistic by the Soviets. After the war, he immigrated to France. The Warsaw monument was judged sufficiently important for a replica to be placed at the entrance to the Yad Vashem complex in Jerusalem. See also James Young, *The Texture of Memory: Holocaust Memorials and Meaning* (New Haven: Yale University Press, 1994), 168; Annette Becker, *"War and Faith": The Religious Imagination in France, 1914–1930*, trans. Helen McPhail (Oxford and New York: Berg, 1998), 132.

66. Designed by the Finnish architects Rainer Mahlamäki and Ilmari Lahdelma and inaugurated in stages between 2013 and 2015.

67. For instance, Witold Pilecki, the author of one of the most remarkable eyewitness accounts on Auschwitz, where he organized the resistance, was executed by the communists in 1948; he was rehabilitated in 1990. See Witold Pilecki, *The Auschwitz Volunteer: Beyond Bravery*, trans. Jarek Garlinski (Los Angeles: Aquila Polonica (US) Ltd., 2012).

68. Letter from Andrzej Olechowski to Jan Karski, May 4, 1994, Yad Vashem archives.

69. "President Obama Announces Jan Karski as a Recipient of the Presidential Medal of Freedom," https://obamawhitehouse.archives.gov/the-press-office/2012/04/23/president-obama-announces-jan-karski-recipient-presidential-medal-freedo.

70. Whence the various accusations of antipatriotism made against the historian Jan Gross. The Order of Merit of the Republic of Poland that he received in 1996 was withdrawn after his book *Neighbors: The Destruction of the Polish Community in Jedwabne, Poland* (Princeton: Princeton University Press, 2001) was published.

71. The title of the first biography, written by E. Thomas Wood and Stanislaw M. Jankowski, *Karski: How One Man Tried to Stop the Holocaust* (Hoboken: John Wiley & Sons, 1994). A film made by Slawomir Grünberg in 2015 featured Wood's interviews of Karski in 1996.

72. Tom Wood, "When Silence Is a Sin: A Hero of the Holocaust Leaves Us Lessons about Duty," Medium.com, January 31, 2017, https://medium.com/@tomwood_94144/when-silence-is-a-sin-88a7853fb230. Ten Karski groups on Facebook reposted the article.

Conclusion

1. Lemkin, critical reading of *Les Mémoires de Mgr Jean Naslian*, 2 vols. (Imprimerie mechithariste, 1955) (our translation).

2. Raphael Lemkin, *Unofficial Man* (unpublished autobiography), quoted in S. L. Jacobs, "Genesis of the Concept of Genocide According to Its Author from the Original Sources," *Human Rights Review* 3, no. 2 (2002): 103.

3. Lemkin, NYPL, typescript pages, 1950s (our translation).

4. Raphael Lemkin, NYPL, microfilm reel no. 2, *Perpetuation of the Psychological Scar*, typescript from the 1950s (our translation).

5. Annette Becker, *Maurice Halbwachs, un intellectuel en guerres mondiales, 1914–1945* (Paris: Noêsis, 2003).

6. Raphael Lemkin, "Perpetuation of the Psychological Scar," n.d., Manuscripts and Archives Division, NYPL, Box 2, Folder 4, Reel 3 (our translation). See also Charlotte Kiechel, "Legible Testimonies: Raphaël Lemkin, the Victim's Voice, and the Global History of Genocide," *Genocide Studies and Prevention: An International Journal* 13, no. 1 (2019): 42–63.

7. Lemkin, "Perpetuation of the Psychological Scar" (our translation).

8. Jean Hatzfeld, *Blood Papa: Rwanda's New Generation*, trans. Joshua David Jordan (New York: Farrar, Straus and Giroux, 2018).

9. Interview in Mushubati, Rwanda, 2016 (our translation). Annette Becker, personal notes.

10. Élise Rida Musomandera, *Le Livre d'Élise* (Paris: Les Belles Lettres, 2014), 72 (our translation).

11. Quoted in Catherine Bedarida, "Il n'y a pas de fin à un genocide," *Le Monde*, May 19, 2005 (our translation). See also Esther Mujawayo and Souad Belhaddad, *SurVivantes* (La Tour d'Aigues, France: L'Aube, "Poche Essai" collection, 2005).

12. Quoted in Jean Hatzfeld, *The Strategy of Antelopes: Living in Rwanda after the Genocide*, trans. Linda Coverdale (New York: Farrar, Straus and Giroux, 2009), 4.

13. Joséphine Kampiré, quoted in Hélène Dumas, *Le Génocide au village: Le massacre des Tutsi du Rwanda* (Paris: Seuil, 2014), 277, 290 (our translation). See Stéphane Audoin-Rouzeau, *Une initiation* (Paris: Seuil, 2017).

14. I quote with affection the French mixed with Yiddish of Philippe Gumplowicz's mom (our translation).

INDEX

George L. Mosse Series in the History of European Culture,
Sexuality, and Ideas

STEVEN E. ASCHHEIM, SKYE DONEY,
MARY LOUISE ROBERTS, AND DAVID J. SORKIN

Series Editors

Of God and Gods: Egypt, Israel, and the Rise of Monotheism
JAN ASSMANN

*Messengers of Disaster: Raphael Lemkin, Jan Karski, and
Twentieth-Century Genocides*
ANNETTE BECKER; translated by KÄTHE ROTH

*Respectability and Violence: Military Values, Masculine Honor,
and Italy's Road to Mass Death*
LORENZO BENADUSI; translated by ZAKIYA HANAFI

The Enemy of the New Man: Homosexuality in Fascist Italy
LORENZO BENADUSI; translated by
SUZANNE DINGEE and JENNIFER PUDNEY

*The Holocaust and the West German Historians:
Historical Interpretation and Autobiographical Memory*
NICOLAS BERG; translated and edited by JOEL GOLB

Collected Memories: Holocaust History and Postwar Testimony
CHRISTOPHER R. BROWNING

Cataclysms: A History of the Twentieth Century from Europe's Edge
DAN DINER; translated by WILLIAM TEMPLER with JOEL GOLB

*Fascination with the Persecutor:
George L. Mosse and the Catastrophe of Modern Man*
EMILIO GENTILE; translated by JOHN and ANNE TEDESCHI

La Grande Italia: The Myth of the Nation in the Twentieth Century
EMILIO GENTILE; translated by SUZANNE DINGEE and
JENNIFER PUDNEY

www.ingramcontent.com/pod-product-compliance
Lightning Source LLC
Chambersburg PA
CBHW062051020426
42338CB00004B/766